365
GAYS
OF THE YEAR

Inspiring | Educating | Creating | Entertaining

Brimming with creative inspiration, how-to projects, and useful information to enrich your everyday life, quarto.com is a favourite destination for those pursuing their interests and passions.

First published in 2023 by White Lion Publishing,
an imprint of The Quarto Group.
One Triptych Place,
London, SE1 9SH,
United Kingdom
T (0)20 7700 6700
www.quarto.com

Design copyright © 2023 Quarto
Text copyright © 2023 Lewis Laney
Illustrations copyright © 2023 Charlotte MacMillan-Scott

A catalogue record for this book is available from the British Library.

ISBN 978-0-7112-7370-2
Ebook ISBN 978-0-7112-7372-6

10 9 8 7 6 5 4 3 2 1

Design by Leonardo Collina

Printed in Malaysia

MIX
Paper | Supporting responsible forestry
FSC™ C007207

LEWIS LANEY

365

GAYS

OF THE YEAR

PLUS 1 FOR A LEAP YEAR
DISCOVER LGBTQ+ HISTORY ONE DAY AT A TIME

ILLUSTRATIONS BY CHARLOTTE MACMILLAN-SCOTT

WHITE LION PUBLISHING

INTRODUCTION

This compendium is an introduction to queer history through the people that made it. My hope is that you learn much from this book featuring brief biographies and bright illustrations of LGBTQ+ icons, and find out about amazing things done by amazing queer people. Perhaps you'll discover people you've never heard of before or maybe you'll spot someone you know, and find out about a heroic thing they did for the LGBTQ+ community, of which you were unaware.

I learnt an abundance of things while researching the book and it made me proud to be part of such an amazing, strong and resilient community who have faced such insurmountable obstacles. One such devastating obstacle is the AIDS epidemic. While it decimated the lives of gay men in the 1980s, 90s and beyond, at the same time it strengthened a community who rose to action through activism, education and care. Sadly, while reading about many people I included in the book, phrases like 'died due to AIDS complications' appeared all too often and it is apparent that a generation of great people never got to fulfil their full potential because of the disease.

I discovered that one of the entries, Flora Murray, a doctor in the early part of the 20th century, worked in the Belgrave Hospital for Children in London, which has since been converted into flats and is somewhere I lived for 10 years! I also learnt that Edward Carpenter, a poet, philanthropist, and a pioneer of sandal-wearing in the UK, lived in my birth town, Chesterfield, for a short while. I chuckled when I read that he apparently left within a year, because he found it dull there. I also loved reading about how Howard Ashman helped form the structure of the Disney musicals my sister and I would watch together as youngsters, and in particular how he managed to get Disney execs to base the animation of Ursula the Sea Witch on cowntroversial drag queen, Divine!

Not only does this book celebrate and shine a light on important queer people throughout history (as well as 12 allies who have supported the community along the way), it also takes the form of an LGBTQ+ calendar, with a different person of note assigned to each date, so you can learn something new every day of the year. The date will have particular significance: whether it be the date they were born, a day upon which they performed a notable act – like when Booan Temple stormed a live 6 o'clock BBC news broadcast to protest against Section 28 (British laws censoring local authorities from 'promoting' homosexuality); or a date that was a first for a queer person – such as Axel and Eigil Axgil becoming the first same sex couple in the world to enter into a civil partnership. Where it wasn't possible to match a person to an exact date, I've placed them in a month that is relevant to them.

The reasons people are featured in this book are wide-ranging. Some are tied to one specific, notable act that is integral to our history, such as Stormé DeLarverie igniting the crowd at Stonewall on 28 June 1969. Many, such as activists Peter Tatchell and Sue Hyde, have spent their lives fighting for the rights of LGBTQ+ people, while others have excelled in their fields and made outstanding contributions to society and just happen to be queer. For example, the discoveries made by archaeologist Mary Anning, the medical advancements pioneered by Martha May Eliot and the hundreds of books written for children by Jacqueline Wilson, are all worthy achievements of anyone, whether they are heterosexual or queer.

For some people in the book, their queer visibility and their determination to live as themselves is their achievement. Mima Simić came out on prime-time Croatian TV in 2007 simply to be 'the first lesbian millions of people… have ever seen'. Marsha P. Johnson, Sylvia Rivera, Pedro Pablo Zamora and Quentin Crisp all bravely lived as their authentic selves in a world full of discrimination, hate and a lack of understanding. As Cliff Joannou, editor-in-chief of *Attitude* magazine, wrote recently; 'Where we are visible, we can't be unseen. And where we are seen, we become examples of hope for countless other LGBTQ+ people.'

Other entrants have advanced queer culture and LGBTQ+ visibility through their arts. Armistead Maupin, Radclyffe Hall and Alan Hollinghurst have penned our stories on the page, while Ryan Murphy, Russell T Davies and Ilene Chaiken have told them on the screen.

There are people included in the book who never publicly came out, those who lived a seemingly heterosexual existence, and many from history where it's difficult to say for sure what letter of the rainbow alphabet they fall under. We now have the language we didn't have years ago; terms like trans, non-binary, pansexual and even queer now provide words that people feel more comfortable using when describing themselves. Years ago, and still today in certain countries, coming out as LGBTQ+ would mean discrimination, ostracisation, arrest and even death, so of course there is a lack of evidence of the queerness of many people. Where it's not always clear-cut, but there is an implication or a discussion, I have made informed conclusions on including people.

Finally, the allies included in this book have all contributed something significant to the lives of LGBTQ+ people and our community. Of course, there are millions of allies out there who deserve our thanks and recognition; those who march beside us at Pride, those who vote for equal marriage in a referendum, those who take us in when we are rejected and those who nurse us when we are sick and dying. I can't fit them all in the book, but we are grateful they are by our sides.

Of course, in any list like this, there will be debate. You — the reader — will possibly disagree with me on some inclusions, and multiple people in the book disagree with each other. Some people are undoubtedly problematic, some have said controversial things (and often regretted them and apologised), while others are victims of their time, having expressed old-fashioned opinions from which we have now moved on. Despite this, every person in the book has an important place in LGBTQ+ history, and whether we agree with everything they have done and said, or not, their contribution has to be recognised.

As I sit down to write this introduction, the Google doodle of the day taunts me with an illustration of Coccinelle, a French celebrity who, Wikipedia tells me, had the first widely publicised post-war gender reassignment case in Europe. Coccinelle is not one of my entries and therefore an example of how this list should not be viewed as either definitive or as a 'best of'. She, like many others not included, lived an extraordinary life and made a unique contribution to queer history, paving the road to where we stand today.

This book only includes 366 profiles so of course there are amazing LGBTQ+ people missing from the list. There just isn't enough space to write about everyone. It's also important to recognise that some people haven't made it into the history books (or on to the internet), so their legacy is sadly lost. Either they or their queerness has been erased over time or was simply never recorded in the first place. The stories of women, people of colour and the financially underprivileged are also often under-recorded; however I strived to make this list as diverse as possible, seeking out lesser-known people and their achievements. Therefore, as we champion the people in this book, let's continue to recognise and lift up all the others who made and are making a difference, no matter how small, or in what way, every day of the year.

Author's Note:
The LGBTQIA+ acronym has grown to encompass more and more letters over the years, and you'll find it used in various forms throughout the book. We've tried to allow people and organisations to describe themselves in their own terms as much as possible, and this also means older acronyms may be used in text referring to historical events.

When using my own voice, I've gone with a commonly used standard (LGBTQ+), but every letter is celebrated here!

THE CALENDAR

THE CALENDAR

THE CALENDAR

THE CALENDAR

THE CALENDAR

THE CALENDAR

THE CALENDAR

E.M. FORSTER

1879–1970

Much of E.M. Forster's writing was informed by his own experience, whether that was his extensive travel, his unhappy time at school or a close friendship confused with love. Forster, whose father died when he was a baby, was raised by his mother and aunts, and spent much of his childhood in Hertfordshire. He studied at King's College, Cambridge and later travelled across Greece, Egypt, Italy, Germany and India.

Forster's romantic encounters included an unrequited love for a 17-year-old Indian student named Syed Ross Masood – sadly, the writer confused Masood's romantic view of their friendship for more. Forster also wrote about sleeping with a wounded soldier in Egypt in his diary in 1917, calling it 'losing R [respectability]'. Then in his late thirties, this was probably the first time he had slept with a man.

Forster's novels include *A Room with a View* (1908), *Howards End* (1910) and *A Passage to India* (1924), all published within his lifetime. His novel *Maurice* (1971), in which he tells a gay love story across classes, was published posthumously in January 1971. Forster had deliberately held off publishing it during his lifetime for fear of persecution at a time when homosexuality was illegal.

LADY PHYLL

B. 1974

Lifelong activist Phyll Opoku-Gyimah is more widely known as Lady Phyll and says the 'Lady' in her name isn't a title: 'It started as a nickname to clarify that I'm not a bloke called Phil.'

Lady Phyll is the co-founder and director of UK Black Pride, an organisation committed to the celebration of Black LGBTQI+ culture in the UK, which hosts an annual event for LGBTQI+ people of African, Asian, Caribbean, Latin American and Middle Eastern descent during Pride Month.

On this day in January 2016, Lady Phyll (respectfully) turned down an MBE in the New Year Honours List, saying she had to stand by her principles: 'I don't believe in empire. I don't believe in, and actively resist, colonialism and its toxic and enduring legacy in the Commonwealth, where – among many other injustices – LGBTQI people are still being persecuted, tortured and even killed because of sodomy laws… that were put in place by British imperialists.'

As well as being co-editor of *Sista! An anthology of writings by and about Same Gender Loving Women of African/Caribbean descent with a UK connection*, Lady Phyll has also served as a trade unionist, been a Stonewall trustee and is now executive director of the Kaleidoscope Trust, a UK-based charity fighting for the rights of LGBT+ people across the Commonwealth.

COLETTE

1873–1954

'A bas les gousses!' ('Down with the dykes!') shouted the audience at the Moulin Rouge on this date in 1907 when Colette, French novelist and performer, staged a pantomime show with her lover Mathilde de Morny. In the show, called *Egyptian Dream*, the two women kissed on stage and depicted themselves as domestic partners — which was how they lived off-stage too.

Colette was best known for her novel *Chéri* (1920), which she adapted into a play, and *Gigi* (1944), also adapted into a play and produced on Broadway in 1951 with Audrey Hepburn in the lead role. Colette's earlier work was not initially credited to her because her first husband,

Henri Gauthier-Villars, a popular writer himself, edited her stories and published them under his own pen name, Willy. He is thought to have locked Colette in a room, forcing her to write.

Once they divorced, Colette began publishing under her own name, at first struggling for success but ultimately lauded as 'the greatest living writer in France' by the writer Paul Claudel. Against the odds, Colette became the first woman president of distinguished Parisian literary organisation the Académie Goncourt, and when she died in 1954, she was honoured by the French Republic with a state funeral, the first for a female writer.

PARIS LEES

B. 1986

Paris Lees made her name as one of the UK's first transgender women to break into mainstream media. In 2013, she was named top of the *Independent on Sunday's* Pink List of the most influential LGBTQ+ people in Britain. On this date in 2018, she became the first openly transgender woman to feature in British *Vogue*, and she subsequently became a contributing editor of the magazine.

   After a troubled start in life in Nottinghamshire, Lees moved to Brighton and then to London, where her career blossomed. She has worked with the organisation All About Trans to change media representation of transgender people, with an aim to bring more positive and powerful trans role models into the public sphere. In a 2012 interview with *PinkNews*, she explained, 'The only story that was being told, for about 40 years, was that of the "classic transsexual", the male-to-female middle-aged misery narrative. Of course, that's a totally valid experience, which many trans people identify with, but it's time for some fresh perspectives.'

   The journalist also created *META* magazine, a digital magazine for trans people to take 'ownership of our own narratives', and in 2012 she released her first book, *What it Feels Like For a Girl*.

BARBARA SMITH

B. 1946

In recognition of a lifetime of activism, writing, theory and other work for Black, queer and feminist communities, Barbara Smith was nominated for the Nobel Peace Prize in January 2005. She was jointly nominated with 999 other women who commit themselves to the cause of peace and justice, often under difficult circumstances.

Smith, along with her twin sister Beverly, had been active in the civil rights movement since high school, campaigning against desegregation, but it was when she started a regional chapter of the National Black Feminist Organization, in Boston, that she really came into her own. This group became the Combahee River Collective, one of the most radical intersectional activist groups of its time.

In 1980, Smith co-founded Kitchen Table: Women of Color Press, the first publishing company run by (and for) women of color in the US. Smith said, 'We publish a work not simply because it is by a woman of color, but because it consciously examines, from a positive and original perspective, the specific situations and issues that women of color face.' The press takes its name from the kitchen as the centre of the home, where women work and communicate with each other. Now in her seventies, Smith still actively champions marginalised voices.

STEPHEN VARBLE

1946-1984

In 2018, almost 34 years after his death, artist Stephen Varble's work went on show at the Leslie-Lohman Museum of Gay and Lesbian Art in New York. To make up for the fact that much of Varble's art had been lost after his death, from AIDS-related complications on this date in 1984, curator David J. Getsy commissioned artist Vincent Tiley to reconstruct several of Varble's costumes. These were some of his most iconic pieces, made from rubbish and assorted objects, pieced together to form glamorous, gender-defying garments.

Varble challenged the status quo of art with his guerrilla performance pieces. While some took place in the street, others involved Varble leading spectators on unauthorised tours of commercial galleries and boutiques in SoHo, taking aim at commercialism, capitalism and gender norms.

While the term 'genderqueer' did not exist at the time, critics and academics now label Varble's work in this way, pointing to his adopted persona, Madame Debris, as well as the non-binary nature of his costumes as signifiers. Believing that art did not need the authorisation of an institute such as a gallery or museum to exist, Varble was a pioneer of 'gutter art', which challenged people to see the beauty in the discarded.

KELLIE MALONEY

B. 1953

In 2014, boxing manager Kellie Maloney entered the UK Celebrity Big Brother house as a contestant, bringing transgender visibility into millions of homes. Earlier that month, she had come out publicly as transgender in the *Sunday Mirror* newspaper, following threats from the press to out her. At the height of her career, Maloney was managing the undisputed heavyweight champion of the world, Lennox Lewis. This role brought her fame, fortune and accolades, such as the Manager of the Year Award from the Boxing Writers' Association of America.

After a hiatus, Maloney returned to the world of boxing, announcing it at a press conference with Cathy McAleer, Northern Ireland's only female professional boxer, on this date in 2020.

Some saw her return as problematic because of derogatory comments she had made in the past about women's boxing, while others believe Maloney to be controversial due to comments made about LGBTQ+ people when she ran as a candidate for the right-wing party UKIP in the 2004 London mayoral elections. She has since apologised for her past comments.

In 2020, the documentary *From Frank to Kellie* told Maloney's personal story of her journey towards being able to live authentically as herself. She now speaks publicly on both boxing and transgender issues.

FRAN LEBOWITZ

B. 1950

Adopted New Yorker Fran Lebowitz rose to fame when Andy Warhol hired her to write a column in his magazine, *Interview*, in the early 1970s. After writing bestselling books, such as her collected essays, *Metropolitan Life* (1978) and *Social Studies* (1981), Lebowitz avoided writing as much as possible, proclaiming she was suffering from writer's block… for forty years! 'I'm really lazy and writing is really hard and I don't like to do hard things,' she told the *Guardian* newspaper in 2021.

Lebowitz, a lesbian and self-proclaimed terrible girlfriend because she loathes domestic life and is not the monogamous type, went on to become a social commentator and performer, who would be paid for voicing her opinions on things. Not so much a comedian, but rather just an opinionated New Yorker, Lebowitz would make witty (and often disgruntled) observations about life in front of an audience.

In 2010, Martin Scorsese directed a documentary about Lebowitz, entitled *Public Speaking*, and 11 years later he also directed and produced a documentary series with and about her. *Pretend It's a City* premiered on Netflix on this date in 2021 and was heralded by *Vogue* as 'one of the best things you will watch this year'.

HARVEY MILK

1930-1978

New York native Harvey Milk moved to San Francisco in 1972. He opened a camera store in the Castro District which quickly became a queer community hub, entered politics and declared his candidacy for the San Francisco Board of Supervisors.

Although he lost this initial race and another in 1975, he grew popular for his wit and candour, becoming a spokesperson for LGBTQ people in the Castro, setting up an association for LGBTQ businesses and helping to organise the Castro Street Fair. Eventually, on this date in 1978, Milk won, becoming California's first openly gay man in public office, and was inaugurated as a San Francisco city-county supervisor.

In his final months, Milk campaigned to prevent the introduction of the Briggs Initiative Proposition 6 – a state law that would prevent LGBTQ people working in public schools. He urged LGBTQ people to come out in a bid to show their friends and family what harm Proposition 6 could do to the people they loved. Going up against Anita Bryant – an anti-gay Christian singer claiming to protect children from the 'evil influence' of homosexuals – brought national media attention to Milk's crusade. Milk was successful and Proposition 6 was defeated.

Tragically, Harvey Milk was assassinated in November 1978 but his legacy and righteous vision lives on, not just in San Francisco, but around the world.

BARBARA JORDAN

1936–1996

On this date in 1967 when Barbara Jordan took up office in the Texas Senate, she became the first African American woman ever elected to it. Five years later, she became president of the Texas Senate in 1972, making her the first Black woman in the US to oversee a legislative body.

As the first African American in the 20th century elected to Congress from the South, Jordan gave an 15-minute opening speech to members of the House Judiciary Committee, as part of the impeachment hearings against President Richard Nixon in July 1974. This televised speech became a career-defining moment for Jordan, with many believing she swayed public opinion in favour of the impeachment. As well as excelling in her political career, Jordan also worked as a lawyer and teacher.

While she never spoke publicly of her relationship with the educational psychologist Nancy Earl, it is believed she was her lifelong companion. The pair travelled together for 30 years, and Earl became Jordan's caregiver when the politician was diagnosed with multiple sclerosis. If we believe this relationship was a romantic one, then Jordan can also be classed as the first LGBTQ+ woman in Congress.

MICHELLE DOUGLAS

B. 1963

When Special Investigations Unit Officer Michelle Douglas was 'released honourably' from her job in 1989 because she was a lesbian, her subsequent legal fight against the Canadian Armed Forces ultimately put an end to discrimination against lesbian and gay service members.

Douglas remained closeted knowing the homophobic culture and practice of the Canadian Army. If outed, she knew policy would restrict her from ever getting a pay rise, a promotion or a transfer. When interrogated about her sexuality and threatened with a polygraph test, she admitted to being gay, was made to leave the army and in January 1990 she filed a lawsuit against the military.

On the eve of her trial in 1992, the military settled, admitted their discriminatory policy and dropped it with immediate effect. They also committed to paying back pay and restoring full rank to LGBTQ+ service members who had suffered because of the policy. 'For me, that was the biggest victory of all, because it had the effect of restoring dignity to people who had been denied it,' Douglas said.

She continued to fight for human rights, becoming executive director of the LGBT Purge Fund, which manages reconciliation projects and memorialisation measures for those affected by the military purge.

SAINT AELRED

1110–1167

Born in Northumberland, UK, Saint Aelred was a Cistercian monk and religious advisor to Henry II of England and David I of Scotland during the 12th century. Some believe that his poetic writings contain thinly veiled glorifications of love between men.

Aelred's book *On Spiritual Friendship* was drawn from his own experiences of living with other monks in the monastery and can be seen as celebrating same-sex love. While some argue his work does not prove Aelred's queerness but rather celebrates the close religious bonds between monks, the pro-LGBTQ+ Anglican organisation, Integrity, has run with this theory and designated Aelred its patron.

In 1147, Aelred became the Abbot of Rievaulx Abbey and according to English Heritage, 'over the next 20 years, the already thriving monastery became a religious, cultural and economic powerhouse'. With Aelred at the helm, the monastery attracted recruits from across Europe, including some who had struggled to settle in other monasteries. Aelred's writings include biographical works of other saints' lives, guides to the monastic life and theological works. Aelred died on this date in 1167 and it is his annual feast day, when both Anglicans and Roman Catholics celebrate his legacy.

DAN LEVY

B. 1983

Dan Levy and his father Eugene Levy created a fictional town with quirky yet lovable residents and, most notably, no homophobia. First aired on this date in 2015, the Canadian TV sitcom *Schitt's Creek* follows the (mis)fortunes of the Rose family after they lose their millions.

Queerness and sexuality are at the heart of its storytelling, expressed with humour and love.'I do drink red wine. But I also drink white wine,' says Levy's character, David, to Stevie, after they share an unexpected intimate moment. 'So, you're just really open to all wines,' she replies, to which he answers, 'I like the wine, and not the label.' In 2018, Levy and other cast members took part in Toronto's Pride Parade, wearing shirts emblazoned with this message.

Schitt's Creek ran for six seasons to global success. The show and its stars won countless awards and broke several records; Dan Levy became the first person to win an award for writing, directing, acting and producing in the same year.

After reading letters he received from the LGBTQ+ community, Levy says, 'television is a really important medium to change those conversations', and he believes it's important 'to find stories that continue to normalise experiences that might not be part of the mainstream'.

JASMIN SAVOY BROWN

B. 1994

On this date in 2022, *Scream* (the fifth instalment in the horror movie franchise) hit cinemas across the US, featuring the series' first queer character, Mindy Meeks-Martin, played by lesbian actress, Jasmin Savoy Brown. Speaking about the character, she pointed out that 'often, a queer character is just "the queer character" and the Black character is "the Black character" and the fact that that's not the case [in *Scream*] is huge'.

The actress has played various parts on television and film but her first major recurring role was in the supernatural drama, *The Leftovers*, which she joined in its second season in 2015. Brown gained even more attention playing the strong-willed teenage queer character of Taissa in the Showtime drama, *Yellowjackets*, which revolved around a plane crash in the 1990s.

The star's talents are not limited to acting, and towards the end of 2021 she delighted fans by sharing her music, releasing her first official music video for 'Crash', in November. In January 2022, Brown and her non-binary *Yellowjackets* co-star, Liv Hewson, began hosting a brand new Netflix LGBTQ+ podcast, *The Homo Schedule*, which celebrated the success stories of queer people and is 'all about queer joy'.

LORI LIGHTFOOT

B. 1962

The former president of the Chicago Police Board, Lori Lightfoot, made history in 2019 when she was elected as Chicago's first Black, female mayor. She also became the first openly LGBTQ+ mayor of the city and upon taking office she pledged to bolster safety and justice for the trans community by improving police training and thoroughly investigating hate crimes.

After graduating from the University of Chicago in 1989, Lightfoot became an attorney and was instrumental in delivering a damning report of misconduct by the city's law enforcement. Overall police reform was a key priority for Lightfoot and once in office she fired the city's police superintendent.

Lightfoot's commitment to helping under-represented communities led to Chicago City Council passing a resolution acknowledging LGBT-owned business enterprises on this date in 2020. During the debate, Lightfoot made an emotional speech, stating powerfully, 'We need not ask anyone's indulgence, patience or forgiveness or acceptance to be who we are and who we love.'

In May 2021, Lightfoot caused controversy by declaring that she would only grant one-on-one interviews to minority journalists, to highlight a lack of diversity.

In 2020, Lightfoot was listed as one of the 'Women of the Year' by LGBTQ+ magazine the *Advocate*, which hailed her as a woman who is changing the world.

JOHN CAGE

1912–1992

On this date in 2004, more than 1,900 people sat in Barbican Hall in London and listened to 4 minutes and 33 seconds of an orchestra sit in silence. The piece they'd 'heard' was '4'33', composed by American experimental composer, John Cage, in 1953. The piece was intended to allow the audience to listen to the ambient sounds that filled the space in the environment they were in. This was, understandably, one of Cage's most controversial pieces.

Throughout his career Cage used experimental techniques to ensure his music pushed boundaries. Influenced by his study of Buddhism and the *I Ching*, many of Cage's compositions included chance music, whereby some element of the music is left to chance when performed.

Cage was also a writer, philosopher and performance artist. He met dancer and choreographer Merce Cunningham while working at the Cornish College of the Arts in Seattle in the late 1930s and the pair became lifelong partners, both in work and romantically.

Cage's experimental methods and the way he used performers in his work influenced not only other musicians, but artists such as Robert Rauschenberg (see 9 Jul). His impact lives on through his influence on late-20th-century rock bands like Stereolab, Radiohead and Sonic Youth.

PETER DOREY

1947-2021

On this date in 1979, a group of gay socialists opened the UK's first LGBTQ+ bookshop in Bloomsbury, London. Gay's the Word was also a community space where all profits were funnelled back into the business. Activists Peter Dorey, Ernest Hole and Jonathan Cutbill co-founded the shop, which is still going strong more than 40 years later. Dorey provided the funding to set up the business, when few financial backers were willing to take such a risk.

Over the years, Gay's the Word has provided a hub for various community groups to meet. These include Black queer groups, Irish gay people in London and, during the miners' strike of 1984–85, the Lesbians and Gays Support the Miners (LGSM) group (later the subject of the 2014 film, *Pride*).

In 1984, thousands of pounds worth of stock was seized by HM Customs and Excise and staff were charged with conspiracy to import 'indecent' material. After much public media attention and a crowd-sourced defence fund which raised more than £55,000, the charges were eventually dropped.

Dorey moved to Brighton in later life but maintained a close relationship with the bookshop. At the shop's 40th anniversary celebration at the British Library in 2019, Hole and he received a spontaneous standing ovation.

ILENE CHAIKEN

B. 1957

Ilene Chaiken has brought female-led stories to the screen in her career as a producer, director and writer, whether through the story of June Osborne in the TV adaptation of Margaret Atwood's *The Handmaid's Tale* (2017–), the lives of a group of lesbians and bisexual women in California in *The L Word* (2004–09), or Pamela Anderson's panned performance in *Barb Wire* (1996).

Chaiken is co-creator of *The L Word*, which aired for the first time on this date in 2004. It was groundbreaking in featuring a mostly queer cast playing lesbian and bisexual female characters, as well as employing a mostly queer team behind the camera, writing, producing and directing the show. The show was criticised for bizarre plot twists, racial stereotyping and the affluence of its characters, but was nevertheless a successful and important show for the queer community, garnering a dedicated following. In 2006, it won the GLAAD Media Award for Outstanding Drama Series.

When speaking about the reboot of *The L Word*, which premiered in 2019, Chaiken highlighted the continuing struggle to get minority stories told on screen, saying, 'The statistics are still grim. It's still a predominantly white male world, and there's still a scarcity of stories of marginalised populations being told.'

GEORGE MICHAEL

1963-2016

'And yes I've been bad, Doctor won't you do with me what you can... I'd service the community (but I already have...),' sang George Michael in his 1998 hit 'Outside', released six months after he was arrested for engaging in a lewd act in a sting operation in a Beverly Hills public restroom. The arrest forced the star into a public outing about his sexuality and he declared he'd been in a relationship with Kenny Goss for two years.

On this date in 1999, LGBT magazine the *Advocate* published an extensive interview with Michael all about it: 'I let people think the issue was my sexuality, not my privacy... the moment there was no privacy, I realized that *that's* all the issue was. Not one part of me has any problem with people knowing I'm gay.'

Michael had soared to success with his musical partner Andrew Ridgeley in their band Wham! in the early 1980s. At a time when record labels and publicists worked to hide the sexuality of LGBTQ+ music stars, Michael remained in the closet as Wham! was pinned up on the bedroom walls of groupies across the world. When Wham! disbanded, Michael went on to become a hugely successful solo artist.

The provocative video for 'Outside', which Michael said was designed to lessen the stigma of cruising, featured outdoor sex between couples (and throuples) of the opposite and same sex. In the video, Michael, dressed as a cop, danced in a public restroom that became a dancefloor complete with glitter balls and sparkly urinals.

JOJO SIWA

B. 2003

When American teen, singer, dancer and YouTuber, JoJo Siwa posted a TikTok of herself singing along to Lady Gaga's queer anthem, *Born this Way*, on this date in 2021, the internet went into a frenzy, trying to figure out if this was a coming out post or not. A few days later the question was answered when Siwa posted again – this time on Twitter – wearing a t-shirt given to her by her cousin, emblazoned with the words 'Best. Gay. Cousin. Ever'. Later that year the star came out as pansexual.

Siwa was a child dance star, rising to fame on shows such as *Abby's Ultimate Dance Competition* and *Dance Moms* – American reality TV shows that chronicled the careers of children (and their mothers) in show business. Her mother taught Siwa her first dance steps and later admitted, 'I would say it's my mission in life to make JoJo a star.'

Siwa's oversized colourful hair bows soon became her signature style and were later produced and merchandised for her fans. Siwa's successful YouTube channel has 12 million subscribers and she has worked with Nickelodeon, released music and toured. In September 2020 she was named one of *Time* magazine's '100 Most Influential People', proving it's possible to conquer the world before you turn 20.

EMILE GRIFFITH

1938–2013

Six-times World Boxing Champion and member of the International Boxing Hall of Fame, US Virgin Islander Emile Griffith killed his opponent, Benny 'Kid' Paret, in a 12-round fight in 1962. At the earlier weigh-in, Paret had taunted Griffith by calling him a *'maricon'*, the Spanish word for 'faggot', and Griffith later said that he 'was very angry in the ring'.

Years later, Griffith expressed his regret but said of the homophobia he was taunted with throughout his career: 'I kill a man and most people understand and forgive me. However, I love a man, and to so many people this is an unforgivable sin; this makes me an evil person.'

While Griffith was part of the LGBTQ+ community in private, he publicly stayed in the closet as this was a time when men could still be arrested for taking part in consensual gay sex and the American Medical Association classified homosexuality as a 'psychiatric disorder'. The boxer later told *Sports Illustrated* magazine, 'I don't like that word: homosexual, gay or faggot. I don't know what I am. I love men and women the same.'

On this date in 2005, directors Dan Klores and Ron Berger released a documentary film about the boxer, called *Ring of Fire: The Emile Griffith Story*.

OLLY ALEXANDER

B. 1990

Yorkshire-born Olly Alexander, best-known as the singer Years & Years, gave a touching and acclaimed performance in Russell T Davies' TV series, *It's a Sin*, which aired its first episode on this date in 2021. The drama followed the story of how AIDS affected a group of friends in the 1980s and 90s, and in the show, Alexander played Ritchie, a young man who moves to London to live his best gay life just as the AIDS epidemic hits. The show won the category of Best New Drama at the National Television Awards, while Alexander was nominated for Best Drama Performance.

Years & Years originally formed in 2010; the five-piece band later became a trio with members Mikey Goldsworthy and Emre Türkmen until their third album, *Night Call*, was released in 2022, and the band split. Alexander is now releasing solo music under the Years & Years name, with relationships and emotions often featuring as the themes of his lyrics.

The singer and actor has spoken openly about being queer since he became famous. He made a documentary called *Growing Up Gay* with the BBC in 2017. It was about mental health in the LGBTQ+ community, and saw him opening up about homophobic bullying, bulimia and self-harm. Alexander continues to speak out for LGBTQ+ rights across the globe.

HANNE GABY ODIELE

B. 1988

On this date in 2017, Belgian model Hanne Gaby Odiele publicly came out as intersex in *Vogue* magazine. She was 28 and modelling for brands including Chanel, Givenchy, Prada and Balenciaga. The star explained she was born with testosterone-producing internal testes, which her body converts to oestrogen, has no uterus or ovaries and that she has one X and one Y chromosome (as is typical with men).

Odiele's parents did not tell her that she was intersex as a child, but she spent much of her childhood in doctor's offices and underwent surgery. After reading about someone similar in a Dutch teen magazine, Odiele figured it out and contacted the intersex girl in the article. Speaking about coming out in *Vogue*, Odiele said she wants to help break down the stigma that intersex people face and encourage parents of intersex children, in particular, to talk about it openly.

Odiele works with the organisation interACT: Advocates for Intersex Youth to help stop the harmful surgeries that many intersex children are subjected to. 'I am proud to be intersex,' she says, 'but very angry that these surgeries are still happening.' In June 2018, Odiele also spoke at the *Teen Vogue* summit to highlight the needs of the intersex community.

MICHAEL CASHMAN

B. 1950

Just before the first gay character appeared on the BBC British soap opera *EastEnders*, British tabloid newspaper the *Sun* ran the headline 'EastBenders' to announce an LGBTQ+ character would be joining the show. Michael Cashman was the actor playing the role of Colin, and when he joined the cast, the press ran defamatory stories about him, as well as homosexuality in general.

In 1987, when Colin kissed his on-screen boyfriend on the forehead, the backlash continued, with the BBC receiving angry letters and phone calls, and bricks were thrown through Cashman's home windows. He was part of the first mouth-to-mouth gay kiss in a British soap, which aired on this date in 1989 and was watched by around 17 million people, and which led to MPs calling for the show to be scrapped.

When Cashman left EastEnders, he took to politics and campaigning for human rights full-time, spurred on by the Conservative Government's legislative attack on LGBTQ+ people during the AIDS crisis in the form of Section 28 of the Local Government Act 1988. He co-founded the LGBTQ+ rights lobbying group, Stonewall, joined the Labour Party and later became the country's first openly gay Labour Member of the European Parliament.

DAN REYNOLDS

B. 1987

Imagine Dragons lead singer, Dan Reynolds, was kicked out of a private university in Utah owned by the Church of Jesus Christ of Latter-day Saints for sleeping with his girlfriend of four years. He felt guilt and shame 'for simply loving someone', and says this was one of the first times he felt empathy for LGBTQ+ people. He also felt conflicted with his Mormon faith when his friend came out as gay and Reynolds realised the church saw this as sinful, while he counted his friend as one of the best people he knew.

In 2017, Reynolds, who regularly drapes himself with the Pride rainbow flag when performing in countries where queer people are persecuted, founded LOVELOUD, a foundation and festival that advocates for LGBTQ+ youth. LOVELOUD has provided grants and support to organisations including PFLAG, the Tegan and Sara Foundation (see 24 Sep) and the Human Rights Campaign.

Reynolds donated his childhood home to the advocacy group Encircle in 2021, to be turned into an LGBTQ+ youth centre. When Reynolds appeared on the cover of *Gay Times* in January 2019, he said, 'I think that it's extremely important for straight males especially, who are the most privileged, to speak out and stand up and say, "We need to be better".'

LIZZO

B. 1988

On this date in January 2020, the American singer and classically trained flautist, Lizzo, won three Grammy awards, including Best Urban Contemporary Album for *Cuz I Love You*. Championed by the rock star Prince early in her career in Minneapolis, Lizzo had previously released two studio albums – *Lizzobangers* (2013) and *Big Grrrl Small World* (2015) – on independent record labels.

Lizzo, whose name comes from an amalgamation of a childhood nickname of Lissa and the Jay-Z song 'Izzo', rejects labels and boxes, telling *Gay Times* magazine in 2018, 'Lately, I've been all about erasing those boxes…' She also told *Teen Vogue* that when it comes to sexuality or gender, 'I cannot sit here right now and tell you I'm just one thing. That's why the colours for LGBTQ+ are a rainbow!'

The star champions body positivity and neutrality, so after receiving racist and fatphobic abuse online when she and Cardi B released their video for 'Rumors' in 2021, Lizzo took to her Instagram account to speak out about the hate. A collective retaliation against the abuse resulted in a wave of empowering TikToks that featured women of various body shapes and sizes lip syncing along to 'Rumors' while embracing their bodies.

TOM OF FINLAND

1920-1991

Mention the name Touko Valio Laaksonen to the gay community or people in the art world and it's unlikely to ring any bells. However, ask them about 'Tom of Finland' and it would be a different story. Touko and Tom are one and the same: the Finnish artist who was a master of homoerotic male art.

Laaksonen produced his highly stylised, usually black-and-white, drawings that depicted men with bulging muscles, usually clad in leather, denim or underwear and all with oversised penises, throughout most of the 20th century. Despite his political opposition to the Nazis, his early inspirations were the jackbooted German soldiers stationed in Finland during World War Two.

His early works were published in American gay proto-porn magazines (both physique and glamour publications) and distributed illegally worldwide in sex shops and leather bars until obscenity laws changed and he gained wider exposure. Laaksonen referred to his art as his 'dirty drawings', but he also hoped that one day his work would hang in the Louvre. 'Of course, in a little side gallery that isn't very important, but nevertheless in the Louvre,' he said.

On this date in 2017, the biopic *Tom of Finland*, starring Pekka Strang, premiered at Gothenburg Film Festival.

DAVID STUART

1967-2022

Born on this date in 1967, David Stuart was a sexual health expert and advocate who worked at 56 Dean Street, a sexual health clinic in London that focuses on the needs of the LGBTQI+ community. The clinic has undertaken pioneering work helping queer people struggling with issues around chemsex – sex that takes place under the influence of psychoactive drugs – primarily among groups of men who have sex with men.

As the clinic's substance abuse lead, Stuart played a key role in developing the first chemsex services in the UK and helped many healthcare professionals to understand how to deal with it in a compassionate way that helped others.

When Stuart died in January 2022, the clinic said, 'His work with our patients has undoubtedly saved many lives and his loss is immeasurable.'

Stuart used his own experiences with drugs to inform his work and in 2007 began volunteering at the Antidote Substance Misuse Service, based at London Friend, an LGBTQI+ mental health and wellbeing charity. He went on to speak at conferences, work with countless healthcare professionals and advise governments on the subject. He is often credited with coining the term 'chemsex'.

CHARLIE CRAGGS

B. 1992

Transgender actor and activist Charlie Craggs campaigned for a trans flag emoji to be included as standard. After years of campaigning, setting up an online petition and hijacking the lobster emoji, Charlie Craggs' battle with the Unicode Consortium was finally over on this date in 2020, when the company announced they would be introducing a trans flag emoji later that year.

Until then, Craggs had called for trans people and their allies to use the lobster emoji as a substitute to show the consortium how much use it would get. Why the lobster? 'Lobsters are low-key kinda trans, they are gynandromorphic (can have both male and female characteristics)', she said.

While at the London College of Fashion, Craggs set up Nail Transphobia, an initiative to break down the barriers that trans people face with the wider public. It involved her and other trans people giving manicures to people who wanted to chat with a transgender person. The recipients were encouraged to ask questions – the aim was for them to leave with a better understanding of trans issues and ultimately become an ally.

In October 2017, Craggs edited a collection of essays and letters written by successful trans women, called *To My Trans Sisters*. In the same year, she was listed as one of the 20 female groundbreakers of 2017 by the *Independent* newspaper in the UK.

CHRIS SMITH

B. 1951

'My name is Chris Smith. I'm the Labour MP for Islington South and Finsbury, and I'm gay.' These were the words spoken by Chris Smith in Rugby on 10 November 1984, as he became the first British MP to publicly come out of the closet. Smith was part of a protest outside Rugby town hall to oppose the council removing the words 'sexual orientation' from their Equal Opportunities policy, essentially opening up queer people in the area to discrimination. Smith later described the brave move as being 'one of the scariest ten minutes of my life'.

As Secretary of State for Culture, Media and Sport in Tony Blair's Labour Government, a position he held from May 1997 to June 2001, Smith was invited to a function at Buckingham Palace with his then-partner Dorian Jabri – an unprecedented move for the time.

On this date in 2005, Smith made history again when he came out as HIV positive in the *Sunday Times* newspaper, becoming the first UK political figure to disclose their positive status to the world. Smith said he'd been moved to speak openly after former South African president, Nelson Mandela, spoke about losing his son to AIDS earlier in the month.

LADY GAGA

B. 1986

With millions of record sales, lead roles in television and film, and countless awards, Lady Gaga is one of the most successful artists of our time. Her career took off in 2008 with her successful single, 'Just Dance', followed by her debut album, *The Fame*. This album earned her a first Grammy Award in the Best Electronic/Dance Album category on this date in 2010.

Her song 'Born This Way' is lauded as a gay anthem and Gaga's status as a gay icon has been cemented through her artistry and her LGBTQ+ activism. In 2011, the star met with President Barack Obama's staffers at the White House to discuss bullying prevention after a fan, Jamey Rodemeyer, tweeted his thanks to Lady Gaga in his final post before taking his own life. Gaga and her mother, Cynthia Germanotta, also run the Born This Way Foundation, which empowers and supports the wellness of young people.

Gaga is bisexual and says that her song 'Poker Face' is about 'poker facing with your sexuality'. She has addressed the issue of bi-erasure saying she has been mis-labelled as a straight ally: 'Anyone that wants to twist this into "she says she's bisexual for marketing", this is a f**king lie. This is who I am and who I have always been.'

JOE ORTON

1933–1967

In August 1967, playwright Joe Orton was found dead in his London flat alongside his long-term lover and collaborator, Kenneth Halliwell. Orton had been brutally murdered by Halliwell, who subsequently took an overdose and died with him. Orton had kept diaries that Halliwell alluded to in his suicide note, saying, 'If you read his diary, all will be explained.' However, the last pages appear to be missing as Orton's final diary entry ends mid-sentence.

At a time when it was illegal in the UK, Orton was not only comfortable with his homosexuality, he revelled in it. According to his diaries, he enjoyed a lot of casual sex.

He told his friend, the actor Kenneth Williams (see 7 Mar), to 'stop worrying, have fun while you can, as long as nobody gets hurt it doesn't matter'.

When Orton and Halliwell spent a stint in prison for defacing books in their local library, and were unable to write together, as they had done previously, Orton found his own style. When released, Orton sold his first manuscript and quickly rose to prominence in the West End. He produced multiple dark comedies and farces for the stage, radio and TV. Among these was *Loot*, a play satirising the Catholic Church, first performed on this date in 1965.

RUPAUL CHARLES

B. 1960

In February 2020, RuPaul Charles put American television interviewer Jimmy Fallon in his place when Fallon described her as the first drag queen to emblazon the cover of *Vanity Fair*. '*A drag queen?*' RuPaul screeched, 'I am the *Queen of Drag.*'

While drag didn't start with RuPaul, she can lay claim to bringing it to the masses globally with her show and its countless regional variations, *RuPaul's Drag Race*. The first series premiered on this date in 2009, on the LGBTQ+ channel Logo in the US. A low-budget production made by gay people for gay people, its popularity quickly snowballed and it picked up Emmy, MTV and GLAAD awards along the way.

RuPaul, who is gay and happy with all the pronouns being used to address her, uses her much-revered voice to promote queer and Black rights. While *Drag Race* comes under the guise of a beauty-pageant-style talent competition, its clear aim is to bring important conversations to the mainstream. The show constantly evolves to reflect the attitudes and needs of LGBTQ+ society by changing language and terms used onscreen, and it inclusively allows transitioning and transitioned contestants to compete. Deemed highly entertaining, the programme effortlessly unites joy and skill with complex conversations around homophobia, racism, hate crime and gender identity.

GERTRUDE STEIN & ALICE B. TOKLAS

1874–1946; 1877–1967

Gertrude Stein enjoyed moderate success as a writer until the publication of *The Autobiography of Alice B. Toklas* propelled her into the bestseller category in 1933. The book, written in the voice of Stein's life partner, Alice B. Toklas, was actually more of a biography of Stein herself.

The pair met in Paris in 1907, when Toklas moved to the city after leaving San Francisco, following its devastating earthquake the previous year, and were together until Stein died of cancer in 1946. They made no secret of their relationship and were accepted by their peers, who included artist Pablo Picasso and writer Ernest Hemingway.

Stein's body of work is extensive, and while the Poetry Foundation acknowledges her influence on art and literature, it says she is 'remembered today, largely as an interesting personality whose works are seldom read'.

Born in Pennsylvania, USA on this date in 1874, Stein lived most of her life in Paris, where she and Toklas held weekend literary salons for writers and artists such as Sinclair Lewis and Henri Matisse. The apartment walls were so adorned with art that the *New York Times* called it the 'first museum of modern art'.

BAMBY SALCEDO

B. 1969

In 2015, a queer Latina teen named Jessie Hernandez was shot and killed in an altercation with Denver Police. On this date, a month after the shooting, the Mexican–American transgender activist, Bamby Salcedo, organised for almost 100 trans people and allies to storm the stage at the National LGBTQ Task Force's annual Creating Change event to protest the killings of queer people and to demand solidarity from the entire queer community. 'If you serve us, you need to include us,' she demanded.

Salcedo's early life in Guadalajara, Mexico, was not easy, with abuse, poverty and drugs all prevalent in her upbringing. After spending time in prison and seeking treatment for her drug addiction, Salcedo turned her life

around and set to work helping others. In 2009, along with a group of transgender, gender non-conforming and intersex (TGI) immigrant people, Salcedo set up the TransLatin@ Coalition (TLC) in Los Angeles, California. The organisation works across 10 states in the US with the primary aim of providing access to resources and services that improve the quality of life of TGI people.

Arguably one of Salcedo's most heart-warming initiatives is Angels of Change, a project that annually produces a calendar featuring transgender youth, helping to develop self-presentation skills in a safe, fun environment. The organisation also bolsters confidence and self-esteem with its non-competitive runway show.

SALLY MILLER GEARHART

1931–2021

In the late 1970s, feminist, activist and science-fiction writer Sally Gearhart campaigned with San Francisco city supervisor, Harvey Milk (see 9 Jan), against California's Proposition 6, a measure that planned to ban gay and lesbian teachers from public schools. It was known as the Briggs Initiative, after conservative state legislator, John Briggs, who sponsored the ballot.

Milk and Gearhart worked together against Briggs. When Briggs linked homosexuals to child molestation during a TV debate, Gearhart smacked down his ill-informed opinion with facts, saying, 'it is more than overwhelmingly true that it is the heterosexual men… that are the child molesters'.

While many are aware of Harvey Milk's legacy, thanks to the biopic *Milk* (2008), Gearhart's story is lesser known. However, people are still discovering her story through the 1993 documentary, *Last Call at Maud's*, which premiered on this date. Gearhart is interviewed in the film, which is an exploration of lesbian culture and the closure of the lesbian bar, Maud's, in San Francisco.

Gearhart and her partner, Jane Gurko, lived for many years in an all-female community close to nature and away from the patriarchy in California's redwood forests, echoing her eco-feminist, science-fiction novel, *The Wanderground, Stories of the Hill Women* (1978).

ALAN L. HART

1890–1962

Twenty years before there was an epidemiological test for tuberculosis (TB), Dr Alan L. Hart was championing work that provided early diagnosis for those suffering with the disease, and discovered that its development could be spotted via X-ray. This ultimately saved millions of lives as more sick people were isolated, thereby lowering the rate of infection.

Hart's gender identity and sexuality were in conflict for years, and as he was assigned female at birth, many perceived his relationships with women to be lesbian affairs. Dressing in masculine clothes and with short hair since childhood, Hart finally received gender confirmation surgery in 1918.

Hart had moved around to avoid his previous identity being discovered, but on this date in 1918 was outed as transgender by the *Spokesman Review*. He found stability with his second wife Enda Ruddick, with whom he remained until his death.

Hart became a successful writer, producing medical novels, such as *The Undaunted* (1936) and *In the Lives of Men* (1937), some of which, boldly for the time, featured queer characters. His literary work was celebrated in 2002 when an exhibition entitled 'The Lives of Men: A Literary Glimpse at the Life of Alberta Lucille Hart / Dr. Alan L. Hart' was held in Portland, Oregon.

JONATHAN MCDONALD VAN NESS

B. 1987

Jonathan McDonald Van Ness (JVN) is familiar to audiences for his role as grooming extraordinaire on the show *Queer Eye*, which first aired on Netflix on this date in 2018.

He was the first male cheerleader at his high school in Quincy, Illinois, and despite being bullied there, he says, 'Really, I think I've always felt comfortable in my skin. It was learning how to deal with other people's reactions to it that took me a minute to get used to.' In his book, *Over the Top*, he talks candidly about his experiences with sexual abuse, sex work, eating disorders and drug abuse. He came out as HIV positive in 2019 and fights to destigmatise and humanise living with the disease by talking about it openly.

Before he rose to fame in *Queer Eye*, Van Ness starred in the web series parody *Gay of Thrones*. The idea arose when he hilariously recapped an episode of TV show *Game of Thrones* in the salon for his client Erin Gibson, who worked with independent comedy studio Funny or Die. Van Ness was only supposed to create one episode, but its popularity ensured that he continued it for years.

KRISTEN STEWART

B. 1990

When Kristen Stewart and her co-star, Robert Pattinson, signed up to star in the *Twilight* saga – what they thought would be a series of indie movies – they didn't anticipate the meteoric rise to fame that the films brought them. Stewart played a teenager (Bella) caught in a love triangle between a werewolf (Taylor Lautner) and a vampire (Robert Pattinson).

Yet, despite the film grossing $69.6 million in its first weekend in the US and Canada, reception for Stewart was mixed. The director later pointed out that this was largely down to 'a huge chunk of the fan base [being] young women and they all wanted to be Bella'.

Years later, Stewart received a very different response to her role as Princess Diana (see 16 Feb) in the film *Spencer*, when she was nominated for an Academy Award on this date in 2022. The *Guardian* newspaper lauded her as 'entirely compelling in the title role' and *USA Today* congratulated her on 'a stellar performance'.

Between playing these two roles, Stewart openly declared she was bisexual, saying she had previously felt a lot of pressure to define her sexuality. She also publicly clarified that 'You're not confused if you're bisexual. It's not confusing at all.'

EVE ADAMS

1891–1943

In 1927, the acting chairman of the US Immigration Service's Board of Review recommended that Eve Adams be deported. Adams, born Chawa Zloczower in Poland, had emigrated to the US in 1912 and settled in New York City. The official reason logged for her deportation, which eventually took place at the end of the year, was 'Disorderly Conduct' and was a result of Adams writing and distributing 'indecent' literature. The US government viewed her as an agitator.

In February 1925, Adams distributed copies of her book *Lesbian Love*, a collection of short stories about women she had met on her travels. All copies of the book, one of the earliest examples of American lesbian literature, were thought to be lost until 1999, when college student Nina Alvarez found a copy in her apartment building.

Adams, also known as Eva Kotchever, held literary salons, called Eve's Hangouts, where lesbians would meet and read poetry. After her deportation to Poland, Adams moved to Paris where she met the German cabaret singer Hella Olstein Soldner. The pair spent the rest of their days together until they were arrested by Nazis, sent to Auschwitz concentration camp and tragically never heard of again. The Parisian street, Rue Eva Kotchever, is named after the writer.

JODIE FOSTER

B. 1962

The sight of Jodie Foster accepting a Golden Globe, while sitting on her sofa with her wife and dog, wearing her Prada pyjamas, was the perfect antidote to the depressing virtual awards ceremonies that the coronavirus pandemic generated in 2021. When she thanked and then kissed her wife, it was the normalisation of a happy, queer celebrity family that lit up screens across the globe.

Foster has had a long and illustrious career in films, which began with her first significant role playing a pre-teen prostitute in *Taxi Driver*, in 1976. On this date the following year, she received her first nomination for an Academy Award for this role and she later went on to win Oscars for playing a rape survivor in *The Accused* (1988) and FBI trainee Clarice Starling in *The Silence of the Lambs* (1991). Foster has also worked as a director for both TV and film.

In January 2013, when she accepted her Cecil B. DeMille award at the Golden Globes, Foster came out publicly. Seemingly out in her private life for many years, this public declaration by a generally very private actress was clearly an important personal milestone for Foster, who continues to have a successful career.

JUSTICE MICHAEL KIRBY

B. 1939

On this date in 2019, former Australian High Court judge Michael Kirby married his partner Johan van Vloten in a civil ceremony in Sydney. The pair had met exactly 50 years to the day before at one of Sydney's few gay venues, in 1969.

In 1996, humanitarian Kirby became the first openly gay judge appointed to the High Court of Australia, the highest court in the country. In office, he earned the nickname 'Great Dissenter', due to his high rate of disagreement with colleagues — more than 50 per cent in constitutional cases.

In 2013, Kirby lead a major inquiry into human rights abuses in North Korea, as part of the UN Human Rights Council. He stated 'a country which so grossly abuses the human rights of its people is inevitably an unstable danger to its neighbours, the region and the world'.

Kirby was out before New South Wales decriminalised homosexuality, which led to some homophobic criticism. In 2002, Senator Bill Heffernan accused him of 'trawling for rent boys'. When this was proved to be a lie, Justice Kirby accepted Heffernan's apology with dignity, saying, '[I] reach out my hand in a spirit of reconciliation. I hope my ordeal will show the wrongs that hate of homosexuals can lead to.'

ETHEL WATERS

1896–1977

After an impoverished childhood, the African American singer and actress Ethel Waters went on to become adored by millions as one of the highest-paid actresses on Broadway, having begun her career singing in Baltimore when she was just a teenager.

Her popularity grew quickly and when she moved to New York City in 1925, she soon became one of the most sought-after Black stars of Broadway.

The star was thrice married to men, the first time when she was just 13 years old, yet she also had relationships with women. Waters was also part of the Harlem Renaissance, a collective of artists, writers and thinkers, of whom many were queer. In the 1920s she was well known in Harlem's lesbian circles, but as her fame grew, she became more discreet, perhaps mindful of her career, and she never publicly acknowledged her lesbianism.

Not only was Waters a success on stage and in music, but she also transferred her talents to film and television, and became the first African American to star in her own television show when *The Ethel Waters Show* aired in 1939. She also became the second African American woman to receive an Oscar nomination, on this date in 1950, for the film *Pinky*.

CHRISTOPHER ISHERWOOD

1904–1986

'Willkommen! Bienvenue! Welcome! Im cabaret, au cabaret, to cabaret!' Novelist, and playwright Christopher Isherwood, embodied queer identity in much of his work. Born in Cheshire, UK, Isherwood studied at the University of Cambridge but was asked to leave in 1925, after writing joke answers in his exam papers. From there, Isherwood travelled in Europe, Asia and the Americas, forging numerous friendships and love affairs that would inform and underpin much of his future work.

In 1951, John Van Druten's play *I Am Camera* – an adaptation of Isherwood's semi auto-biographical novel *Goodbye to Berlin* – opened on Broadway, featuring the character Sally Bowles in the Berlin Kit Kat Klub. This inspired the Kander and Ebb musical, *Cabaret*, which opened in 1966. The show won eight Tony Awards and was later adapted into the movie *Cabaret*, released on this date in 1972. The film, directed by Bob Fosse and with Liza Minnelli in the lead role, won eight Academy Awards.

Just before he turned 50, Isherwood fell in love with Don Bachardy, a young college student from LA. Their relationship would inspire Isherwood's masterpiece novel, *A Single Man*, later made into a film by Tom Ford (see 11 Dec). Bachardy and Isherwood remained lovers until the writer's death in 1986.

XIAN

B. 1989

Homosexuality has only been legal in China since 1997 and the Chinese Society of Psychiatry classified it as a mental disorder up until 2001. Despite these changes, most queer people still struggle for acceptance from their families in China and same-sex marriage is not recognised.

For these reasons, many LGBTQ+ activists in the country operate underground, use aliases or try to fly under the radar. Xian is one such person. If you search for the lesbian activist online, you won't find much information.

However, over the years, Xian has set up online and in-person networks for queer people to connect. She founded Tongyu (meaning 'Common Language' in English), the most famous and authoritative lesbian organisation in mainland China, which now offers support and resources to other queer organisations across the country.

As well as helping to organise the Beijing Lala Salon, which offers cultural activities to the lesbian community there, Xian also helped set up the Beijing LGBT Center, founded on this date in 2008.

ALLA NAZIMOVA

1879-1945

The debate about whether only queer actors can play queer parts authentically is ongoing, and many productions now involve an all-LGBTQ+ ensemble. However, when Russian actress Alla Nazimova enlisted an all-queer cast and crew for her film adaptation of Oscar Wilde's *Salomé*, released on this date in 1923, it was considered a very bold move.

The actress, who moved to the US in 1905 and quickly became a Broadway star, was open about her relationships with women, despite her faux marriage to fellow gay actor Charles Bryant. Theirs was a lavender marriage — a term used in Hollywood at the time for marriages of convenience when actors and/or studios wanted to hide the sexualities of stars.

Nazimova briefly became one of the highest-paid actresses in Hollywood films, but the Motion Picture Production Code of 1930 extinguished her light. It banned anything viewed as immoral, and Nazimova's risqué style and persona, including the parties she held for Hollywood lesbians at her home on Sunset Boulevard, became too much of a liability for the studios.

Nazimova is credited with coining the covert term 'Sewing Circle', used to refer to the group of queer Hollywood women including actresses such as Greta Garbo and Tallulah Bankhead.

DIANA, PRINCESS OF WALES

1961–1997

Diana Spencer, Princess of Wales was the first wife of King Charles III (then Prince Charles) and was perhaps the first member of the British royal family who was an out and proud LGBTQ+ ally.

In April 1987, the princess opened the UK's first HIV/AIDs unit at London's Middlesex Hospital, famously speaking to and greeting patients with a handshake. One such handshake was photographed by the media and featured in newspapers across the globe. This simple, human gesture helped break down stigma, changed people's attitudes to the disease and provided a welcome morale boost to the gay community during its darkest days.

The princess visited HIV/AIDs patients in both the UK and US. On this date in 1993, Diana gave a powerful speech about the 'aching loneliness and rejection' of those with AIDS to delegates at the First Management Forum Conference on AIDS in London.

Both the princess's sons have carried on their mother's legacy as an LGBTQ+ ally. In 2016, William became the first member of the British royal family to be photographed for the cover of a gay publication, and in 2019 Harry worked with Mermaids, a charity that supports transgender youth.

PROUD ALLY

MISS MAJOR GRIFFIN-GRACY

B. 1940

'Fuck my shoes. Put on my dress,' says Miss Major Griffin-Gracy as she explains her fatigue at people thinking they understand what it's like to walk a mile in her shoes. 'Wear my hair… run from the police by leaping over cars, changing clothes while you're running so that you're dressed different… and they don't recognize you.'

Born in Chicago, Miss Major Griffin-Gracy came out to her parents as trans around 12 years of age. When they kicked her out, she left Chicago and became part of the trans community in New York City, where she took part in the Stonewall riots. She believes the Stonewall uprising was historically whitewashed by cis white gays and lesbians, wanting to erase the Black and Brown transgender women who fought for justice.

Griffin-Gracy has helped countless trans women rebuild their lives after incarceration and as a former executive director of the Transgender, Gender Variant and Intersex Justice Project (TGIJP), advocated for incarcerated transgender people. In February 2021 the organisation Decriminalize Sex Work proclaimed Major their hero of the month.

Her legacy project is House of GG. Opened in 2018, it is a permanent home in Arkansas where transgender people can come, feel safe and be part of a trans community working for social justice.

AUDRE LORDE

1934-1992

'Black, lesbian, mother, warrior, poet.' This is how librarian, lecturer, human rights activist and poet, Audre Lorde, described herself. Born on this date in 1934, in New York, Lorde published her first poem in *Seventeen* magazine while still at high school. She went on to write many books, poems and essays that dealt with race, class, sexuality and gender.

Lorde's work dealt with the intersectionality of her identity as a Black lesbian feminist mother, and called on people (white feminists, in particular) to confront racism and oppression, and to celebrate difference rather than simply tolerate it. Speaking about the fight for queer rights for *everyone* in the community, Lorde pointed out 'there is no such thing as a single-issue struggle, because we do not live single-issue lives'.

Among many accolades, Lorde won a National Book award for *A Burst of Light* in 1989, and was made poet laureate of New York from 1991–1992. She documented her experience of breast cancer in *The Cancer Journals* in 1980. Heralded as a milestone in illness narrative publishing, Pulitzer Prize-winning author, Alice Walker said of it, 'This book teaches me that with one breast or none, I am still me.' Lorde suffered with cancer for many years and died aged just 58.

DAVID BOWIE

1947–2016

British singer, songwriter, actor and trailblazer of glam rock, David Bowie released his 26th and final studio album, *Blackstar*, on his 69th birthday in 2016. Sadly, two days later he died.

Bowie was well-known for his constant reinventions and performances as characters or alter-egos. Perhaps his most famous incarnation was as the gender-bending alien rock star Ziggy Stardust. Wearing make-up and extraordinary outfits, Bowie's characters would blur the lines of gender and sexuality. This was groundbreaking for a male star at the time, with only a handful of other glam rock artists, like Marc Bolan, trying out similar styles.

In line with this ambiguity, he told the music magazine *Melody Maker* that he was gay but told *Playboy* he was bisexual. Later, he said he'd regretted coming out as bisexual as it affected his career in America. While his first wife Angie supports his claims of bisexuality, some journalists would continue to ask the star for clarification on the subject for years.

As well as producing a huge back catalogue of music, Bowie acted, produced music and collaborated with musical icons such as Mick Jagger, Bing Crosby and Queen. On this date in 2014, Bowie became the oldest person ever to receive a Brit Award for Best British Male.

PAUL FAIRWEATHER

B. 1957

When Paul Fairweather visited bars and clubs in Manchester's gay village in 1988, asking them to turn off their music so he could speak, he wasn't immediately popular with the revellers there. However, once they heard what he had to say about Margaret Thatcher's Tory government's plan to introduce the legislation that became known as Section 28 and prohibited the 'promotion of homosexuality', they listened intently.

At the time, Fairweather worked for Manchester City Council as one of their Gay Men's Officers, helping the LGBTQ+ community with city services and ensuring the needs of gay people in the city were being acknowledged. Along with a group of activists from the North West Campaign for Lesbian and Gay Equality, Fairweather organised and promoted a protest against Section 28. On this date in 1988, the march took place through Manchester City Centre with 20,000 people in attendance – one of the biggest LGBTQ+ rallies the UK has ever seen.

Fairweather recalled that the protest organisers used to meet in a secret office in the town hall attic. 'We were in a local government office, organising a demonstration against the government...' he said. 'What we were doing was completely illegal.'

RIKKI BEADLE-BLAIR

B. 1961

In May 2021, the *Guardian* newspaper ran a piece about the British filmmaker Rikki Beadle-Blair, with the headline 'The brilliant stage and screen writer who should be a household name'. They were referring to the fact that he remains relatively unknown, despite writing, directing, producing and starring in countless productions throughout his 40-year career.

Beadle-Blair, who is gay, wrote the screenplay for *Stonewall*, the 1996 film that centres around a group of queer characters with multiple ethnicities in New York in the weeks leading up to the Stonewall riots. Putting drag queens and non-binary people of colour front and centre of the film, Beadle-Blair's script is considered to be more representative than Roland Emmerich's 2015 film of the same name.

On this date in 2001, Beadle-Blair's pioneering TV show, *Metrosexuality*, aired on Channel 4 in the UK. It was groundbreaking for the plethora of sexualities it represented, as well featuring racially diverse, gender nonconforming and disabled characters.

In 2016, when Beadle-Blair was awarded an MBE, he felt conflicted about whether to accept it but in the end he did, saying, 'When I recommend a writer, and I've got MBE after my name, it helps them get grants and interviews, and it helps them get seen.'

CARLOTTA

B. 1943

When Australian soap opera *Number 96* first aired in 1972, it launched with the infamous tagline 'Tonight, Australian TV loses its virginity'. While the show was racy and its storylines led with shock, it can be credited with featuring LGBTQ+ characters well before its British and American contemporaries. One such character was Robyn Ross, played by transgender showgirl Carlotta. Her first appearance was on this date in 1973, and while her stint in the show was brief, it was groundbreaking when the character told her onscreen partner that she was 'not a girl'.

Carlotta, also known as Carol Byron, was already part of the famous showgirl dance troupe, Les Girls, in Sydney's Kings Cross area before her stint in *Number 96*. Her profile grew and led to the Les Girls show bosses (falsely) advertising her as the recipient of 'Australia's first sex change!'

Carlotta became a national star, at one point leaving Les Girls and performing in her own half-a-million-dollar stage production. She wrote her autobiography and a TV movie was made about her life, but perhaps one of her biggest legacies goes uncredited, as she and others will tell you that she was a major inspiration for the Oscar-winning film *The Adventures of Priscilla, Queen of the Desert* (1994).

RUSSELL T DAVIES

B. 1963

On this date in 1999, UK's Channel 4 aired a daring new commission. Russell T Davies' seminal queer drama, *Queer As Folk*, grabbed headlines and courted controversy from the start – a scene in its first episode led Becks beer to drop its sponsorship of the show.

The first of its kind, the drama revolved around characters in the Manchester Gay Village who were almost all LGBTQ+. The show offered cultural reference points and representation historically denied to the LGBTQ+ community and in a time before gay marriage, depicted strong friendships and had chosen families at its heart. It grew in cult status and put Davies firmly on the map as an unashamed writer of quality queer drama.

As well as a two-part second series for *QAF*, Channel 4 commissioned Davies' to write *Cucumber*, another drama centred around LGBTQ+ characters. He later moved to the BBC to help resurrect *Dr Who* and in 2019 penned the dystopian drama *Years and Years*.

Davies has spoken about how he tries to cast gay actors in gay roles. He did this in *It's A Sin* (2021), the critically acclaimed drama starring Olly Alexander (see 22 Jan), set during the AIDS epidemic of the 1980s and 1990s.

ELVIRA SCHEMUR (ELYA)

2000-2022

The war in Ukraine began on this date in 2022. In March 2022, a Russian missile struck a regional administration building in Kharkiv, Ukraine and killed 21-year-old Elvira Schemur (often known as Elya), who was volunteering there. Schemur was a Ukrainian law student and an LGBTQ+ activist, who took part in three Kharkiv Prides and was reported to be 'actively engaged in human rights interventions'.

In February 2022 Ukrainians were forced to defend their country against Vladimir Putin's army, as Russia invaded. LGBTQ+ citizens lived in fear of what would happen next, with the shadow of the Russian regime's homophobia looming over them. Speaking about the war in his country, openly gay Ukrainian soldier Viktor Pylypenko said he believed 'Russians had drawn up a "kill list" targeting LGBTQ activists in Ukraine. The first thing Russia will do is rid civil society of activists... Human rights are the number one enemy for Putin's regime.'

Maksym Eristavi, a board member of Kyiv Pride, remembered Schemur as 'an activist and a patriot', who participated in 'all possible actions and democratic events of Kharkiv'. As tributes poured in for Schemur, she was described as a 'kickass volunteer', 'brave and courageous' and as someone who motivated those around her.

CLAUDE CAHUN

1894-1954

When the *New York Times* featured Claude Cahun in their 2019 series of 'Overlooked Obituaries,' profiling people whose deaths they'd not reported, it highlighted their gender ambiguity, saying, 'Here she's a man. There she's a woman. Sometimes she's a little of both.' Cahun, born Lucy Renee Mathilde Schwob, was a French Surrealist whose photographic, sculpture and written work challenged gender and sexual norms.

It is thought that Cahun's photographic works were mostly collaborations with their long-term partner Marcel Moore (born Suzanne Malherbe), as Cahun set up scenes and posed in front of the camera while Moore operated it. The pair fled from France to Jersey in 1938, and there they worked together as resistance fighters during World War Two, distributing anti-Nazi propaganda in the form of poetry and literature, signed as '*der Soldat ohne Namen*' ('the soldier with no name'). In 1944, their activities were discovered and they were imprisoned and sentenced to death. Luckily, they escaped execution when the island was liberated from Nazi occupation in 1945.

For years, Cahun's work remained rarely seen or discussed, but it has enjoyed renewed interest in the 21st century. In 2012, an exhibition of their work began in Paris and travelled to Barcelona before opening in Chicago on this date.

FRANKIE KNUCKLES

1955–2014

When *Rolling Stone* magazine wrote about the death of Frankie Knuckles on its website, there were many accolades for the DJ/producer, including 'Godfather of House Music' and 'one of the dozen most important DJs of all time'.

Born in the Bronx as Francis Warren Nicholls, Jr, Knuckles began DJing in New York City in the 1970s before moving to Chicago and honing his style at the Warehouse. His sets became hugely popular, widening the audience of the club, which had predominantly been Black, gay men, like himself, and House Music was born – the name coming from a shortened form of 'Warehouse'.

In 1983, Knuckles opened his own club, the Power Plant, and by the mid-80s he began recording and releasing music, primarily on the independent label, Trax Records. He worked with Jamie Principle on *Your Love*, which later became the foundation of the Candi Staton and The Source hit, *You Got The Love*.

After a stint in London, Knuckles moved back to New York and formed Def Mix Productions with David Morales. He worked with many big 80s and 90s stars, including Michael Jackson, Chaka Khan, En Vogue and Diana Ross. On this date in 1997, Knuckles was awarded the Grammy for Remixer of the Year, Non-Classical.

CECILIA CHUNG

B. 1965

Cecilia Chung, a transgender immigrant from Hong Kong, who has worked with the LGBTQ+ and HIV communities in San Francisco for over 40 years, says that as a teenager she thought she might be gay but by the time she was 22, she realised she was actually transgender.

Chung has an impressive CV, which includes being appointed to the Presidential Advisory Council on HIV/AIDS by President Barack Obama in 2013. Prior to this she was the first transgender woman and first Asian person to be elected to the Board of Directors of the San Francisco Lesbian, Gay, Bisexual, and Transgender Pride Celebration committee.

Chung was also a member of San Francisco's Transgender Discrimination Task Force in the 1990s, and in 2005 became the first Deputy Director of the Transgender Law Center, the largest American transgender-led civil rights organisation in the US.

Chung's achievements seem all the more remarkable given that when she began transitioning in 1992, she lost her job, was made homeless and became a sex worker to survive. Her incredible story inspired a character in the docudrama series, produced by Gus Van Sant and Dustin Lance Black, *When We Rise*, which premiered on TV on this date in 2017.

LUIZ MOTT

B. 1946

Luiz Mott founded the first queer support group in Bahia on this date in 1980, called Grupo Gay da Bahia (Gay Group of Bahia). It offers help and advice to LGBTQ+ people in the Brazilian state and organises events such as Pride. The organisation also publishes regular statistics on LGBTQ+ murders in Brazil; in 2017, it found that a queer person was killed every 25 hours in the country. The information it gathers is instrumental in bringing visibility to homophobic attitudes and violence in Brazil because there are no government statistics on hate crimes.

Openly gay since the 1970s, Mott is an expert in anthropology and has written extensively on Afro—Brazilian culture, the history of religion, AIDS, homosexuality and homophobia. He believes he has found evidence of homosexual desire in a number of indigenous Brazilian tribes. In 1993, he published a biography of Rosa Egipcíaca da Vera Cruz – an enslaved African-born woman who wrote *Sacred Theology of the Love of the God of Light Shining in the Pilgrim Souls* in the 1700s, the oldest book written by a Black woman in Brazil.

In 1995, Mott was awarded the Felipa de Souza Award by the International Gay and Lesbian Human Rights Commission, in recognition of his activism.

PEDRO PABLO ZAMORA

1972–1994

In 1994, 21-year-old Pedro Zamora, born on this date, moved into a house with six other housemates to have their daily lives filmed for the MTV reality show: *The Real World: San Francisco*.

Following a diagnosis aged 17, Zamora was HIV positive and even before his exposure on the show brought widespread awareness of him and his illness, he was an educator on the subject, giving lectures in schools, speaking on radio and TV shows, and even testifying at Congress.

Zamora was chosen out of more than 25,000 applicants to live in front of the camera. Jon Murray, co-executive producer of the show recalled, 'We've hit the jackpot. Not only is this kid HIV positive, but he can speak eloquently of it.' The series ran for 20 episodes from June 1994 and brought international attention to the realities of HIV/AIDS and LGBTQ+ issues. Zamora was the first person to be featured on a reality TV show living openly with the disease and his commitment ceremony to his partner Sean Sasser, which also featured on the show, was the first same-sex ceremony shown on American TV.

Sadly, Zamora died shortly after the last episode of *The Real World: San Francisco* aired.

ALAN BELL

1970–1990

At its height, *BLK* was a monthly magazine for LGBTQ+ African Americans distributed right across the US and into Canada. It started out as a small newsletter, put together by graphic designer Alan Bell for the members of his Black gay man's safer-sex club, Black Jack, in Los Angeles.

Bell had previously published the weekly gay and lesbian newspaper *Gaysweek* (between 1977 and 1979) in New York, and after relocating to LA and opening Black Jack, he realised the need for printed matter on local venues and HIV information for the Black LGBTQ+ community.

Bell's first foray into printing and design came as a child, when he watched his father use a hand press for business cards at his kitchen table. He went on to study journalism at high school and later became the editor of his school's newspaper.

When asked about the legacy of *BLK*, whose last issue was published on this date in 1994, Bell said he hoped that in 5,000 years' time people would read the magazine and 'there will be some record, some sense of... Black gay and lesbian people who lived in this time... That a record of our activities... what we did... will be there, in the future, for future people to see.'

LEYNA BLOOM

B. 1993

In July 2021, model and actress Leyna Bloom became the first transgender woman to feature on the cover of the American magazine, *Sports Illustrated*. Chicago-born Bloom, who has a Filipina mother and an African-American father, dedicated her cover appearance to 'all ballroom femme queens past, present and future'.

When she was chosen for the role of Wye (a trangender woman in the New York ballroom community) in the movie *Port Authority* in 2019, her real-life associations with the ballroom scene contributed to the credibility of the film. Co-casting director, Damian Bao, said, 'There's nothing more authentic to pay tribute than to cast someone from that community and she embodies the spirit of the character.'

In April 2018, Bloom took to Twitter in a campaign to become Victoria's Secret's first trans lingerie model. She called out the brand's lack of representation of not just trans models but also models with curves and models of colour. While Bloom's wish to model for Victoria's Secret has so far been unsuccessful, on this date in 2019 she featured as part of the Tommy Hilfiger X Zendaya SS19 show in Paris. It featured an all-black runway cast, including singer Grace Jones, with Bloom as the only transgender woman of colour to walk Paris Fashion Week that season.

ADOLF BRAND

1874–1945

Delve into queer history in pre-Nazi Germany, and the likelihood is that you'll soon come across the sexologist Magnus Hirschfeld and his Scientific-Humanitarian Committee, the first public homosexual rights organisation to exist. However, the lesser-known publisher, writer and anarchist, Adolf Brand, was also an important queer figure in Germany around the same time.

Brand created and published the magazine *Der Eigene* (*The Unique*), thought to be the first regular homosexual periodical, running from this date in 1896 to 1931, when the rise of the Nazis made it too risky to continue publishing. The magazine was dedicated to 'masculine culture' and love between men, made up of literature, poems, art and essays.

Brand advocated for pederasty – physical love between a younger and older man, such as was common in ancient Greece, where they believed it was the epitome of masculinity and brotherly love. Brand and his peers rejected the psychological and medical model used to describe same-sex relations that Hirschfeld used, often associated with femininity.

Brand also founded Gemeinschaft der Eigenen, an organisation for like-minded men who took part in camping and trekking, and sometimes nudism. Popular in 1920s Germany, this evolved into Freikörperkultur, a culture advocating the health benefits of nudism under sports teacher Adolf Koch.

ERIC MARCUS

B. 1958

'I think about the stories that I captured for *Making Gay History* – for my original book – and what would have happened if I hadn't recorded them. Most of them would not have been remembered,' says Eric Marcus about his vast audio collection of interviews with iconic queer activists. Luckily, he did keep them after publishing his book in 1992, and turned them into a seminal podcast and website on queer history, with the same name.

Marcus interviewed many people in this book, including Sylvia Rivera (see 24 Jun), Hal Call (see 30 Nov) and Jean O'Leary (see 11 Oct), and in doing so captured a unique record of American LGBTQ+ history.

Of the podcast he says, 'People who listen have a chance to find out who their ancestors were.' He donated his entire *Making Gay History* research collection to the New York Public Library with the agreement that they digitise it.

Marcus has authored numerous books, including *Breaking the Surface*, the *New York Times*' bestselling biography of gay Olympic diver Greg Louganis (see 8 Aug), which was published on this date in 1995.

In 2016, Marcus founded the Stonewall 50 Consortium, which brings together non-profit institutions and organisations that produce programmes, exhibitions and educational materials related to LGBTQ+ history and culture.

TRUMAN CAPOTE

1924–1984

Truman Capote lived his life as an openly gay man and was never one to shy away from notoriety. He moved in celebrity circles, mixing with actors, authors and royalty, and sustained a long-term, on-off, relationship with fellow novelist and playwright, Jack Dunphy, for most of his life.

Breakfast at Tiffany's (1958) is arguably Truman Capote's most famous novella. Later made into a hugely successful film starring Audrey Hepburn, Capote reportedly hated the film, primarily because he had wanted Marilyn Monroe to play the lead.

Capote spent six years writing another of his most famous works, *In Cold Blood*.

The 1966 novel tells the true story of the murder of the Clutter family from Kansas. Capote interviewed police, friends and neighbours of the four victims, and once published, the book became an instant bestseller and came to define the non-fiction novel. Writing it took a huge toll on Capote. He said, 'It scraped me right down to the marrow of my bones. It nearly killed me. I think, in a way, it did kill me.'

The biopic *Capote* largely focused on the writing of *Cold Blood*, and Philip Seymour Hoffman won an Academy Award for his portrayal of the author on this date in 2005.

MICHELANGELO BUONARROTI

1475–1564

Michelangelo was born in the Republic of Florence on this date in 1475. As was common for artists at the time, he worked in various mediums, expressing his art through painting, drawing, architecture and poetry. The artist considered himself primarily a sculptor.

One of his most famous sculptures is *David* (1501–04), an enormous, beautiful marble statue of the biblical figure, David, which originally stood in front of the entrance of the Palazzo Vecchio. Along with many other Michelangelo sculptures, this can now be viewed in the Galleria dell'Accademia in Florence.

Michelangelo's painting on the ceiling of the Sistine Chapel stretches 500 square metres, took four years to complete (1508–1512) and is viewed by around five million visitors a year.

It is now widely believed that Michelangelo was gay, with historians citing the hundreds of love poems he wrote to Tommaso dei Cavalieri, a nobleman in his twenties who he met in Rome, as evidence. Michelangelo, who never married, would pair the poems with homoerotic drawings and gift them to Tommaso. The artist's love of the male form is evident in his work and in 2015 an Italian LGBTQ+ tour company began offering tours of the Vatican focusing on the sexualities of Michelangelo and his peers.

KENNETH WILLIAMS

1926-1988

Kenneth Williams' voice was particularly unique for someone born and educated in working-class north London. His phrases such as 'Ooh Matron' and 'Stop messing about!' were instantly recognisable, and on the BBC radio show, *Hancock's Half Hour*, he entertained audiences with his comical character voices for years. His face later became known to the masses from his regular appearances in the *Carry On* films, in which his camp innuendos were a standard.

Diaries that Williams kept for over 40 years were published after his death, largely confirming that he lived an almost asexual life, with a string of unconsummated relationships documented. His last diary entry was famously made on the night of his death in April 1988, when he overdosed on barbiturates, and read 'Oh – what's the bloody point?'

On the radio show, *Round the Horne*, which first aired on this date in 1965, Williams and fellow performer Hugh Paddick brought the secret gay language of Polari to the masses via the dialogue of their characters, Julian and Sandy. At times, the show boasted listening figures of up to 20 million – some of whom were aware of what they were listening to and some who definitely were not.

LI TINGTING

B. 1989

Li Tingting is a queer feminist and LGBTQ+ rights activist in China, a country where she has had her phone tapped, police have turned up at her parents' house and her activities have led to time in prison.

Tingting's work has included trying to change the rape culture in China, where there is not just a lack of support for victims, they are stigmatised as well. She has also walked through the streets of Beijing dressed in a wedding dress splattered with blood, carrying a placard reading 'Love is not an excuse for violence' to protest against domestic violence.

Tingting planned to campaign against sexual harassment on public transport, by putting stickers on buses and trains across Chinese cities to coincide with International Women's Day on this date in 2015. However, Tingting and four other women activists were arrested the day before, interrogated for 24 hours and then held in a detention centre for 37 days.

Tingting's plight garnered international attention for the issues she campaigns for, with even Hillary Clinton tweeting her support. Later that year, the first legislation against domestic violence was passed in the country, finally putting the law on the side of abused women in China.

JAMES DEAN

1931–1955

James Dean had one of the most short-lived careers of any Hollywood star, appearing in just three films over a period of less than two years. His untimely end came when he collided with another car at an intersection in California and he died, aged 24.

At the time of his death, only one of his films, *East of Eden* (1955), had been released, premiering in New York on this date in 1955. His iconic portrayal of disaffected youth in this movie, and also in *Rebel Without A Cause* (1955), became the defining representation of the troubled American teenager. Dean had crafted his art around this new movement of young adulthood emerging after World War Two

that was setting the tone for fashion, popular music, TV and films.

Dean's sexuality has long been debated. Some biographers claim he was bisexual, others believe he was gay but in the closet, while some even paint him as a sex worker or say he had sadomasochistic sexual relationships with older men. Screenwriter William Bast claims the pair had an on-off relationship and were about to move in together before Dean died. Despite the diverse views of Dean, what seems undeniable is an appetite for life, and given the absence of his voice due to his early death, no doubt the speculations continue.

RON AUSTIN

1929–2019

When members of CAMP (Campaign Against Moral Persecution) were thinking of organising a political protest in 1978, it was Ron Austin, born on this date in 1929, who came up with the idea of a street party. What took place later that year was the origin of the Sydney Gay and Lesbian Mardi Gras.

The group of marchers (now known as the 78ers, after the year the first march took place) gathered at Taylor Square in Sydney on 24 June, with little more than a sound system mounted on the back of a truck. They marched the streets until police confiscated the truck and began not only arresting but also beating the participants. Afterwards, the names, addresses and occupations of those arrested were published in the *Sydney Morning Herald*, which lead to many losing their jobs and accommodation.

Throughout his life, Austin remained an active member of CAMP, as well as the Gay Task Force and the Pride History Group. He was also a founding member of 'Phone a Friend', an LGBTQ+ phone counselling service that still exists today as QLife.

Austin marched annually in the Sydney Mardi Gras Parade until his death. The Ron Austin Award for best float is awarded annually in his honour.

LORRAINE HANSBERRY

1930–1965

On this date in 1959, history was made when the play *A Raisin in the Sun* by Lorraine Hansberry, opened on Broadway — the first play by an African American woman to be produced there. Hansberry, then 28, went on to become the youngest American and the first Black playwright to win a New York Critics' Circle award for the show. The play tells of a Black family's struggle against racism, and drew on the experiences of harassment Hansberry and her family endured when they moved to a white neighbourhood in Chicago in 1938.

Throughout her life Hansberry was active in the Black civil rights movement and campaigned for human rights internationally. She also wrote for *Freedom*, the Harlem-based leftist newspaper focused on Black issues from 1950. Her second play, *The Sign in Sidney Brustein's Window*, featuring themes of homosexuality and suicide, premiered in 1964.

In 1957, the year she separated from her husband, publisher Robert Nemiroff, Hansberry began contributing letters to the *Ladder*, the magazine of the lesbian group, Daughters of Bilitis. Some historians see these letters, along with Handberry's 'Notes on Self' where she lists 'My Homosexuality' as something 'What I Love' and 'What I hate', as the playwright's admission to being a 'heterosexually married lesbian.'

JOSH HUTCHERSON

B. 1992

Josh Hutcherson is an actor and producer best-known for his role as Peeta Mellark in the *Hunger Games* film series. Hutcherson, who describes himself as 'mostly straight' but believes 'defining yourself as 100 per cent anything is kind of near-sighted and close-minded', is also an LGBTQ+ advocate. He has said that having gay uncles who died of AIDS around the time he was born inspired him to be a supporter of gay rights.

The actor has worked with multiple organisations that help the queer community, including Straight But Not Narrow. This grassroots, non-profit organisation focuses on educating straight youth and young adults to positively influence their perception of, and behaviour towards, their LGBTQ+ peers. On this date in 2011, Hutcherson appeared in a Straight But Not Narrow video launching their first campaign. Driven by the fact that more than half of closeted LGBTQ+ youth in America use the internet to connect with fellow LGBTQ+ individuals, Hutcherson launched a campaign called 'Power On' in 2014. The initiative encouraged people to donate unused electronic devices to be refurbished and given to LGBTQ+ youth from rural areas and low-income households.

In 2012, Hutcherson became the youngest person to receive a Vanguard Award, from GLAAD, given to those who 'have increased the visibility and understanding of the LGBT community'.

LESLIE FEINBERG

1949-2014

Leslie Feinberg was a trans, butch lesbian, communist and activist, who helped begin the early conversations around trans and gender non-conforming language. Feinberg used the pronouns zie (for she) and hir (for her), but also believed the intention and the location of when a pronoun was used to be important. 'It matters whether someone is using the pronoun as a bigot, or if they are trying to demonstrate respect,' zie/she said.

Feinberg was best-known for hir/her novel *Stone Butch Blues*, a groundbreaking fictional work published in March 1993, which dealt with the complexities of gender and being trans in 1970s America. It was winner of the 1994 American Library Association Stonewall Book Award and a 1994 Lambda Literary Award. When Feinberg died, the *New York Times* obituary described *Stone Butch Blues* as a 'landmark in the contemporary literature of gender complexity'.

Feinberg was a longstanding member of the Workers World Party, a revolutionary Marxist–Leninist political party in the US, and wrote for its newspaper for many years. As part of the party, zie/she helped organise multiple anti-racist rallies against the Ku Klux Klan and white supremacists, as well as taking part in community work against anti-abortion groups.

LARRY KRAMER

1935–2020

During the late 1970s and 1980s, American author Larry Kramer was not a popular man. His 1978 novel, *Faggots*, detailed the sexual exploits of gay men in New York and these gay men did not like how they were depicted. 'The straight world thought I was repulsive, and the gay world treated me like a traitor,' Kramer later explained; he was even banned from his local grocery store.

As AIDS ravaged the gay community, Kramer tried tirelessly to raise awareness among both officials and the community, neither of whom seemed willing to act. On this date in 1983, the gay newspaper the *New York Native*, ran a 5,000-word piece entitled '1,112 and Counting', written by Kramer. It lambasted health officials and accused gay men of killing each other through their lack of action.

Kramer and a group of others set up the Gay Men's Health Crisis to raise funds for research into the disease and offer support (primarily via a counselling hotline) to people affected. *The Normal Heart*, Kramer's autobiographical play about a frustrated activist's role in an HIV-advocacy group, first premiered in New York City in 1985. Performed many times on stage, it was later adapted for television and starred Julia Roberts and Mark Ruffalo.

RYAN MURPHY

B. 1965

Time magazine called him 'the king of the streaming boom', the *New Yorker* called him 'the most powerful man in TV', but many queer people think of Ryan Murphy as the man who brought marginalised characters to the mainstream on TV. 'I made gay sidekicks the leads,' he says. In 2018, Murphy signed a $300 million deal – rumoured to be the biggest of its kind in television history – with Netflix to create television series, feature films and documentaries.

Murphy rose to fame with his series, *Nip/Tuck*, in 2003, but it was his all-inclusive high-school comedy-drama, *Glee*, first aired in 2009, that set him on his ride to world TV domination. When two of the teenage gay characters had their first kiss, on this date in 2011, it was notable for simply serving the plot rather than being used as a shock tactic to court ratings – as so many gay kisses on TV had previously been.

Murphy continued to put queer characters front and centre of his shows, such as *American Horror Story* (2011–), *The Politician* (2019–20), *Ratched* (2020) and *Pose* (2018–21). *Pose*, the story of the queer ballroom community in New York City in the 1980s and 90s as it was ravaged by AIDS, broke boundaries by having the largest transgender cast of any commercial scripted TV show.

ANNA GRODZKA

B. 1954

In 2008, Polish politician Anna Grodzka co-founded the Trans-Fuzja Foundation, a non-profit organisation that supports the trans community and educates the public about transgender issues.

Born on this date in 1954, Grodzka was the first openly transgender person elected to the Polish Parliament in 2011, as part of the left-liberal party, Palikot's Movement. Upon election she declared, 'Today, Poland is changing. I am the proof.' Since then, she has been a member of the Green Party and the Polish Socialist Party.

During her time in Parliament, she sought to improve tenant rights with an amendment to the Tenant Protection Act. She also submitted the Gender Accordance Act, aimed to simplify legal procedures for people whose gender identity differs from the sex listed on their birth certificate. The act passed in 2015 and became the country's first gender recognition legislation.

The politician, who has received death threats and had the windows of her parliamentary office smashed, released a book about her life in 2013 named *Mam na imie Ania (My name is Ania)*. She said she hoped it would help people understand transgenderism better, 'because nothing is more important to transgender people than the understanding and acceptance of those they are closest to'.

HOLLY JOHNSON

B. 1960

When William Johnson was a teenager in Liverpool, UK in the 1970s, his schoolmates threw bricks at him because of how he styled himself. His father didn't want him to leave the house on account of his appearance and attitude. Aged 14, Johnson adopted the name 'Holly', after Holly Woodlawn, a transgender Puerto Rican actress and friend of Andy Warhol, and the musician Holly Johnson was born.

Johnson gained local fame as the bassist in the punk band *Big in Japan* in the late 70s, but it was as lead vocalist in the pop band *Frankie Goes to Hollywood* that he rocketed to stardom. Johnson unashamedly blurred gender lines in his appearance and art, thrusting divine decadence, punk and queerness to those even glancing his way.

The band's debut single 'Relax', released in 1983, was an instant hit despite causing controversy at the BBC when DJ Mike Read refused to play the song. Later banned by the BBC, the song still reached number one and became one of the UK's bestselling singles of all time.

After his HIV diagnosis in 1991, Johnson withdrew briefly from music and penned an autobiography, which was released on this date in 1994. The book, entitled *A Bone in My Flute* and featuring a picture of Johnson by queer artists Pierre et Gilles on the cover, became a bestseller.

CAMILLE CABRAL

B. 1944

Camille Cabral is a French–Brazilian transgender activist who made history when she became the first trans and migrant woman to be elected as a councillor in Paris, France, with the Green Party on this date in 2001.

Originally from northern Brazil, Cabral arrived in Paris in 1980 to complete her medical studies and went on to work in the dermatology department of the Saint-Louis hospital. She later conducted an action research project on the prostitutes of the Bois de Boulogne for the French Agency for the Fight against AIDS. This was the start of her long-time activism in this area.

As a result of her work with transgender prostitutes in Paris, Cabral set up PASTT – Prévention Action Santé Travail pour les Transgenres (Prevention, Action, Health and Work for the Transgender Community), an organisation that assists people living with HIV and defends the rights of transsexuals and sex workers. PASTT operates a mobile health and advice service from a bus that travels to places where trans prostitutes operate. Cabral believes PASTT is the only organisation of its kind in the world; one that operates a broad range of services including HIV prevention, integration and accommodation, and fights for transsexual rights and against discrimination.

THE BRIXTON FAERIES

1974-1981

In the 1970s, Brixton in south London, UK was a hotbed of radicalism. A slew of empty properties were taken over by hippies, feminists, Black Panther members and the South London Gay Liberation Front (GLF). The GLF occupied an empty shop in the area now known as Poet's Corner and in March 1974 opened the South London Gay Community Centre — what is thought to be the first gay community centre of its kind in the UK.

The centre was run and funded by a cooperative largely made up of gay men who lived in squats close by. It offered counselling, information and advice to gay people, regularly hosted gay discos and even had its own wrestlers' group. The South London Gay Liberation Theatre Group also operated from here, producing several plays and street theatre performances that focused on social and political issues affecting LGBTQ+ people and women. The theatre group later became known as the Brixton Faeries.

People lived communally, sharing resources. Ian Townson, one of the community centre founders, said the residents were those 'determined to come out into the clear light of day with a public statement of gay identity... Some consciously saw this as an opportunity to attack "straight" society through adopting an alternative lifestyle that challenged the prevailing norms of the patriarchal nuclear family and private property.'

JANE LYNCH

B. 1960

Before becoming a regular in Christopher Guest's mockumentary films, beginning with *Best in Show* in 2000, American actress Jane Lynch had mainly performed on stage, in commercials and in secondary roles on TV and film. In 2009, her fame skyrocketed when she was cast as high school coach Sue Sylvester in the musical comedy series *Glee*, which ran from 2009 and ended on this date in 2015.

Glee, about a glee club at a fictional high school, was a trailblazer in portraying LGBTQ+ issues and characters on TV. It featured long-standing queer cast members and addressed issues such as coming out, gay marriage and homophobia in school.

Lynch, who is openly gay and married her partner, Jennifer Cheyne, in 2021, has spoken about feeling like her lesbianism was a disease when she was young. 'I had a journal and I remember I wrote, "I am gay. No one can ever know this." And I went four blocks away and threw it out in somebody else's garbage.'

As well as receiving a Primetime Emmy Award and a Golden Globe for her role in *Glee*, in 2010 she was also honoured with the 14th annual Achievement Award for her contributions to LGBT film and media, by Outfest, the Los Angeles gay and lesbian film festival.

MADONNA

B. 1958

Michigan-born singer, songwriter, actress, activist and one of the most successful women on the planet, Madonna has been a long-time ally to queer people. Her ballet teacher, Christopher Flynn (one of the first gay men she met), instilled confidence in the young star, telling her she had something to offer the world. With openly gay friends such as Keith Haring (see 2 Sep), Sandra Bernhard, Rosie O'Donnell and Rupert Everett, Madonna has consistently supported the rights of LGBTQ+ people.

In 1991, she brought the real lives of gay men to the big screen in her documentary of her tour, *Truth or Dare* (released as *In Bed with Madonna* in the UK), which featured her gay dancers kissing and discussing sex. Her album, *Like a Prayer*, was released on this date in 1989 amid the AIDS epidemic and included a pamphlet with safe-sex advice entitled 'The Facts About AIDS'.

Madonna has not only provided a soundtrack to the lives of millions of queer people, but also fought for their rights: appearing on the *Ellen DeGeneres Show* to speak about the bullying of gay teens, dressing up as a boy scout at the GLAAD awards to protest the Boy Scouts of America's ban on homosexuals and using her platform to encourage people to vote in favour of marriage equality.

PROUD ALLY

HOWARD ASHMAN

1950–1991

Working as the artistic director at an off-Broadway theatre in the 1970s, Howard Ashman met his partner in music, the composer Alan Menken. The pair, who first achieved success with their musical *Little Shop of Horrors* in 1982, went on to write music together until Ashman's death. They worked at Disney, where Ashman wrote lyrics for the animated musicals *The Little Mermaid* (1989), *Beauty and the Beast* (1991) and *Aladdin* (1992). Ashman is credited with playing a major part in Disney's revival at this time.

On this date in 1990, Ashman and Menken won an Academy Award for best original song for 'Under the Sea' from *The Little Mermaid*. Drawing on his theatre experience, he championed the importance of an 'I want' song, where the lead sings about their hopes and dreams, allowing the audience to root for them, as with Ariel's 'Part of Your World' in *The Little Mermaid*.

Ashman continued working when he became sick with AIDS, but never saw final cuts of his work in *Aladdin*. Receiving a posthumous award on his behalf for best original song in *Beauty and the Beast* in 1992, Ashman's partner, architect Bill Lauch, importantly pointed out in his speech, 'This is the first Academy Award given to someone we've lost to AIDS.'

PYOTR TCHAIKOVSKY

1840–1893

When Russian composer Pyotr Tchaikovsky died in 1893, it was reportedly from cholera. Years later, a rumour surfaced via a chief prosecutor for the Russian Senate, who had allegedly told his wife that a 'court of honour' had instructed Tchaikovsky to commit suicide to avoid a homosexual scandal. Some believe he died of poisoning, but these allegations cannot be proven.

Despite Russia's homophobic cultural politics and anti-gay propaganda, the Tchaikovsky Museum in Klin, near Moscow, allowed their vast collection of the composer's letters to be published in 2018. These letters contain many admissions of the composer's love for young men and even reference his dalliances with rent boys. The editor of the collection,

Marina Kostalevsky, pointed out that while Tchaikovsky's queerness had long been accepted in the West, 'it is still a subject of heated and often ugly public debate' in Russia.

Tchaikovsky started writing *Symphony No. 1* – his earliest notable work – in March 1866. The composer created masterpieces that featured western European musical tradition while remaining authentically Russian. Despite this, Russian musicians attacked him for being insufficiently nationalistic and because of the West's view of homosexuality as a deviant illness, during the 20th century Tchaikovsky's work was unfairly criticised and labelled as neurotic. Some of his most famous works are the scores he created for the three full-length ballets, *Swan Lake* (1877), *The Sleeping Beauty* (1890) and *The Nutcracker* (1892).

BOB KOHLER

1926–2007

A lifelong activist, Bob Kohler was a co-founder of the Gay Liberation Front and ensured that it pushed for more than gay rights: GLF was anti-imperialist, anti-capitalist, fought sexism and racism and aligned itself with the Black Panther Party. Kohler was arrested for taking part in political activity on this date in 1999, aged 73! And at 75, he stood outside the housing agency in New York for hours to help those affected by an illegal denial of emergency housing by the mayor's office.

After serving in the navy as a young man, Kohler opened a talent agency that specialised in representing African American actors.

This was an act of defiance in itself, since it was during the era of the Jim Crow racial segregation laws.

Described as the old white man with blue eyes who would always show up at a rally or picket when needed, Kohler fought against racial injustice and for LGBTQ+ rights in equal measure. He said, 'I do not equate my oppression with the oppression of Blacks and Latinos. You can't. It is not the same struggle, but it is one struggle. And, if my being here as a long-time gay activist can influence other people in the gay community, it's worth getting arrested.'

PEDRO ALMODÓVAR

B. 1949

Pedro Almodóvar's first film *Pepi, Luci, Bom*, both written and directed by the filmmaker, was typical of a hedonistic wave of culture that swept through Madrid (and other cities) following the death of dictator Francisco Franco in 1975. Released in 1980, the film featured drug use, bondage, sex and violence — issues that Almodóvar has never shied away from in his lengthy career. He has a unique style, involving high camp melodrama, death, colour, deviance and comedy, and his plots often focus on female characters, where sexuality and LGBTQ+ issues are frequently prevalent.

Known for cultivating Spanish talent for Hollywood, his films have propelled the likes of Penélope Cruz, Antonio Banderas and Javier Bardem to stardom. His first big hit came when *Women on the Verge of a Nervous Breakdown*, released on this date in 1988, won five Goya Awards and was nominated for Best Foreign Language Film at the Oscars.

Almodóvar and his younger brother Augustin set up a production company in the late 1980s and subsequently all his movies have been produced under it, enabling him to write, direct, cast and produce them exactly as he wants. The director now has two Oscars, five BAFTAs and a Golden Globe to his name.

ELAINE NOBLE

B. 1944

During her election campaign for the Massachusetts House of Representatives in 1975, Elaine Noble was harassed in person and on the phone and her campaign headquarters were vandalised. Despite this, Noble won and served two terms (1975–1979), becoming the first openly lesbian or gay candidate elected to a state legislature in the US. When later asked about the significance of being elected, she said '...I viewed it as being elected in spite of being gay, not because of it. Now people get elected because they are gay... Kind of nice.'

Noble was a member of lesbian civil rights organisation the Daughters of Bilitis, and a key organiser in Boston's first official Pride in 1971. She also championed the busing system in Boston, which assisted with the desegregation of public schools by transporting white students to black schools and vice versa across the city.

On this date in 1977, Noble met with aides to President Jimmy Carter at the White House, along with other LGBTQ+ activists including Jean O'Leary (see 11 Oct) and Frank Kameny (see 17 Jun) as part of the first National Gay Task Force. It was the first time lesbian or gay people had been invited to the White House to discuss policy issues relating to them.

BILLIE HOLIDAY

1915-1959

Billie Holiday, the wild lady of jazz, had a troubled life. She was born into poverty and was the victim of an attempted rape aged just 11. She struggled with alcohol and drugs, and endured a string of abusive relationships with men involved with crime and drugs. Despite singing, performing and recording music throughout her short life, the story goes that Holiday died with only cents in the bank and her entire fortune of a few hundred dollars strapped to her leg.

It's reported that Holiday was openly bisexual and had a long relationship with actress Tallulah Bankhead, known for her appearance in Alfred Hitchcock's 1944 film *Lifeboat*.

Holiday's first singing gig came when she auditioned to dance in a New York night club as a teenager but was asked to sing instead. Holiday's performance style was unique and hugely influential to the genre of jazz. She played around with tempo, often being told she sang too slow, and her tone was described as both 'velvet' and sounding like a horn. On this date in 1948, after losing her legal right to work anywhere that sold alcohol, Holiday played a sold-out show at Carnegie Hall to over 2,700 people.

ALAN CUMMING

B. 1965

Scottish actor Alan Cumming appeared in popular Scottish TV programmes such as *Take the High Road* and *Taggart* in the 1980s, but it was the TV film *Bernard and the Genie* that gave him his big break. This was followed by *The High Life*, a comedy series he co-wrote and co-starred in with Forbes Masson. Countless appearances in TV dramas, comedies, theatre performances and film roles ensued.

One of Cumming's most lauded stage roles was the Emcee in *Cabaret*, first in London's West End and then on Broadway in New York, where he won a Tony and Drama Desk Award for his performance. In 2018, Cumming starred in the US TV police drama, *Instinct*,

the first show of its kind to feature a gay leading character. After it was cancelled, Cumming said, 'Because of [*Instinct*] millions of people will have seen a same-sex marriage portrayed for the first time and I hope we changed and opened some minds in the process.'

As an LGBTQ+ rights advocate and a campaigner against male circumcision ('It's genital mutilation'), Cumming identifies as bisexual and has been married to both men and women. On this date in March 2005, Cumming received the Vito Russo Award from GLAAD for his work towards eliminating homophobia within the entertainment community.

URVASHI VAID

1958-2002

On this date in 1990, US president George H.W. Bush gave his first speech on AIDS since taking office, and was heckled by Urvashi Vaid, the former executive director of the National Gay and Lesbian Task Force, who held up a sign reading, 'TALK IS CHEAP, AIDS FUNDING IS NOT'. As staff attorney at the National Prison Project of the American Civil Liberties Union (ACLU), Vaid initiated the group's work on HIV/AIDS in prisons.

In 2012, her book *Irresistible Revolution* challenged LGBTQ+ rights activists to aspire beyond the narrow framework of equality for queer people, advocating for a more substantive politics with race, class and gender at its foundation.

Throughout her career, Vaid has been an author, an attorney, a strategist, a community activist, an academic, a researcher and co-founder of many organisations such as the National LGBTQ Anti-Poverty Action Network and the National LGBT/HIV Criminal Justice Working Group. Interviewed in 2002 she said, '…politics is a tremendously empowering and interesting process… I find political organizing and community political action a really satisfying process… it doesn't discourage me, even when it looks totally bleak, and even when you lose.'

In 2009, Vaid was named one of *Out* magazine's 50 most influential people in the US.

ANNE LISTER

1791–1840

On this date in 1834, diarist and industrialist Anne Lister and her partner Ann Walker were privately blessed in a church in York, UK, at a time when such acts were not just rare for queer people, but could even result in prosecution.

Walker was not Lister's first love; her diaries (of which there are 26 volumes) reveal that she had a long on-off passionate affair with Mariana Belcombe, the daughter of a physician. These diaries, extensively detailing her day-to-day life, current politics, social events, her loves and her sex life (although Lister wrote the more salacious parts in code) would ultimately become her legacy. When a relative deciphered the code after Lister's death, he was advised to burn the diaries but luckily hid them instead, and they were eventually published (in part) in 1988.

Born into a wealthy family, Lister inherited well and became a formidable businesswoman when she entered the world of coal mining. On account of her status, her masculine appearance and her public relationship with Walker, she was often referred to as 'Gentleman Jack'. In 2019 a UK television drama of the same name, starring Suranne Jones, was aired and won a Royal Television Society Award for Best Drama Series the following year.

KARINE JEAN-PIERRE

B. 1977

When White House Principal Deputy Press Secretary Karine Jean-Pierre gave a press briefing aboard Air Force One on this date in 2021, she made history. Not only was she the first Black woman to hold such a briefing in around 30 years, she was also the first LGBTQ+ person to ever do so. A few months later, on 26 May, Jean-Pierre made history again when she became the first openly gay spokeswoman and only the second Black woman to deliver a briefing from the podium of the White House briefing room.

Jean-Pierre, who was previously chief of staff for then vice-presidential candidate Kamala Harris, told reporters, 'It's a real honor to be standing here today. I appreciate the historic nature... being in this building is not about one person. It's about what we do on behalf of the American people.'

Jean-Pierre was born in Martinique to Haitian parents who emigrated to New York when she was five years old. She graduated from New York Institute of Technology and went on to gain an MPA from the School of International and Public Affairs, Columbia University in 2003.

In November 2019, Jean-Pierre published her book *Moving Forward*, a part-memoir of hope and hard work.

JAYNE OZANNE

B. 1968

After years of struggle to reconcile her faith with her sexuality, British Christian evangelical Jayne Ozanne came out as gay to her friends and family in 2009. Six years later, she came out publicly in an article in *Christian Today* and also in a *Sunday Times* newspaper feature a few days later. As a high-profile Christian and founding member of the Archbishops' Council, Ozanne was catapulted into the limelight concerning issues of faith and sexuality. She began to campaign for better inclusion of LGBTQ+ people in the Church and to lead a fight to ban conversion therapy.

She set up the Ozanne Foundation, which campaigns for and advises on issues including same-sex marriage, conversion therapy and queer issues relating to faith around the world. Ozanne's work on the attitudes towards conversion therapy helped the UK government to agree to banning it for LGB people. Regrettably, Boris Johnson's Conservative Government failed to include trans people in the ban, and writing in the *Guardian* newspaper, on this date in 2022, Ozanne called on the then prime minister to commit to do the right thing.

When Ozanne met Pope Francis in 2019, she presented him with a copy of her memoir, *Just Love*, and the *2018 Faith & Sexuality Survey*, which examined religious beliefs and their impact on acceptance of people's sexual orientation in the UK.

KATHY KOZACHENKO

B. 1954

When someone told Kathy Kozachenko's teenage son of the important place his mother held in the queer history books, he Googled it, learning only then that she was the first openly gay person elected to political office in the United States. Kozachenko's discretion could explain why Harvey Milk (see 9 Jan) is often misrepresented as the first openly gay person elected to office in the US.

On this date in 1974 Kozachenko was elected to the Ann Arbor City Council in Michigan. She ran as an openly gay woman for the Human Rights Party, although LGBTQ+ rights were not central to her manifesto. When asked about her quiet legacy, she said, 'I was and am a social justice advocate, of which LGBTQ rights comes in.'

Kozachenko fought for a range of issues from the genocide of Native Americans to rent control. 'I don't think I was brave, because I was in a college town where it was cool to be who I was,' she says. 'On the other hand, I stepped up and did what I felt needed to be done at the time.'

When her two-year term came to an end, Kozachenko didn't run again, but continued her activism and was a key organiser in the 1979 March on Washington for lesbian and gay rights.

THOMAS BEATIE

B. 1974

'This was pre-Chaz Bono. This was pre-Caitlyn Jenner. This was before anyone knew anything… exposing the importance of fertility for trans people was a huge eye-opener,' says Thomas Beatie, the transgender man from Portland, Oregon who shot to fame when he became pregnant and told his story to the world on *The Oprah Winfrey Show* on this date in 2008.

The 'pregnant man', as Beatie was labelled by the press, decided to carry a child after his wife, Nancy, was unable to become pregnant because of a previous hysterectomy. 'Who hires a surrogate if they are perfectly capable of carrying their own child?' Beatie asked at the time. The couple garnered major attention at a time when there was very little trans visibility in mainstream media and were subjected to ignorance and transphobia by the public and even those in the public eye.

When the couple separated, a court in Arizona tried to prevent their divorce by questioning whether their marriage was legal in the first place, citing Beatie's pregnancies as evidence he was not a male and, therefore, their marriage was invalid (at the time same-sex marriage wasn't legal in Arizona). After many battles, the couple were able to divorce in 2014 and Beatie later remarried.

DIEGO GARIJO

B. 1980

When drag queen and bare-knuckle fighter Diego Garijo is asked what hurts more, waxing or taking a punch in the face, he says the punches don't bother him but 'breaking an acrylic fingernail. It's a nightmare.'

Garijo was brought up by his mother and surrounded by gay cousins as a child in Mexico. He was later smuggled into America and spent the early part of his life involved in crime and drugs. Garijo got back on track by dedicating his life to Mixed Martial Art fighting (MMA), competing professionally and winning seven fights before being forced into retirement by a detached retina. Undeterred, Garijo took up bare-knuckle boxing when it became legal in the US.

Garijo's drag alter ego is known as Lola. Lola came about when Garijo was taking a course on emotional intelligence that required him to do something outside of his comfort zone and after taking dance classes, waxing his body and learning to walk in heels he never looked back.

In an interview released on this date in 2021, when asked about his future, Garijo said that as well as art, painting and poetry he wanted to continue to do drag, compete in a few more fights and 'most importantly [wage] a war against toxic masculinity!'

MERCE CUNNINGHAM

1919-2009

American Merce Cunningham's work as a dancer and choreographer was anything but traditional. His works came from various stylistic philosophies, including collaboration and chance. He collaborated with groundbreaking artists from every discipline, including architects, musicians and painters.

His primary collaborator was composer John Cage (see 16 Jan), who was also his life partner. The pair used what is known as the chance process for much of their work, which resulted in regular musical forms and narrative being abandoned. They believed music and dance, while being performed together, could be independent of one another.

On this date in 1944, Cunningham's work *Triple Paced* was first performed at the Humphrey-Weidman Studio Theatre in New York. It was the first joint concert of solo music and dance given by Cunningham and Cage.

To mark the centenary of Cunningham's birth, the *Guardian* called on four of his disciples to share memories of the dancer. All commented on how quiet he was when rehearsing, barely critiquing, yet encouraging fellow performers to have fun and allowing them to go on their own journeys. He said, 'I don't tell people what to do. If they don't ask me questions, they're not ready to hear the answer.'

SUZI RUFFELL

B. 1986

Comedian and podcaster Suzi Ruffell was born in Portsmouth, UK, into what she describes as a 'large, loud, rough-and-tumble, a bit dodge in the nicest possible way' family. Struggling at school due to dyslexia, Ruffell would listen to her dad and uncle tell stories in the pub and see how everyone loved it. Here she realised that being funny would be better than being good at school.

Ruffell began stand-up comedy in 2008 and has performed sell-out shows at the Edinburgh Festival and supported comics such as Katherine Ryan and Joe Lycett. In 2018, her first headliner show, *Keeping it Classy*, was recorded for *Live from the BBC*.

Ruffell co-hosts a podcast, *Like Minded Friends*, with her friend and fellow comedian Tom Allen. Described as two homo comedians talking about life, love and culture, Ruffell says, 'A lot of gay stuff in the media is downbeat — AIDS, homophobia, discrimination — so Tom and I thought we would talk about the joyous things, to celebrate who we are.' Her other podcast, *Out with Suzi Ruffell*, which first aired on this date in 2020, explores the inspiring lives of LGBTQIA+ people and invites listeners to share their own stories, 'making this a genuinely inclusive, as well as intelligent, show', according to the *Guardian*.

THE CHEVALIER D'ÉON

1728-1810

On this date in 2022, a short BBC documentary by Jono Namara aired about the extraordinary duplicitous life of the Chevalier d'Éon, known as 'the world's first transgender spy'.

D'Éon was born in France in 1728 and lived publicly as both a male and female. Born into a noble family, they officially served as secretary to the French ambassador to Russia. However, the Chevalier was actually employed by the most covert spy service in France, *le Secret du Roi* (the King's Secret). While living in Russia, the Chevalier was able to express their gender non-conformity when attending 'metamorphosis balls', where people dressed up as the opposite sex.

The Chevalier was later sent to England as a spy and there rumours circulated that they were born a woman but raised as a man in order to receive a family inheritance. Interest was so great that bets about their sex were even placed on the London Stock Exchange. On returning to France, the Chevalier was officially declared a woman at the age of 49. After their death in 1810, however, doctors examining the body proclaimed that they found 'male organs in every respect, perfectly formed'. Whatever their medical details may have revealed, the Chevalier had lived their life, never conforming to just one identity, appearing publicly as both a man and woman.

MIMA SIMIĆ

B. 1976

In 2011, Mima Simić was named the Croatian LGBT person of the decade by the Zagreb Pride Committee. While she has many strings to her bow, including being a film critic, an activist, a teacher and a translator, it is arguably her decision to out herself on Croatia's hugely popular game show, *Who Wants To Be A Millionaire*, on this date in 2007, which brought her notoriety. Simić says that her decision to come out on the show on Easter Sunday, in a country that is approximately 80 per cent Catholic, was a pragmatic, activist mission as she was 'basically being the first lesbian millions of people of Croatia and the ex-Yu region have ever seen'.

Croatia's 'dangerous liaison' with the Catholic Church makes it difficult to push for LGBTQ+ rights, says Simić. When she was a host at Split Pride in 2011, the event was marred by violence and fascist homophobia, that many believe was supported by the church and local government.

In 2019, Simić became the first openly lesbian politician in Croatia, when she ran for the European Parliament. She continues providing visibility for lesbians in mainstream media and splits her time between Zagreb, Topanga in California and Berlin, where she lives with her partner, Marta Šušak, the founder of the first student LGBTQ+ initiative in Croatia.

SHANE ORTEGA

B. c. 1990

On this date in 2015, Sgt Shane Ortega came out in the *Washington Post* as the first person in the US military to transition while on active duty. Ortega, who at that time had served two combat tours in Iraq and one in Afghanistan, discussed issues faced by transgender people in the military and highlighted how rules had stated he should wear a woman's 'dress blues' for official occasions. 'Administratively I shouldn't exist,' he said. 'But I do exist, so that's still the problem.'

Ortega is a two-spirit, Haudenosaunee-Tuscarora Native American whose parents both served in the military. He believes there is a toxic masculinity in the military, which is worse for trans women as a 'loss of masculinity [is] viewed as a negative thing'.

Ortega campaigned for the repeal of the 'Don't Ask, Don't Tell' policy that was in place until 2011 and which effectively forced LGBTQ+ people to serve in silence or risk being discharged. He then fought for the community again in 2017, when President Donald Trump announced via Twitter that there would be a ban on transgender people serving in the military. The law came into place in 2019, but was repealed in January 2021 by President Joe Biden.

LIZ CARR

B. 1972

In November 2010, when actress, comedian and disability rights activist Liz Carr tied the knot with her longtime partner Jo Church, in a 'Day of the Dead' themed civil partnership ceremony, she dubbed it a 'wheelie special wedding'. Alluding to her use of a wheelchair owing to arthrogryposis multiplex congenita, the star, who has campaigned for disability rights for over 25 years, talks openly and honestly about her condition.

Carr is part of the group 'Abnormally Funny People', an entourage that uses comedy to highlight the issues faced by people with disabilities. She also wrote and performed in *Assisted Suicide: The Musical*, which she dubbed a 'TED talk with show tunes'.

Carr starred in the popular TV crime drama *Silent Witness* for eight years, and was one of very few disabled women on primetime television at the time. After the Covid-19 pandemic, she returned to the stage to play Emma Brookner in Larry Kramer's *The Normal Heart* at the National Theatre in London. Her performance of the character, who is based on Linda Laubenstein, one of the first doctors to recognise the HIV and AIDs epidemic, led to Carr receiving the Laurence Olivier Award for Best Actress in a Supporting Role on this date in 2022.

JOHANNA ELBERSKIRCHEN

1864–1943

Johanna Elberskirchen, born in Germany on this date, wrote countless essays, publications and books on subjects including women's suffrage, education, medicine, naturopathy, gender, politics and sexuality. Like many women then denied access to university in their home countries, Elberskirchen studied medicine and law in Switzerland before returning to Germany and settling near Berlin. Here, she and her partner Hildegard Moniac opened a homoeopathic practice.

Elberskirchen, who lived openly as a lesbian, believed that sexual freedom was biologically natural and that sex drives and urges were biologically the same for men and women, but that women's were repressed by men, marriage, patriarchy and financial restrictions. While there was much discourse over gender and sexuality at this time, particularly in Germany, Elberskirchen's beliefs were seen as particularly radical as she went so far as to claim that 'we are all homosexuals… More precisely: we are all bisexual' in her publication 'Love Among the Third Sex' (1904). As well as her writings and work at Magnus Hirschfeld's Institute for Sexology, Elberskirchen also lectured internationally on sexuality and social reform.

It is believed that Elberskirchen's ashes were secretly buried in the grave of her partner Hildegard Moniac, which now bears plaques to commemorate them both.

PETER TATCHELL

B. 1952

'Dr Carey supports discrimination against lesbian and gay people. He opposes lesbian and gay human rights. This is not a Christian teaching.' These are the words Peter Tatchell projected from the pulpit at Canterbury Cathedral on this date in 1998, when he and other members of the campaign group OutRage! interrupted the then Archbishop of Canterbury's Easter sermon. At the time Dr George Carey opposed LGBTQ+ rights reforms proposed by the New Labour government. Tatchell highlighted that Carey also opposed LGBTQ+ foster parents and equal opportunities for queer people in the workplace.

Tatchell was found guilty for his stunt in line with the 1860 Ecclesiastical Courts Jurisdiction Act (ECJA), which effectively curtailed free speech and the right to protest in a place of worship. The judge sentencing Tatchell expressed a witty disapproval of the ECJA by only fining the offender £18.60 — a clear reference to the year the ECJ Act became law.

Australian-born Tatchell, who has lived predominantly in the UK, began as a prominent member of the Gay Liberation Front in the 1970s, joined the Labour party in the 80s and then co-founded OutRage! in the 90s.

Tatchell later created The Peter Tatchell Foundation, whose mission embodies Tatchell's life's work: to speak out for human rights.

JEAN PAUL GAULTIER

B. 1952

Jean Paul Gaultier acquired his first job as a design assistant at Pierre Cardin in 1970, despite a lack of formal fashion education. By 1976, he'd launched his own collection, fusing streetstyle, classic tailoring and gay club culture to create his signature style. His clothes playfully blur the lines between masculine and feminine. Gaultier created skirts for men, and it wasn't unusual to see women in pin-striped suits walking the runway alongside trans models at his theatrical fashion shows.

In the 1980s, the Gaultier/Madonna (see 21 Mar) partnership was formed and the singer went on to wear many of the French fashion designer's clothes. The conical bra-and-corset outfit Gaultier made for the queen of pop's 1990 *Blond Ambition* tour defined her look during that period. The tour began on this date that year and exposed Gaultier's designs to millions across the globe.

After Gaultier lost his partner, Francis Menuge, to AIDS in 1990, the designer worked to help spread awareness of the disease and created T-shirts emblazoned with the words 'Safe Sex Forever'. He revived the slogan in 2021 on socks, donating proceeds to Sidaction, a French organisation that sponsors HIV and AIDS research.

MIRIAM MARGOLYES

B. 1941

British-Australian actress Miriam Margolyes makes it well-known that she disagrees with her good friend Sir Ian McKellen (see 6 Aug) on the subject of coming out. 'He feels that you should come out [to give encouragement to others]. And I say, it depends who you're coming out to,' says Margolyes, who believes that coming out to her parents was detrimental to her mother's health.

At the same time, Margolyes herself didn't struggle to accept her sexuality and doesn't shy away from it, saying, 'I think it gives you an identity because you can say "I am a lesbian". I still think it's an absolutely terrific thing to be…'

Margolyes' impressive CV has seen her star on screen, stage and radio for more than 45 years. Her accolades include a Best Supporting Actress BAFTA and a Sony Radio Award for Best Actress (both in 1993).

On this date in 2021, the short film, *Wings*, starring Margolyes and Virginia McKenna, was released internationally. Spanning six decades, it charted the love story of two Land Army girls during World War Two, and it won the Best Drama Short Film accolade at the Out On Film Awards in 2020.

LEONARDO DA VINCI

1452-1519

Italian renaissance painter, Leonardo da Vinci, was born to unmarried parents on this date in 1452. In his early teenage years, he trained as an artist's apprentice under Andrea del Verrocchio in Florence, in painting, sculpture and the technical-mechanical arts. He lived and painted in Florence, Milan, Rome and France, working for dukes, kings and even the pope. Among his most famous works are *Lady with an Ermine* (*c.* 1489–91), *The Last Supper* (*c.* 1495–98) and, of course, the *Mona Lisa* (*c.* 1503–06).

The question of Da Vinci's sexuality has been on the lips of historians for decades and many modern scholars and art theorists believe him to have been gay, a view supported by an accusation of sodomy with a 17-year-old sex worker, and tales of a complicated shifting triangular relationship that Da Vinci seems likely to have had with two of his assistants. Some biographers, and even Austrian psychoanalyst Sigmund Freud, suspect the artist was gay but celibate.

Although best-known for his paintings and sculpture, Da Vinci was also hugely adept in the fields of architecture, science and engineering. Thousands of pages of his notebooks show his writings and sketches on subjects including geology, anatomy, flying and optics, and are littered with inventions for objects such as bicycles and airplanes.

DORA RICHTER

1891–1933

After being arrested multiple times in pre-Nazi Berlin, for the 'crime' of cross-dressing, Dora Richter was released into the care of German physician and sexologist Magnus Hirschfeld, founder of the Institute of Sexual Research. Richter, assigned male at birth, was then able to continue living and working as a woman at the institute as a domestic maid.

It is thought that Richter, born on this date in 1891, was the first trans woman to undergo genital reconstructive surgery, including a vaginoplasty. The first part of this new and experimental surgery took place in 1922, when the testicles were removed by Dr Erwin Gohrbandt to evaluate the effects that reduced testosterone would have on Richter's body. Nine years later her vaginoplasty was completed successfully.

As with many LGBTQ+ people who had lived full lives under the liberal Weimar Republic, Richter's life was cut short by the rise of Hitler. On 6 May 1933, Nazi troops and supporters stormed the institute and ransacked the building, destroying years of study and attacking staff and residents. Tragically, Richter was never heard from after this and it is presumed she was killed in the attack. Yet, her bravery in undertaking the pioneering surgery created a legacy that paved the way for future generations of transgender people.

WANDA SYKES

B. 1964

Actress, comedian, writer and producer Wanda Sykes has starred in films such as *Monster-In-law* and the *Ice Age* series. She's also had countless roles in TV shows, including *Black-ish* and *Curb Your Enthusiasm*, as well as hosting *The Wanda Sykes Show* and multiple comedy specials of her own. She has won Emmy Awards for her work on the *Chris Rock Show* and *Inside the NFL*.

While queerness often features in her comedy, along with being Black and a mother, Sykes didn't publicly come out until she was 44 years old, when she was on stage at an equality rally in Las Vegas in 2008. A year later, she became the first African American woman and first openly LGBTQ+ person selected to be the featured entertainer for the annual White House Correspondents' Association dinner.

In 2018, Sykes was working on the reboot of the American sitcom *Rosanne* when the show's namesake, Barr, posted a racist tweet about President Barack Obama's former adviser. Sykes immediately announced on Twitter that she was leaving the show and within hours the network cancelled the sitcom; Barr blamed Sykes, amongst others, saying her tweet made ABC network nervous.

On this date in 2010, Sykes received the Stephen F. Kolzak Award at the 21st Annual GLAAD Media Awards in Los Angeles, for her work towards eliminating homophobia.

LUCÍA SÁNCHEZ SAORNIL

1895-1970

Lucía Sánchez Saornil was a Spanish feminist and anarchist who disagreed with other anarchists. Specifically, Saornil disagreed with the sexist men in the Confederación Nacional del Trabajo (CNT), an anarchistic union-based organisation aimed at empowering the Spanish labour force. She was part of the CNT during the early part of the 20th century but Saornil and other female members felt women's issues were being largely ignored, so they set up their own anarchist federation.

With Mercedes Comaposada and Amparo Poch y Gascón, Saornil set up Mujeres Libres (Free Women) in Madrid and Barcelona in April 1936.

The organisation set out to empower working-class women, offering education, childcare and sexual-health advice, and also trained women as nurses to aid the Civil War. It grew to 30,000 members and played a large part in the Spanish Revolution and Civil War (1936–39).

Saornil was a lesbian, who wrote political works as well as poetry exploring the subject, primarily under a male pen name to evade obscenity charges. Saornil spent the end of her life with her lover América Barrosa, moving between Spain and France trying to evade the fascism and traditional Catholic attitudes that denied their love.

RITA MAE BROWN

B. 1944

Rita Mae Brown's debut novel, *Rubyfruit Jungle*, published in 1973, was heralded as a lesbian coming-of-age story with which readers could identify. When it was republished years later, the *Washington Post* called it 'The breakout lesbian novel'. Despite similarities between the main character, Molly, and the author, Brown said it was fictional but that it 'parallels aspects of my life, or at least intellectual concerns I had at the time'.

Always open about loving both men and women, Brown became a member of the National Organization for Women (NOW) but was disheartened by its lack of inclusivity and action for lesbians. She later became a founding member of The Furies, a lesbian feminist collective that published *The Furies: Lesbian/Feminist Monthly* magazine, where some of her radical lesbian poetry appeared in print.

Brown was a co-founder of the Student Homophile League, one of the first college campus LGBTQ+ groups in the US. Originally set up in 1966, it was officially granted approval by Columbia University on this date in 1967.

Brown, who had a long-term relationship with tennis star Martina Navratilova (see 9 Sep), has published many books, including a mystery series co-authored with her cat, Sneaky Pie. She has also written for television and been nominated for two Emmy Awards.

FREDDIE MERCURY

1946–1991

Seven months after the death of Freddie Mercury – frontman of rock band Queen – from AIDS-related complications, some of the world's most successful music artists, including his Queen bandmates John Deacon, Roger Taylor and Brian May, came together to put on a tribute concert like no other. It took place on this date in 1992 at Wembley Stadium, where seven years previously in 1985, Freddie had given the performance of his life at Live Aid. The concert, which reached an estimated audience of one billion people, aimed to raise funds and awareness for AIDS research.

Mercury released 14 albums with Queen, as well as his own solo album.

The band won countless awards and their *Greatest Hits* album sold 25 million copies in 1982.

There are conflicting reports about Mercury's sexuality. Some claim he was bisexual, others that he was a closeted gay man. At the end of his life Mercury lived with hairdresser Jim Hutton, who was his partner for seven years and, along with close friends, nursed him during his illness. Mercury remained close to his long-term lover, Mary Austin, after they ended their relationship of many years in the 1970s. He left his house to Austin and entrusted her to bury his ashes in an undisclosed location.

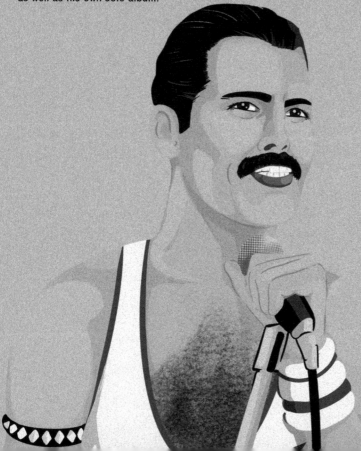

DICK LEITSCH

1935-2018

Dick Leitsch's 'Sip-in', an ingenious act of civil disobedience, on this date in 1966, was instrumental in creating safe spaces for gay men and lesbians in New York. His goal was to challenge a discriminatory State Liquor Authority (SLA) policy which dictated that a bar deemed to be a 'disorderly house' could lose its licence; under unwritten guidelines, queer people were deemed to be inherently 'disorderly'.

Although in 1960s New York, bars were one of the few places that queer people could socialise, they were not wholly safe. Patrons risked being barred in line with SLA's policy or entrapped for 'homosexual solicitation' by plain-clothed policemen. As the New York president of the Mattachine Society, a

pre-Stonewall organisation, Leitsch fought both issues, reminding society that gay and lesbian Americans lacked basic civil rights protections.

Taking inspiration from the 'sit-ins' of the civil rights movement, Leitsch, along with two other members of the Mattachine society, Randy Wicker (see 19 Sep) and Craig Rodwell, took a journalist and photographer to a staged Sip-in. They visited New York City bars and proclaimed their homosexuality when they ordered a drink. The fourth venue they visited refused them, giving Leitsch the evidence needed to challenge the SLA. The Commission on Human Rights was brought in, adding pressure to the SLA which later changed its policy: homosexuals would no longer be viewed as disorderly patrons.

HAVELOCK ELLIS

1859–1939

Born in Croydon, UK, Havelock Ellis enrolled in St Thomas's Hospital Medical School to study as a physician. His aim wasn't to practise medicine but to understand the body better, in order to become a sexologist.

Ellis studied homosexuality (although he used the terms 'inverts' or 'inversion' to describe same-sex attraction), transvestitism, auto-eroticism (masturbation), psychedelics and fetishes, among other sexually related subjects. He was one of the first medical professionals who did not consider homosexuality to be an illness or deviant behaviour, and his research included interviews with both heterosexual and homosexual couples. Ellis aimed to show that same-sex desires were common biological manifestations in both humans and animals.

Ellis was married to the women's rights activist and proclaimed lesbian, Edith Mary Oldham Lees. The pair often lived separately and had an open marriage, with Ellis reportedly suffering from impotence and/or having no interest in sexual relations of his own. Many might now refer to him as asexual.

His major work, *Studies in the Psychology of Sex*, was published in numerous volumes from April 1897 to 1910 and was co-authored with writer and historian John Addington Symonds. It was praised for paving the way for homosexuality to be seen as less immoral by society.

GERALDINE ROMAN

B. 1967

In 2016, Geraldine Roman made history by becoming the first transgender politician to win a congressional seat in the Philippines. Upon her victory she said, 'What triumphed was the politics of love, acceptance and respect.' Born on this date in 1967, Roman is part of a political family dynasty: both her father and mother have previously served as members of the House of Representatives.

In a devoutly Catholic country where abortion and even divorce are banned, Roman succeeded against the odds, even going so far as to include LGBTQ+ issues in her political agenda. Within months of becoming elected she made a powerful speech expressing her commitment to getting the Anti-Discrimination Bill passed, after it had languished for almost two decades. The bill finally passed in September 2017.

Roman faced criticism for filing a Civil Partnership Bill as opposed to one that would bring about equal marriage, but she pragmatically explained that she believes the Philippines is not yet ready for same-sex marriage. 'Should we fight for something that will never win at this point in time? Or... for something that will give us practically the same rights and obligations and that has more certainty of being passed into law?'

KATE MCKINNON

B. 1984

Comedian and actress Kate McKinnon is best-known for her work on *The Big Gay Sketch Show*, an LGBTQ+ US comedy show produced by Rosie O'Donnell which debuted on this date in 2007, as well as her legendary impressions on the prime-time sketch show *Saturday Night Live* and appearances in films such as *Ghostbusters* (2016) and *Bombshell* (2019).

McKinnon, who graduated from Columbia University in 2002 with a degree in theatre, became the first openly gay female cast member in *Saturday Night Live*'s 37-year run, when she joined in 2012. Speaking about being a lesbian comedian, she said, 'As minorities, we're on the fringe, and there's just something so wonderful about that perspective, something so inspiring.'

When McKinnon presented Ellen DeGeneres (see 30 Apr) with the Carol Burnett Award at the Golden Globes in 2021, she spoke about being a queer teenager in the 1990s and said 'the only thing that made it less scary was seeing *Ellen* on TV'.

In 2016, and again in 2017, McKinnon won the Outstanding Supporting Actress in a Comedy Series Primetime Emmy for her performances on *Saturday Night Live*. Her most popular impressions on the show include Ruth Bader Ginsburg, Hillary Clinton and Ellen DeGeneres.

LANI KA'AHUMANU

B. 1943

In 1976, Lani Ka'ahumanu left her husband, enrolled on a Women's Studies course at San Francisco State University and came out as a lesbian. A few years later she came out as bisexual, after which she felt shunned by many in the lesbian community of which she had become a part. This led her on a mission to heighten the visibility and acceptance of bisexual people within the queer community.

In 1983, Ka'ahumanu formed BiPOL, the first bisexual political action group in the US, and later co-founded the Bay Area Bisexual Network (BABN) in 1987. In 1990, 450 people attended the first National Bisexual Conference in San Francisco. Set up by Ka'ahumanu, its aim was to 'Educate, Advocate, Agitate, and Celebrate'.

In 1991, along with bisexual author and activist, Loraine Hutchins, Ka'ahumanu co-edited *Bi Any Other Name*. A collection of essays, poetry and art by bisexual people, the book became known as the 'bisexual bible' and was nominated for a Lambda Literary Award.

After successfully leading a campaign to have 'Bi' included in the March on Washington for Lesbian, Gay and Bi Equal Rights and Liberation, Ka'ahumanu spoke at the event on this date in 1993, the only bisexual person to do so.

OSCAR WILDE

1854–1900

Tragically, the criminal trial of playwright Oscar Wilde, which began on this date in 1865, is as famous as his literary works. Hugely popular, Wilde's plays were filled with wit, satirising society and exposing many Victorian hypocrisies.

At the height of his success, although married to Constance Lloyd, Wilde had a very public relationship with Lord Alfred 'Bosie' Douglas, the son of the 9th marquess of Queensbury. The marquess accused Wilde of being a 'posing sodomite', a claim Wilde refuted. The playwright sued for libel, but then lost his case. Unfortunately for Wilde, evidence that proved the marquess' accusation came to light during the libel trial and led to his own arrest and trial for gross indecency with men. Wilde was found guilty and sentenced to two years' hard labour.

During the trial Wilde gave a speech that modern readers might now see as a public fight of gay rights in Victorian England. He spoke of 'The love that dare not speak its name' and proclaimed: '[it] is such a great affection of an elder for a younger man… as you find in the sonnets of Michelangelo and Shakespeare… It is beautiful, it is fine, it is the noblest form of affection. There is nothing unnatural about it.'

JANG YEONG-JIN

B. 1958

The North Korean government claims that homosexuality does not exist in the country because the people there live with 'sound mentality and good morals'. Indeed, when Jang Yeong-jin, the only known gay defector from North Korea, escaped the dictatorship, he claimed he didn't realise he was gay 'or even [know] what homosexuality was'.

Yeong-jin originally escaped the country into China in 1996, but when he was unable to find a way to cross to South Korea, he returned to the North. He later risked his life by crawling across the border, through the demilitarised zone (DMZ) — a 4-kilometre patrolled and mined territory — to the South, where he arrived on this date in 1997. It was only then, after reading a magazine article, that Yeong-jin learned what being gay meant. Until then, he hadn't understood why he felt unhappy in his arranged marriage and didn't love his wife.

Since leaving North Korea, Yeong-jin has written an autobiography, *A Mark of Red Honor*, and moved to the US. His relocation was prompted, at the age of 62, by finding love with a Korean–American restaurateur through a dating site. The pair spent lockdown with each other during the Covid-19 pandemic, and got engaged after two months of living together.

LENA WAITHE

B. 1984

Chicago-born producer, screenwriter and actor, Lena Waithe, puts Blackness front and centre of her work. One of her earliest jobs was as a producer for the comedy-drama *Dear White People*, about racial tensions at an Ivy League university, which premiered on this date in 2017.

In September that year, Waithe became the first Black woman to win the Outstanding Writing for a Comedy Series Emmy Award, for the episode she wrote for the TV show *Master of None*. She wrote and starred in the episode 'Thanksgiving', which was partially based on her own experience of coming out as a lesbian to her mother.

She also created the Showtime drama, *The Chi*, a coming-of-age drama series set in the South Side of Chicago, also based on her own experiences of growing up in the city. Still running, it premiered in 2018. Waithe wrote the script for the 2019 film *Queen & Slim*, which echoes the Bonnie and Clyde 'love on the run' movie of the 1960s and deals with America's racial divide. She was also executive producer of the 2021 horror-drama series *Them*, in which a Black family suffers extreme racism (among other traumas) when they move to a new neighbourhood.

JEANNE MANFORD

1920-2013

On this date in 1972, the *New York Post* published a letter entitled 'I have a homosexual son and I love him'. The letter was written by Jeanne Manford, whose gay son, Morty, was violently attacked while handing out flyers about gay rights in New York City earlier that month. Police had seemingly failed to intervene during the incident and Manford expressed her outrage at this in her letter, which received attention and public support for the issue.

Manford didn't stop there: later that year, she marched alongside Morty in New York's Christopher Street Liberation Day parade with a handmade sign reading 'Parents of Gays Unite in Support for Our Children'. She and her husband Jules went on to found what is thought to be the first support group for parents of gay children in the US, Parents of Gays (POG), which later became PFLAG (Parents and Friends of Lesbians and Gays).

PFLAG still operates today, with chapters across the country offering support and advice to queer people and their friends and families. In February 2013, Manford was posthumously awarded the 2012 Presidential Citizens Medal by President Barack Obama.

PROUD ALLY

ELLEN DEGENERES

B. 1958

Ellen DeGeneres is arguably one of the most famous lesbians in the US, if not in the world. *The Ellen DeGeneres Show* ran for 19 years until May 2022, during which time it won over 30 Daytime Emmy's, and while the show latterly received some negative press, DeGeneres' humour and personable character has enabled her to have one of the most successful television careers in America.

Starting out as a stand-up comic, in 1994 DeGeneres landed her own sitcom, *Ellen*, which was hugely popular and aired on ABC for four years. On this date in 1997, the lead character came out as gay, mirroring DeGeneres' real life, when she gave a coming-out interview on *The Oprah Winfrey Show* and featured in a famous 'Yep I'm Gay' cover on *Time* magazine in April 1997. Sadly, there was a career backlash for her, with her sitcom ratings declining and the implementation of a parental advisory at the beginning of each episode.

The show was monumental in US television history and a bold, brave move by DeGeneres. The queer community applauded her, however, and in 1998 the show won the Outstanding TV Comedy Series GLAAD Award, while DeGeneres herself was recognised with the Stephen F. Kolzak Award.

STEPHEN FRY

B. 1957

Actor, writer, comedian, voice-over artist, activist — Stephen Fry's credits are too plentiful to catalogue here. He rose to fame with his comedy partner, Hugh Laurie (who Fry met while studying English at Cambridge), when working with Ben Elton on a show called *There's Nothing to Worry About!* in the early 1980s. Fry and Laurie were later given their own show on the BBC, *A Bit of Fry & Laurie*, in 1986.

Although Fry struggled with his sexuality in early life, and even abstained from sex for 16 years, he eventually embraced being gay and became an open advocate for LGBTQ+ social and political issues. In 2007, the *Independent*

on Sunday Pink List named Fry the second most influential gay person in Britain.

Fry, aged 40, portrayed Oscar Wilde (see 26 Apr) in the film *Wilde*, which premiered on this date in the US in 1998, opposite Jude Law as Wilde's lover Bosie. The film earned Fry widespread critical acclaim and a Golden Globe nomination.

Fry, who has bipolar disorder, is also a mental health advocate, and in 2006 he released a documentary on the subject, entitled *Stephen Fry: The Secret Life of the Manic Depressive*, which won the International Emmy Award for Best Documentary in 2007.

ROMAINE BROOKS

1874–1970

In May 1910, American modernist painter Romaine Brooks held her first exhibition at the Durand-Ruel gallery in Paris, a city where she spent most of her life among other artists. The show included a nude portrait called *Azalées Blanches* (*White Azaleas*), which was unusual at the time because both artist and nude subject were female.

Brooks painted the portraits of numerous women, including a self-portrait in 1923 that became one of her most famous works. Many of her subjects were depicted wearing typically masculine clothing or seemingly blurring the lines of societal gender norms. The artist, who inherited a fortune enabling her to be financially independent, was a lesbian and styled herself in an androgynous way. Cassandra Langer, the author of *Romaine Brooks: A Life*, described her as 'one of the first modern artists to depict women's resistance to patriarchal representations of the female in art'.

Her painting *La France Croisée* (1914), featured a subject modelled on the dancer and actress Ida Rubinstein (with whom Brooks was in a relationship), wearing a red cross in front of the burning city of Ypres. It was produced to show the artist's opposition to World War One, and copies were sold to raise money for the Red Cross.

GLYN FUSSELL

B. 1980

Glyn Fussell and his friend Amy Zing set up their queer club night, Sink The Pink, at the Bethnal Green Working Men's club in London in 2008, as a response to 'too many bland and non-inclusive nights out'. The impact their creation had on the clubbing landscape over the next 14 years was unprecedented, as *Dazed* magazine called them 'the genderfucking drag collective changing London'.

The night, made up of a collective of creative misfits, dancers, drag queens, DJs, singers and artists, became the 'not to be missed' event on the clubbing calendar, not just in London but also internationally, as Fussell took the troupe all over the world from New York to Singapore. Fussell also helped set up Mighty Hoopla in 2017 — a fabulous pop-extravaganza of a festival, made up of over 200 performers and now attended by 25,000 people annually.

On this date in 2022, Fussell released his first book, *Sink the Pink's Manifesto for Misfits*, with contributors such as Mel C, Yungblud and Lady Phyll (see 2 Jan) telling their stories. Fussell described the book as a way of spreading the Sink the Pink message of inclusion and empowerment to misfits all over the world, saying, 'I want to make sure the misfits conquer the earth!'

PHYLLIS LYON & DEL MARTIN

1924–2020; 1921–2008

Phyllis Lyon and Del Martin – the lesbian activists who started what is thought to be the first lesbian rights group in America – got married twice! First in 2004, when the mayor of San Francisco issued city marriage licences to same-sex couples, despite gay marriage not being legally recognised, and for the second time on 16 June 2008, when they became the first same-sex couple to tie the knot in San Francisco, when it was legalised in California.

In 1955, the couple, along with several other women, bravely set up a political and social lesbian organisation, the Daughters of Bilitis; the name was inspired by a collection of lesbian poetry by Pierre Louÿs entitled 'Songs of Bilitis'. The group allowed women to connect with other lesbians, and members received a newsletter, the *Ladder*, which was the first printed lesbian magazine in the US.

Martin and Lyon were feminists and active members of the National Organization for Women. In 1979, the pair set up Lyon–Martin Health Services to provide health care to marginalised women of colour and trans patients.

On this date in 2021, the San Francisco Board of Supervisors voted unanimously to give the couple's former home in San Francisco landmark status.

VIRGINIA WOOLF

1882–1941

When the body of the British writer, Virginia Woolf, was recovered from the River Ouse in April 1941, the *New York Times* printed part of a suicide note she left to her husband in which she said she '…cannot go on any longer in these terrible times. I hear voices and cannot concentrate on my work.' Sadly, the author had been plagued by depression throughout her life.

Woolf's writings included *Jacob's Room* (1922), *Mrs. Dalloway* (1925) and the novel, *Orlando* (1928), which is widely thought of as 'the first trans novel in English'. It features a main character who lived for centuries and changed sex from male to female. It also deals with the issue of primogeniture and inheritance, an issue that Woolf's lover, Vita Sackville-West, had experienced when she was unable to inherit Knole House in Kent — which is explicitly featured in the book — because she was female.

Woolf's most autobiographical novel, *To The Lighthouse*, was published on this date in 1927. Her works were written in a stream-of-consciousness style — a narrative device that Woolf pioneered.

Orlando and *A Room of One's Own* (1929) both discussed gender and the struggles women faced because of a patriarchy that restricted their access to education, personal finance and property. Woolf's writing is still revered today and studied the world over.

KAYTRANADA

B. 1992

Born in Port-au-Prince, Haiti, but brought up in Montreal, Canada, Louis Kevin Celestin is more widely known as record producer and DJ Kaytranada (one half of the hip-hop duo, The Celestics).

The self-proclaimed shy loner who created a lot of his early music in his bedroom, before putting it out on Soundcloud, has collaborated with artists including Estelle, Craig David and Pharrell, and DJed for Madonna's New York Pride party in 2021.

The musician has spoken about how he didn't really know about gay culture and queer history when he came out, saying he had to learn a lot: 'I'm just gay and I love hip-hop. I love Mobb Deep, and I'm happy to be gay. I hear their homophobic raps and I'm like, "Yeah, it's sad, but the beat is crazy."'

Kaytranada released his debut album, *99.9%*, on this date in 2016 and it earned the accolade of Apple Music Canada's Best Album of the year, as well as the 2016 Polaris Music Prize. When his second album, BUBBA, received the Best Dance/Electronic Album award at the 63rd Grammy Awards in 2021, Kaytranada became the first Black winner in the category.

SAMUEL BARBER

1910-1981

American Samuel Barber was one of the most lauded composers of the 20th century, with an impressive catalogue of compositions and steeped in honours and awards, including two Pulitzer Prizes for Music. His second, for his *Concerto for Piano and Orchestra* (1962), was announced on this date in 1963.

Barber's long-time partner in life and music was librettist and director, Gian Carlo Menotti. The pair met at Philadelphia's Curtis Institute of Music in 1928 and stayed together for 40 years. Menotti wrote the libretto for Barber's Pulitzer Prize winning opera, *Vanessa*, and the musical duo lived and worked together in a house just north of New York City for 30 years, remaining close even after they separated.

Barber was a perfectionist — so much so that he ordered his publisher to destroy the score for a symphony he had created for the US Air Force, but with which he was unhappy. Years later, in 1984, it was discovered that not all of the symphony had been destroyed and parts of it were used for a recording by the New Zealand Symphony Orchestra in 1988.

LILY TOMLIN

B. 1939

American comedian, writer, actress and long-time LGBTQ+ activist, Lily Tomlin first found success on the US television sketch show *Rowan & Martin's Laugh-In*, which she joined in its third season in 1970.

Tomlin has enjoyed a long career, appearing in movies such as *Nashville* (1975), for which she received an Academy Award nomination for Best Supporting Actress, *9 to 5* (1980) alongside Dolly Parton and Jane Fonda, and *Tea with Mussolini* (1999), featuring Cher, Judi Dench and Maggie Smith. As well as her own TV specials, Tomlin has appeared in popular shows such as *Will and Grace* and *Desperate Housewives*. The actress found renewed success in the autumn of her career when she was reunited with Jane Fonda in the hit comedy *Grace and Frankie* (2015), where the two women play wives whose husbands fall in love with each other. Her role in the show, which premiered on this date in 2015, earned Tomlin four Emmy nominations and a Golden Globe nomination.

Tomlin and her partner, Jane Wagner, have been long running benefactors of the Los Angeles LGBT Center, a place that helps to house homeless LGBTQ+ youths and seniors, and provides medical services and STI testing to the queer community.

DANA INTERNATIONAL

B. 1969

The Eurovision Song Contest has long been a celebration close to the hearts of the queer community, earning its nickname 'The World Cup for Gays'. The relationship between the competition and LGBTQ+ people was firmly cemented on this date in 1998 when Dana International, an out trans Israeli singer, won the globally aired contest and brought trans visibility to the mainstream.

Dana International, real name Sharon Cohen, had reassignment surgery in England in 1993, and began her music career on her return home to Israel. Her popularity was immediate, and she became Israel's Best Female Artist of the Year award the following year.

After an initial failed attempt to represent her country at Eurovision in 1995, she successfully reapplied in 1998 with the song 'Diva'. Her entry was not without objections: she reportedly received death threats from orthodox religious members of Israeli society before the competition. However, she won and paved the way for others, including Conchita Wurst, a bearded drag queen from Austria, who took the crown in 2014. Dana International's legacy is fully embraced by the competition who invited her back to perform at the contest's 50th anniversary in Copenhagen in 2005.

CHAZ BONO

B. 1969

When the writer, musician and actor Chaz Bono made an intimate documentary about his transition, it was at a time when trans issues and stories were not often told honestly on television. *Becoming Chaz*, which aired on American television on this date in 2011, gave the star a chance to show the world his journey. It included footage of his mother, Cher, one of the most famous entertainers in the world, discussing the concerns she had for her child surrounding his transition.

Speaking to Oprah Winfrey about his journey, Bono, who had previously come out as lesbian in the LGBTQ+ magazine the *Advocate*, said he'd felt like his body was betraying him and was now much happier. Later that same year, he took part in the 13th series of the US TV show, *Dancing with the Stars*. This was the first time an openly transgender man had taken part in such a major network television show focusing on something unrelated to being transgender.

Bono is an LGBTQ+ activist, has been a spokesperson for the Human Rights Campaign and served as the Entertainment Media Director for GLAAD, who awarded him the Stephen F. Kolzak Award in 2012.

GIANNI VERSACE

1946–1997

Born to a dressmaker mother who allowed him and his sister, Donatella, to play in the fabric baskets of her seamstress studio, it seems Gianni Versace was destined to become a successful fashion designer.

He started the Versace brand, which became known for sleek designs that showed flesh and celebrated Classical Greek and Roman motifs, as well as courting and using celebrities to showcase its clothes. Editor-in-chief of *Vogue*, Anna Wintour, pointed out that Versace 'was the first to realize the value of the celebrity in the front row, and the value of the supermodel'. Versace was a pioneer in fusing fashion with celebrity pop culture in the way we see so commonly now.

On this date in 1994, the relatively unknown model and actress Elizabeth Hurley wore a black Versace dress held together with oversized gold safety pins to the premiere of the film *Four Weddings and a Funeral*. This garnered unprecedented global press coverage and the dress became Versace's career-defining creation.

Versace held family in high regard. His brother Santo ran the business when it began and became president. Donatella, his muse, was always by his side, and when he was murdered in Florida in 1997, she took up the company reigns and continued its success.

STEPHEN SPENDER

1909–1995

Stephen Spender, the British poet and novelist, was often in interesting company. Firm friends with Christopher Isherwood and W.H. Auden (see 13 Feb and 29 Sep) from their Oxford University days, he later rubbed shoulders with writers such as T.S. Eliot, Dylan Thomas and Virginia Woolf (see 5 May).

Spender's poetry, much like Auden's, was pioneering in that it presented England's gritty industrial landscape of the 1930s to its readers, addressing political issues in an accessible way. Spender was a member of the Communist Party for a time and some of his early works, such as the poem *The Funeral* (1955) and his essay *Forward from Liberalism* (1937), deal with communism.

He married twice, both times to women, but having often written of his love of boys in letters and in his diaries, Spender's sexuality has been much discussed. His autobiographical work *World Within World* (1951) disclosed details of a homosexual relationship he had with a man who fought in the Spanish Civil War. Spender also co-founded the Homosexual Law Reform Society on this date in 1958, a group that campaigned for British sodomy laws to be overturned.

In 1965, Spender became the first non-American to be appointed poetry consultant to the US Library of Congress (now called Poet Laureate).

EDWARD CARPENTER

1844–1929

Writer and philosopher Edward Carpenter's legacy is substantial and his collection of autobiographical notes *My Days and Dreams*, published in May 1916, has left us great insight into the man and his works. Not only did he leave an extensive catalogue of poetry, philosophy and essays on animal rights, but he also influenced others and their work. It is thought that the 'simple life' he lived in Derbyshire with his lover, George Merrill, influenced the queer novel *Maurice* (1971) of his friend, E.M. Forster (see 1 Jan).

A fan of the German sexologist, Magnus Hirschfeld, Carpenter advocated free love and sexual liberation. In a brave move for the time, Carpenter wrote that gay relationships should be celebrated, not persecuted, in his 1906 book, *The Intermediate Sex*. Practising what he preached, Carpenter had an open relationship with Merrill and had numerous male lovers.

For a time after his death, Carpenter's works were not widely available. However, as society became more liberal, his writings on issues such as environmentalism, vegetarianism and sexual liberalisation became more popular.

As an ode to his leftist works and the fact that he and his partner spent time making and selling sandals in Millthorpe, Derbyshire, Carpenter has often been referred to as 'The Saint in Sandals'.

MAX SPOHR

1850-1905

German publishing magnate, Max Spohr was an early advocate for sexual freedom, publishing renowned German sexologist Magnus Hirschfeld's pamphlet, *Sappho and Socrates*, in 1896, after the sexologist had previously struggled to find a publisher. From that point onwards, the pair became friends.

Hirschfeld is often described as the pioneer of the modern study of sexuality, in particular homosexuality. On this date in 1897, Spohr and Hirschfeld, along with lawyer Eduard Oberg and writer Franz Joseph von Bülow, founded the Scientific-Humanitarian Committee (Wissenschaftlich-humanitäres Komitee) in Berlin. The organisation advocated for homosexuality

to be accepted as a natural way of life and conducted groundbreaking studies, publishing their findings in countless books and periodicals.

Before publishing Hirschfeld's pamphlet, Spohr had published other LGBTQ+ works — he was one of the first people to do so in the country. Reports suggest he faced prosecution for obscenity on numerous occasions.

There doesn't seem to be any evidence that Spohr was gay, bisexual or queer himself, and in 1880 he married Elisabeth Hannöver-Jansen, with whom he fathered three sons. Spohr was honoured as an ally and businessman, 96 years after his death, when officials in Leipzig named a street after him.

PROUD ALLY

ROBERTA COWELL

1918-2011

In November 1944, a British warplane crash-landed in Germany. Its pilot was taken into captivity, initially held in an interrogation centre and ending up in Stalag Luft I, a prisoner-of-war camp. In 1945, the Germans abandoned the camp and the Red Army liberated the POWs, including the pilot, on the night of 30 April.

That pilot was Roberta Cowell, the first known person to undergo gender-reassignment surgery in Britain. Before being a fighter pilot, Cowell was a professional racing driver, a husband and a father to two daughters.

In her autobiography, Cowell wrote that she believed her 'nature was essentially feminine and in some way my world was out of joint'. She suffered with depression, sought psychiatric help and said through psychoanalysis found 'my unconscious mind was predominantly female'. On this date in 1951, Cowell had a vaginoplasty, performed by plastic surgeon Sir Harold Gillies. Betty, as she later became known, briefly returned to racing, and won the 1957 Shelsley Walsh Speed Hill Climb.

Cowell became estranged from her children, yet when her daughter Diana was informed of her death, she called her mother 'an extraordinary woman'.

MARY ANNING

1799–1847

On this date in 2022, Mary Anning made a comeback in her home town of Lyme Regis, UK, when a long-campaigned-for commemorative statue was delivered to the town, 175 years after the pioneering palaeontologist and fossil collector's death.

Anning began collecting fossils as a child and at the age of 12, discovered a 5.2-metre-long skeleton, which was later identified as a marine reptile that lived 201–194 million years ago.

Despite her multiple momentous findings, which contributed to the early understanding of prehistoric life on the Jurassic Coast, Anning was often uncredited in scientific papers written at the time. Her work is thought to have partly influenced the theory of evolution put forward by Charles Darwin.

In the 2021 film *Ammonite*, actress Kate Winslet portrayed Anning as queer, with the story focused on her relationship with a married middle-class woman, Charlotte Murchison, who Anning taught to fossil hunt. While there's no direct evidence that the unmarried Anning was gay or bisexual, director Francis Lee said, 'It is well documented that she had close friendships with women… and where Mary had been virtually written out of history because of her gender and social status, it didn't feel right to give her a relationship with a man.'

PATRICIA HIGHSMITH

1921–1995

Patricia Highsmith was an American writer, well-known and revered for her thrillers. Alfred Hitchcock made her 1950 novel, *Strangers on a Train*, into a film the year after it was published, and her series featuring the character Tom Ripley ran up to five novels over 36 years.

Her 1952 novel, *The Price of Salt*, a semi-autobiographical lesbian love story, was originally published under a pseudonym. It centred around a woman Highsmith had met while working in Bloomingdale's at Christmas and was notable because it had a happy ending. Highsmith, often reported to be an odd and difficult person, had been working there to save up money for psychoanalysis in the hope she might one day live a heterosexual life.

The book, re-titled *Carol*, was republished years later under Highsmith's own name, and more than 60 years after it was written, the film of *Carol* was released with Cate Blanchett and Rooney Mara in the lead roles. It premiered at Sundance on this date in 2015 and won the Queer Palm at Cannes the same year.

Highsmith lived an isolated existence in later life, happiest at home with her pet snails and cats.

JEAN-MICHEL BASQUIAT

1960-1988

On this date in 2017, Jean-Michel Basquiat's 1982 painting of a skull, *(Untitled)*, was purchased for $110.5 million at Sotheby's, at the time the sixth-most expensive-work ever sold at auction.

The Brooklyn-born artist began his career creating street art in New York with friend, Al Diaz, and quickly went on to immerse himself in the New York Hip Hop scene of the late 1970s and early 80s. After selling his postcards to Andy Warhol, Basquiat formed a band called Gray, with filmmaker Michael Holman, dated Madonna (see 21 Mar) and starred in the film *New York Beat*.

His art soon gained notoriety and he quickly created a vast portfolio of work, showing at exhibitions alongside artists such as Keith Haring (see 2 Sep), Nan Goldin and Andy Warhol (see 3 Jun). As he became more famous, he partied as hard as he worked and sadly died as a result of heroin use at just 27 years old.

According to Jennifer Clement, author of *Widow Basquiat*, the artist was 'attracted to people for all different reasons'. While he eluded labels, Clement said: 'They could be boys, girls, thin, fat, pretty, ugly. It was, I think, driven by intelligence.' The artist's ex-lover, Suzanne Mallouk, has also spoken openly about the artist's bisexuality.

ALIX DOBKIN

1940–2021

Throughout 2014 and 2015, the *Guardian* ran a regular feature called 'The 101 strangest records on Spotify'. Included in this list were two records by lesbian folk singer Alix Dobkin; according to the newspaper, *Lavender Jane Loves Women* and *Living With Lesbians* are 'both bloody great'. Dobkin's music was written and performed for a female-only audience, her feminist politics running through everything she did. However her performances in women-only spaces included events like Michigan's Michfest that had a transgender exclusionary door policy, which obviously renders Dobkin's legacy within the LGBTQ+ community problematic for many.

Dobkin, who died on this date in 2021, was originally married to Sam Hood, proprietor of a famous Greenwich Village café, but after hearing Germaine Greer interviewed on the radio by Liza Cowan in 1970, Dobkin managed to get herself on the same show, met Cowan and the pair fell in love.

Dobkin set up her own label, Women's Wax Works, to release her first album in 1973. It was entirely produced by women, right down to the people who pressed the vinyl. A powerful voice in the lesbian feminist movement for decades, she focused her activism and music on 'the lives, concerns and perspectives of women who love women'.

JASON COLLINS

B. 1978

'I'm a 34-year-old NBA center. I'm Black. And I'm gay,' the 7-foot, 255-pound US basketball player Jason Collins told the world in an article in the May 2013 issue of *Sports Illustrated*. It made him the first active male athlete in a major American professional team sport to come out publicly.

In the weeks following publication, Outsports.com reported that around 187 professional athletes talked about issues surrounding LGBTQ+ athletes, and on this date, the Gay, Lesbian and Straight Education Network (GLSEN) presented him with the Courage Award. As a direct result, the NBA donated $100k+ to GLSEN and the Matthew Shepard Foundation, both LGBTQ+ youth charities.

In 2014, *Time* magazine included Collins as one of its '100 Most Influential People', and featured the star on some regional editions of this issue. When Derrick Gordan became the first player in Division I college men's basketball to come out in April 2014, he cited Collins as an inspiration.

In 2014, Collins announced that he was retiring from the game after a 13-year professional career playing for teams such as the Atlanta Hawks and the Boston Celtics, but said 'I will continue to speak out and push for people to live their authentic life, continue to speak up for diversity and inclusion.'

JAMES DALE

B. 1970

When James Dale spoke publicly about being gay, while discussing the health needs of lesbian and gay teenagers at a social work conference in 1990, the Boy Scouts of America (BSA) expelled him from his position as an assistant scoutmaster, explicitly stating that Dale's homosexuality was the reason for his expulsion.

Dale challenged the BSA in the New Jersey Superior Court, alleging they had violated the state statute prohibiting discrimination on the basis of sexual orientation in public places. A ruling favouring Dale was originally reached but then overturned when the BSA appealed to the Supreme Court of America.

After a 10-year fight, Dale was not successful and understandably disappointed by the result. Nevertheless, he felt his actions had been worthwhile, saying, 'There has been an incredible amount of progress, and the 5-4 loss in the Supreme Court shows how far we've gone... If I could do it all over again, I would do it exactly the same way.'

Years later, on this date in 2015, BSA president Robert Gates said he would no longer revoke the charters of chapters that want to defy the ban on gay adult scout leaders, effectively giving each group the right to decide whether to allow gay scoutmasters.

CARLA ANTONELLI

B. 1959

Carla Antonelli, who describes herself as 'a true left-wing woman', is a trans Spanish actress, activist and politician from Tenerife in the Canary Islands. She fought for the rights of sex workers and challenged her own party, the Spanish Socialist Workers' Party (PSOE), on their gender laws.

She was instrumental in pushing the Law of Identity and Gender Expression through the Assembly of Madrid, which aimed for the depathologisation of transsexuality (meaning transsexuality should not be classed as an illness) and to protect trans youths.

In 2017, when asked about the transphobic abuse directed at her from far-right Vox Party members in the Madrid Assembly, Antonelli explained, 'What has happened is a drop of water in a glass that is about to overflow. A glass that is too full of humiliations, insults and disqualifications… that we are a danger for feminism and for Spaniards… is an outrage and an absolute injustice towards a group of people who have had it and have it very difficult throughout their history and who are trying to raise their heads. We are not numbers, we are people.'

On this date in 2011, Antonelli became the first trans person elected to a legislature in Spain. She was re-elected in the 2015 and 2019 regional elections.

BOOAN TEMPLE

B. c. 1959

Section 28, also called Clause 28, was a piece of legislation brought in by the UK Conservative government that prevented the 'promotion' of homosexuality in schools. At the time, 75 per cent of the population said they thought that gay relationships were almost always wrong – appealing to this sentiment, the vaguely worded clause also spurred the LGBTQ+ community into action.

On 23 May 1988, the night before Section 28 became law, four women, including carpenter Booan Temple, invaded a live BBC news broadcast, wearing 'Stop the Clause' t-shirts and even handcuffing themselves to equipment. At the time, Temple was part of an all-female local council team that was '… involved in lots of things: rape crisis, women's reproductive rights, the "stop the strip-search" campaign… so as this legislation was proposed, the idea that we had to do something grew'.

Temple and her comrades felt that their cause wasn't getting air-time and so they decided to obtain it themselves. The on-air invasion garnered publicity for the women but they were primarily mocked as 'loony lesbians'. The group were arrested but never charged, and when they were released they made their way to the House of Commons to join the protest as the law passed at midnight.

Section 28 was finally repealed in 2003.

GERRY STUDDS

1937-2006

Gerry Studds was the first openly gay congressman in the US. As a Democrat he served constituencies in Massachusetts for 24 years, one which, before him, had been solidly Republican.

Studds came out after a previous sexual relationship with a 17-year-old male congressional page became public 10 years later. The congressman was censured for sexual misconduct; he defended the relationship as consensual but admitted to a 'very serious error in judgment'. Despite this scandal, he was re-elected multiple times.

Studds was an environmental advocate who created numerous state parks and protected areas and worked with the fishing industry to improve stock. Later in his career, he introduced the Marine Mammals Protection Act.

The significance of Studds' openness about his sexuality was highlighted by Congressman Barney Frank, who said, 'The important thing about what Gerry did was the reaction to it. And the reaction to it was that there was no reaction… Americans understand that they really aren't homophobic, they just thought they were supposed to be.'

After coming out, Studds championed gay rights and on this date in 2004, he and his partner Dean Hara were among the first couples to marry under the new Massachusetts law legalising gay unions.

PETER ACKROYD

B. 1949

British biographer, novelist and critic Peter Ackroyd was born and raised on an East Acton council estate, in West London. He was brought up in a devout Roman Catholic family, but despite the strongly held religious beliefs of the faith, knew from an early age that he was gay.

Ackroyd's interests are embedded in London's history and culture, especially that of queer culture, which can be seen in his book *Queer City: Gay London from the Romans to the Present Day*, published on this date in 2017. In the book, Ackroyd explores queer culture, which has always existed in the city. He also delves into the language of homosexuality, explaining the origins of terms such as 'faggot', which was originally used to describe a bundle of wood that would be formed to make a fire – the term thus implying that those accused of sodomy could be burned to death.

Having studied at the University of Cambridge University in the UK and Yale University in the US, Ackroyd has won many awards and honours for his writing, including two Whitbread Awards and the *Guardian* Fiction Prize for his 1985 novel, *Hawksmoor*. He was nominated for the Man Booker Prize in 1998 and in 2003 became a Commander of the Order of the British Empire (CBE).

REGINA FONG

1946–2003

Reginald Bundy, born on this date in 1946, trained as a dancer and worked both in front of and behind the curtain in London's West End shows. In the early 1980s, he joined up with Rosie Lee and Gracie Grab It All to form drag trio The Disappointer Sisters, performing across London bars and clubs. Then, in 1985, Reg created his long-standing character, Regina Fong.

Fong appeared regularly at The Black Cap, a gay cabaret pub in north London, in a flame-red wig, blood-red ballgown and 'Jungle Red' nail polish. She roused her cult followers (the Fongettes) into song and often spun the tale that she was a member of the Romanoff family, who had escaped St Petersburg with three Fabergé eggs hidden most intimately about her person. Throughout her career, she hosted Pride events, charity and awards galas, and even fronted a late-night youth TV show called *Club X*.

When Fong died in 2003, the Black Cap held a night in her honour and *QX Magazine* described her as a performer who '...can be credited with redefining the gay cabaret scene with characterisations that appealed to the broadest spectrum of gay men, lesbians and clued-up straights, too... fondly remembered as, perhaps, the greatest drag act of them all'.

GARETH THOMAS

B. 1974

Rugby player Gareth Thomas made his debut for Wales on this date in 1995. In 2005, he became captain of the British & Irish Lions, while on tour in New Zealand, and by the end of his career in 2007, he had made history by becoming the first Welshman to win 100 caps in Rugby Union.

In December 2009, he made history once again by coming out as gay in a UK national newspaper. Explaining why he hadn't been open about his sexuality before, Thomas said, 'It [rugby] is the toughest, most macho of male sports, and with that comes an image… I could never have come out without first establishing myself and earning respect as a player.'

Since then, Thomas has worked with various individuals, including Prince Harry, and charities such as the Terrence Higgins Trust, to break down the stigma of being HIV positive, after he revealed his own positive status in 2019.

Thomas married his husband in 2016 without publicly announcing the occasion until years later, and in 2020 he was appointed Commander of the Order of the British Empire (CBE) in the Queen's Birthday Honours List for services to sport and health.

LEE MOKOBE

B. 1995

Lee Mokobe is a slam poet whose work addresses social injustices and explores queer identities through the lens of a Black transgender immigrant in the US and South Africa. Mokobe is South African and was the youngest ever and first African coach at the Brave New Voices Festival, the largest ongoing spoken word event in the world.

In 2011, Mokobe co-founded Vocal Revolutionaries, a not-for-profit organisation aimed at improving the lives of youth in Cape Town. As well as helping young people find their voices using poetry, digital art and music, Vocal Revolutionaries offers safety, shelter and food to orphans and abandoned youth. The organisation's website says it is 'giving youth the space to use their voices as tools for social and personal transformation'.

On this date in 2015, Mokobe spoke at the TEDWomen conference in California, performing their work about what it feels like to be transgender. The poem beautifully captures Mokobe's lived, queer experience, with lines such as 'tightroping between awkward boy and apologetic girl, /and when I turned 12, the boy phase wasn't deemed cute anymore…'

YVES SAINT LAURENT

1936–2008

Fashion designer Yves Saint Laurent left his home in Algeria to travel to Paris, France when he was 17. Soon after, his sketches were published in French *Vogue* and caught the eye of Christian Dior, who hired him; he was put in charge of haute couture at the label at just 21.

In 1960, Saint Laurent established his own fashion house with lover and business partner Pierre Bergé. The pair created iconic looks such as *le smoking* (a smoking suit) and the jumpsuit.

Although Saint Laurent struggled with drug and alcohol addiction throughout his life, his excesses, including a self-proclaimed wild and plentiful sex life, did not affect his productivity. He turned out two haute couture and two prêt-à-porter collections a year. It's thought that the bullying and homophobia he endured as an adolescent, coupled with conscription to fight in the Algerian war, contributed to the designer's substance abuse in later life.

Although his sexuality was an open secret for years in the fashion world, Saint Laurent came out publicly in the French newspaper *Le Figaro*, in 1991. On this date in 2008, Bergé and he exchanged vows in a civil union, just a few days before Saint Laurent died.

CHRISTOPHER MARLOWE

1564–1593

The circumstances surrounding the fatal stabbing of British playwright Christopher Marlowe on this date in 1593, have often been debated. Some say it was a simple bar brawl over the payment of a bill, others suggest it was an assassination ordered by Queen Elizabeth I, while some point to it being a dispute over a boy. Both in life and death, Marlowe, a contemporary and friend of William Shakespeare, sparked controversy and speculation about his sexuality.

Marlowe, a successful and popular playwright and poet, was often in trouble with the law, particularly on account of him being an atheist and suspected spy.

His plays include *The Tragicall History of Doctor Faustus* (*c.* 1592) and *Edward II* (1592), a work about King Edward in which Marlowe appears to encourage the audience to interpret the relationship between the king and nobleman Piers Gaveston as homosexual.

In March 2017, the British Library in London put on public display a document written by Richard Baines, an Elizabethan double agent and Catholic priest, who claims that Marlowe declared Jesus Christ was gay. The document also states that Marlowe believed the only purpose of religion was to intimidate people and that 'all they that love not tobacco and boys were fools'.

ZANELE MUHOLI

B. 1972

The work of the non-binary, South African artist and visual activist, Zanele Muholi, focuses on sharing Black LGBTQIA+ South African lives and experiences with the world. They believe their role as artist and activist are intrinsically linked, saying, 'Art needs to be political — or let me say that my art is political. It's not for show. It's not for play.'

The artist's ongoing photography project, *Faces and Phases*, is made up of hundreds of powerful portraits of Black lesbian, transgender and non-binary individuals, taken from 2006 onwards. The participants stare straight into the camera, forcing the viewer to hold their gaze.

Muholi, who was born in Durban, South Africa, and now lives in Johannesburg, won an Infinity Award from the International Centre of Photography in 2016. They see their work as an opportunity 'to re-write a Black queer and trans visual history of South Africa for the world to know of our resistance and existence at the height of hate crimes in SA and beyond'.

Muholi's retrospective exhibition at the Tate Modern in London ran during the global Covid-19 pandemic and the resurgence of the Black Lives Matter movement, from November 2020 and ending on this date in 2021.

MATTHEW ASHTON

B. 1974

'I'm really proud that I work for a company that wants to make a statement like this and really wants to include everybody,' said Matthew Ashton, the LEGO® Group's vice president of design, as the company launched its first LGBTQIA+ set on this date in 2021. 'Representation is so important. I grew up in the 80s and was obviously a gay kid. There was a lot of negativity back then around being gay,' he said. So Ashton set out to design a product with a clear spirit of support and inclusivity.

The set was named *40516 Everyone is Awesome* and included a diferent monochrome character for each of the 11 colours of the Progress Pride flag. Ashton said that when the idea for the set was initially discussed at LEGO® headquarters in Denmark, he'd already made a prototype for himself that sat on his desk, which became the blueprint for *40516 Everyone is Awesome*.

During his two decades at LEGO®, Ashton has been an executive producer on the LEGO® movies and a head judge for the TV show *LEGO® Masters UK*. In autumn 2021, he collaborated with Bobby Berk, from TV show *Queer Eye*, to create a LEGO® set of the Fab Five presenters from the show.

PATRICK O'CONNELL

1953–2021

Patrick O'Connell was the founding executive director of Visual AIDS, a New York-based organisation that supports artists living with HIV and AIDS. It 'utilizes art to fight AIDS by provoking dialogue, supporting HIV+ artists, and preserving a legacy'.

In 1989, Visual AIDS started 'Day Without Art', in which hundreds of galleries, arts organisations and museums throughout the US covered artworks or temporarily removed them from display and replaced them with information about HIV and safer sex.

One of the group's most successful awareness campaigns, spearheaded by O'Connell, was the Red Ribbon Project in 1991, designed to be a public participatory artwork. It involved getting people together (in the beginning artists, friends and colleagues of Visual AIDS members) to cut and fold thousands of snips of red ribbon. After celebrities wore the ribbons on this date at the 1991 Tony Awards, they became a ubiquitous sign of both protest and awareness of the pandemic.

Of the red ribbons, O'Connell said, 'People want to say something, not necessarily with anger and confrontation all the time… This allows them. And even if it is only an easy first step, that's great with me.'

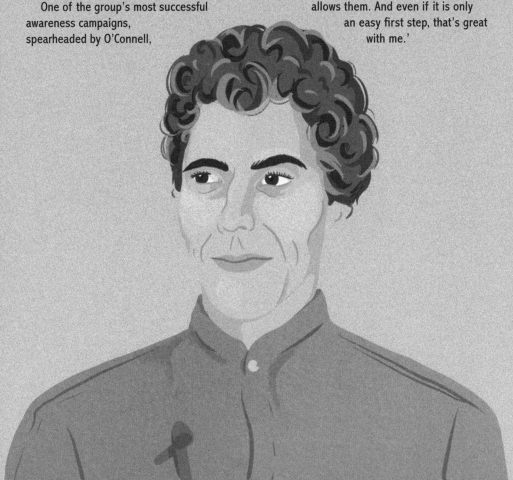

ANDY WARHOL

1928–1987

Anyone can view Andy Warhol's grave online, 24 hours a day, seven days a week, as part of a project called *Figment*, via Warhol.org. This seems a fitting tribute for the man obsessed by fame who said, 'In the future, everyone will be world-famous for 15 minutes.'

Warhol was born to Slovakian immigrant parents. He moved to New York in 1949 and began working successfully as a commercial illustrator and art director. He became a central figure in the Pop Art movement in the 1960s and created a unique workspace in New York City, The Factory, a hang-out for artists and celebrities. On this date in 1968 the radical feminist and author of *SCUM Manifesto*, Valerie Solanas entered The Factory with an unfounded grudge against the artist and shot him. He survived, but with long-lasting injuries.

Warhol's most famous works include photographic silkscreens of celebrities such as Jackie Kennedy, Marilyn Monroe and Elvis Presley; however the artist, who was openly gay, never shied away from producing queer art. Some of his early work included erotic drawings of men, and in 1975 he produced a portrait series of trans women and drag queens named Ladies and Gentlemen.

PHILIPPA YORK

B. 1958

Scottish-born Philippa York is a former professional road racing cyclist and now sports journalist, who came out publicly as transgender in 2017 after transitioning some years earlier.

When competing, York was one of the most celebrated British cyclists in the 1980s and early 1990s, winning the King of the Mountains prize in the Tour de France in 1984. York's other wins include the Mountains classification in the 1987 Giro d'Italia, the 1989 Tour of Britain and the 1990 Critérium du Dauphiné Libéré, which culminated on 4 June.

York stepped back from sporting and public life after 2002, completing her transition in private. When she announced her public comeback in 2017, she revealed she would be part of ITV4's Tour de France commentary team and said her family's 'support [and] encouragement and the shift in modern society's attitudes, means that this will be a step forward for everyone'.

York, who now lives in Dorset, UK, returned to cycle in Scotland in 2020 for the first time in 20 years, as part of The Great Tour, a fundraising challenge. She returned again in 2021 as the village of Lennoxtown unveiled a mural in her honour.

ARTHUR SMITH GRAHAM

1871–1928

In cult author Frederick Rolfe's novel, *Nicholas Crabbe: A Romance*, the character Theophanes Clayfoot lives in a beautiful Cornish estate and steals the affections of a man from the protagonist. In fact, Clayfoot is based on Arthur Smith Graham, the son of a wealthy merchant family, and the Cornish estate represents Smith's real-life home, Great Ambrook.

Graham commissioned and created a unique Italian walled garden at Ambrook, designed in his vision by the architect Thomas Henry Lyon. The garden was set away from the house, and had 15-foot high walls most of the way around. This secluded space was designed to provide privacy for Graham, who was homosexual (as was Lyon). At a time when fellow Oxonian Oscar Wilde (see 26 Apr) was jailed for homosexual crimes, Graham wanted somewhere he could discreetly socialise away from prying eyes. Complete with tennis courts, pools and a summerhouse, the garden provided a private area where the owner could entertain his friends.

After Graham's death and Ambrook had changed hands numerous times, the walled gardens had become neglected. Only recently has care and restoration been undertaken, after they were given a Grade II listing on the Register of Parks and Gardens on this date in 2014.

LA VENENO

1964–2016

La Veneno, aka Cristina Ortiz Rodríguez, was interviewed on the late-night Spanish TV show *Esta noche cruzamos el Mississippi* (*Tonight We Cross the Mississippi*) in 1996 and was later enlisted as a regular guest due to her instant popularity. Her brash but lovable personality and sense of humour endeared her to the public. She went on to act, sing and model, and became the most visible trans person in Spanish pop culture at a time when life was incredibly difficult for the country's LGBTQ+ community.

La Veneno's life was often troubled and in 2003 she was convicted of insurance fraud and arson, after her home burnt down. She denied the charges, accusing her boyfriend, Andrea Petruzzelli, as the perpetrator, but was found guilty and, horrifically, sent to a men's prison to serve her sentence.

In 2020, the HBO TV drama *Veneno* aired, which starred three transgender actresses each playing La Veneno at different periods in her life. 'There were no women who looked like her at the time. I was so starstruck when I saw her,' said Jedet, one of the actresses who played the star. The show aired to critical acclaim and won Iris and Premio Ondas Awards.

On this date in 2021, an episode of *Drag Race España* paid tribute to La Veneno with a runway challenge themed around her iconic looks.

LIBERACE

1919-1987

Known as Mr Showmanship or simply Liberace, Władziu Valentino Liberace – the American singer and pianist known for his flamboyant appearance and dazzling performances – was one of the most popular performing artists in the US from the 1950s to 1970s.

Often dressed in sequins and fur, and sitting at a rhinestone-covered grand piano adorned with a glittering candelabra, Liberace's performances were dazzling and schmaltzy. His skills as a pianist were impressive and his constant TV appearances, magazine interviews and concerts made him not only hugely popular (particularly with middle-aged women), but also incredibly rich.

On this date in 2013 the movie *Behind the Candelabra* was released, chronicling the turbulent five-year relationship Liberace had with Scott Thorson, his former chauffeur. When Thorson sued Liberace in 1982, exposing their relationship, the singer denied he was gay and the pair eventually settled out of court. Despite lovers, biographers and friends all testifying that he was gay, Liberace never came out and contested at least two court cases on the matter, demonstrating what was at stake at the time for someone so successful.

LEO HERRERA

B. 1981

Leo Herrera is a queer Mexican writer, activist and filmmaker whose work focuses on the American queer experience. While his primary medium is film, he became popular on social media for political commentary during the Covid-19 pandemic, creating memes to communicate his thoughts.

One of his most well-known projects, *Fathers*, is a sci-fi documentary and multimedia series that imagines the AIDS pandemic never happened, and therefore a whole generation of missing queer people had lived to change the world. In one of the films, Herrera visualises a surviving Vito Russo (see 21 Aug) as becoming the president of the United States!

Herrera began reading about queer history as a teenager in Phoenix, Arizona and after he and his gay brother moved to San Francisco, they began making films with their friends.

Fathers was seen as controversial by some who felt it was distasteful to 'erase' the AIDS pandemic, but while Herrera worried about this when developing the project. He also admitted intending to cause anger, saying, 'I'm one of those people that thinks art should make you a bit uncomfortable.'

On this date in 2019, *Behind The Lens*, a behind-the-scenes documentary by Claudia Escobar that features the making of *Fathers* and profiles Leo's background, won an Emmy.

LAVERNE COX

B. 1972

Laverne Cox has many groundbreaking claims to fame. She was the first openly transgender actor to have a recurring role on a primetime television show (playing Candis in the ABC drama *Dirty Sexy Money*). She was also the first openly transgender actress to be nominated for a Primetime Acting Emmy for *Orange is the New Black*. And on this date in 2014 she became the first openly transgender person to grace the cover of American news magazine, *Time*.

That issue of the magazine featured an article called 'The Transgender Tipping Point', in which Cox talked about her experiences as a transgender woman and about the importance of visibility. She pointed out that 'When people have points of reference that are humanizing, that demystifies difference.' The feature is heralded for bringing the transgender perspective to millions of Americans who might otherwise have been left ignorant.

Cox is an LGTBQ+ activist and in 2020 was an executive producer of the film *Disclosure*; a documentary screened on Netflix that uncovered and exposed how trans people are represented in film and on TV. 'Some folks, they just don't understand. And they need to get to know us as human beings,' she says.

HARVEY FIERSTEIN

B. 1954

Actor and writer, Harvey Fierstein was cast in Andy Warhol's (see 3 Jun) play *Pork*, aged just 16. He went on to write (and star in) *Torch Song Trilogy*, a collection of three plays dealing with queer characters and relationships, usually performed together in three acts. The Broadway production, which opened on this date in 1982, earned Fierstein the accolades of Best Play and Best Actor in a Play at the Tony Awards in 1983. The play was made into a film of the same name in 1988.

Fierstein's other writing credits include the books for *La Cage Aux Folles* (1983) and *Kinky Boots* (2012). In film, Fierstein played the gay brother of Robin Williams' character in *Mrs Doubtfire* (1993). Albeit only in a sidekick comedic role, the character was an openly gay man in a relationship, portrayed positively in a mainstream Hollywood film in the 1990s.

In 2002, Fierstein delivered camp comedy gold as he played the part of housewife Edna Turnblad in the Broadway musical *Hairspray*, based on John Waters' 1988 film. The show was a huge hit and Fierstein won Best Performance by a Leading Actor in a Musical at the 2003 Tony Awards.

FLORENCE GIVEN

B. 1998

The website of British artist, author and activist, Florence Given, boasts that she became 'the youngest author to hold a position in the top five of the *Sunday Times* bestseller list for a consecutive 12 weeks in a row' with her debut book, *Women Don't Owe You Pretty*. Published on this date in 2020, the book is an illustrated work in which Given encourages the reader to challenge out-dated narratives supplied by 'the patriarchy'.

Given, who identifies as queer, uses her art and her Instagram platform, which she started when she was 17, to promote discussion and raise awareness on issues such as sexuality, gender and race. She fills her feed with typographic images showing slogans such as, 'It's a wonderful day to dump him', and illustrations of naked women of various body types alongside feminist messages.

In January 2022, Given launched the podcast *Exactly. With Florence Given*, in which she explores sex, social media, feminism, relationships and body image. She previously worked with Always, the menstrual hygiene brand, on their #EndPeriodPoverty campaign to help get free period products to young women. When interviewed by the *Evening Standard* in 2020, she said, 'I want women to learn to love the sh*t out of themselves and put themselves first.'

JESSICA KELLGREN-FOZARD

B. 1989

London-born Jessica Kellgren-Fozard began making YouTube videos in 2011, covering a range of subjects including 'vintage fabulousness', LGBTQ+ issues, living with disabilities and chronic illnesses, deafness and, more recently, parenthood, as she and her wife became parents in the summer of 2021. She was nominated for a DIVA Rising Star of the Year Award in 2019.

Kellgren-Fozard was diagnosed with hereditary neuropathy with liability to pressure palsies (HNPP) when she was 17. This can make gripping objects difficult and causes numbness of the skin and severe fatigue, among other things. She also has mixed connective tissue disease (MCTD), an autoimmune disorder that causes the body's defence system to attack itself. The YouTuber speaks openly and honestly about her condition online and to the media. In a *Guardian* interview in 2018 she explained that the fact that her disabilities are not always visible to others is a hindrance, as strangers are less accepting and even think she's making it up.

On this date in 2018, Kellgren-Fozard shared a YouTube video that taught people how to sign queer words and phrases using British Sign Language (BSL). At time of writing, it has been viewed by almost 90,000 people.

ROXANE GAY

B. 1974

Roxane Gay's collection of essays, *The Bad Feminist*, became a *New York Times* bestseller when it was released in 2014. The American author and academic has also written short stories, the comic book series, *World of Wakanda*, and the Lambda Literary Award-winning memoir, *Hunger*, released on this date in 2017, which explores intimacy and sensitivity around food and bodies.

After dropping out of Yale University in her Junior year, Gay, who came out as lesbian and then later as bisexual, supported herself by working on phone sex lines. She also blogged, saying 'through writing, I was, finally, able to get respect for the content of my character'. The trauma of being sexually assaulted by a group of boys when she was 12 years old manifested itself in Gay through compulsive eating. She wanted to be physically large, not weak, to make herself 'repulsive' to men.

While at Michigan Technological University, Gay worked on the literary magazine, *PANK*. As well as writing essays and fiction, she contributes to the *New York Times*. Among other aspects, Gay's writing deals with relationships, sex, sexual assault, feminism, body image, race and gender, often drawing from her own experiences. Of her own reading habits Gay once said, 'I also read romance novels, because they are fun, and they are sweet... The world is shit, so — I need that happy ending.'

LUKE POLLARD

B. 1980

UK Labour candidate Luke Pollard became the first out gay MP for Plymouth Sutton and Devonport after winning his seat in 2017 from the incumbent Conservative. He has since worked as the Shadow Secretary of State for Environment, Food and Rural Affairs, as well as Shadow Minister for the Armed Forces.

Pollard spoke out against Brexit party MEP Ann Widdecombe's homophobia when she claimed that science might one day 'produce an answer' to being gay. 'Being gay isn't a disease to be cured,' he said. He was also praised for his dignified response to criminals who graffitied his office with homophobic slurs in 2019. Pollard responded by saying that 'we must also seek to build bridges and not walls'. On Valentine's Day 2021, Pollard posted a picture of himself with his boyfriend on social media, only to receive a torrent of homophobic abuse. Pollard responded with positive comments about his relationship and said the abuse was a reminder that the fight for equality 'is not yet up'.

On this date in 2022, he made a speech advocating for the inclusion of trans and non-binary people in a Bill banning conversion therapy, saying, 'Regardless of who you are and who you love, you have the right to be loved. You have the right to be safe...'

JOBRIATH

1946-1983

The *Gay Times* described Jobriath, born Bruce Wayne Campbell, as 'the world's first openly gay musician to be signed to a major record label'. Tipped to be the next David Bowie, Jobriath was a glam rock performer with music and stage success already under his belt from a stint in the musical *Hair* in New York. After he was signed by music mogul Jerry Brandt, a huge publicity campaign for his debut album *Jobriath* ensued. The album was released on this date in 1973, but a planned three-night debut concert run at the Paris Opera never happened, and Jobriath's music sales didn't materialise.

The singer's struggle with drug abuse worsened after his music career failed and he faded into obscurity. Later, in 1979, he told a magazine that Jobriath was dead and he was now living as Cole Berlin. Sadly, in 1983, he was found dead at the Chelsea Hotel in New York as a result of AIDS-related complications.

In 2004, pop legend Morrissey became 'obsessed' with Jobriath and released his music on CD under his own label. In 2021, discussion surrounding Jobriath's legacy emerged once more with the release of Kieran Turner's *Jobriath A.D.*, a documentary film chronicling the life of the singer.

BENJAMIN BRITTEN

1913–1976

Benjamin Britten was a revered British composer, conductor and pianist. His opera, *Peter Grimes* (1945), brought him international acclaim and set him on course to produce some of the most well-known operatic works of the 20th century. These included *The Rape of Lucretia* (1946), *Billy Budd* (1951) from the Herman Melville novella of the same name, and *Gloriana* (1953), written for the coronation of Queen Elizabeth II.

Early in his career, while working on a documentary film, Britten met the poet W.H. Auden (see 29 Sep), who became a mentor, friend and collaborator on future projects, such as the two-act operetta *Paul Bunyan* (1941). Around this time, he also met tenor Peter Pears, the man who went on to become his life partner in both love and work. From this point on, much of Britten's work was produced for Pears to perform.

In 1973, Britten wrote his final opera, *Death in Venice*, adapted from the Thomas Mann novella of the same name. This would be a work close to the composer's heart, as it dealt with themes of homosexuality and illness – at the time, Britten required heart surgery. The opera opened on this date in 1973 and, as usual, Britten's partner, Peter Pears, took the lead tenor's role.

FRANK KAMENY

1925–2011

Gay rights activist, Frank Kameny, who is said to have invented the slogan 'Gay is Good', enjoyed being referred to as 'the world's oldest living homosexual... or the great-grandfather of the gay movement'.

Kameny was an astronomer for the US Army Map Service and was fired for being homosexual, then referred to as 'immoral, sexual perversion'. This led to his involvement in public protest. He tried repeatedly to sue the government in federal court for his dismissal, until the Supreme Court declined to hear his case in 1961.

Along with Barbara Gittings (see 15 Dec), Kameny was also responsible for organising the Annual Reminder that took place each 4 July. These were civilised pickets made up of respectably dressed homosexuals, protesting quietly outside Independence Hall in Philadelphia, carrying signs requesting their rights. These began in 1965, four years ahead of the Stonewall riots. 'There would not have been Stonewall if the mindset hadn't already been established by us,' believes Frank.

On this date in 2009, Kameny was invited to the White House to meet President Barack Obama as he signed a Memorandum extending employment benefits to gay partners of US government workers. In the same year, the US government officially apologised to Kameny for firing him from his job in 1957.

SALLY RIDE

1951–2012

It wasn't until after her death that the world learned that Sally Ride, the first American woman in space, was the life partner of 27 years to Tam O'Shaughnessy, the children's science writer and former professional tennis player. Ride, who went to space on this date in 1983, had kept her relationship with O'Shaughnessy a secret.

As a child, Ride herself played tennis and even ranked in the top 20 nationally on the junior tennis circuit. She later gained a Bachelor of Science in Physics and a Bachelor of Arts in English from Stanford University, and by 1978 was accepted into the astronaut corps where she was thrilled to be one of six women, saying,

'It made it clear that NASA was committed to really bringing more gender diversity into the astronaut corps.'

After retiring from NASA, Sally and Tam wrote multiple children's books with space exploration at the heart of their stories. The pair later set up Sally Ride Science, a non-profit organisation that motivates children from all backgrounds, especially girls, to take an interest in science, technology, engineering and maths (STEM).

In 2013, Ride was honoured posthumously with a Presidential Medal of Freedom, presented to O'Shaughnessy by President Barack Obama.

WILLEM ARONDEUS

1894–1943

'Homosexuals are not cowards!' was the final message that Dutch artist, author and resistance fighter Willem Arondeus asked his lawyer to relay to the world, as he was executed by the Nazis.

Arondeus was commissioned to paint a mural for Rotterdam City Hall in 1923. He later wrote two novels, as well as a biography of the painter Matthijs Maris, but it would be his illegal underground publication *Brandarisbrief* and his subsequent fight against the Nazi regime that would be his legacy.

When the Nazis invaded the Netherlands, Arondeus helped to falsify identity papers for Dutch Jews, as part of the resistance.

The Nazis checked documents against public records in the Municipal Office in order to identify forgeries; so to counteract this, Arondeus and his fellows came up with a plan to bomb the office in Amsterdam and destroy the records.

The successful attack took place on 27 March 1943, destroying 800,000 identity cards. Yet, just a few days later Arondeus was caught. In June 1943, he was tried and sentenced to death. He was posthumously awarded the Resistance Memorial Cross and, on this date in 1986, Yad Vashem (The World Holocaust Remembrance Center) recognised Arondeus as Righteous Among the Nations.

JIMMY SOMERVILLE

B. 1961

Born and raised in Glasgow, where he discovered disco music in a straight basement club, singer Jimmy Somerville left Scotland for the bright lights of London before he turned 20. There, he co-founded the synth-pop group Bronski Beat with Steve Bronski and Larry Steinbachek.

The band's debut single, 'Smalltown Boy', resonated with queer people struggling to feel represented in 1980s Britain, as it told the story of a young gay man running away from home to find acceptance. It reached number three in the UK charts. The band performed their single on the Channel 4 music show *Ear Say* on this date in 1984.

He proudly put his gayness at the heart of his music when he named Bronski Beat's debut album *The Age of Consent*, referencing the LGBTQ community's battle with Margaret Thatcher's government over equalising the age of consent for gay men. The band also headlined the 'Pits and Perverts' benefit concert in 1984, organised by queer activists in support of the miners' strike. This was portrayed in the film *Pride* (2014).

Somerville left Bronski Beat to form The Communards with pianist Richard Coles and the pair had a huge hit with 'Don't Leave Me This Way' in 1986. Somerville went solo in 1988.

BENEDICT FRIEDLAENDER

1866–1908

Sexologist and scientist, Benedict Friedlaedner was born in Berlin, Germany in 1866. He studied mathematics, physics, botany and physiology at university in the city, graduating with a PhD in zoology aged just 22.

While Friedlaender published works on sociology and science, it is his work and advocacy for homosexual love for which he is most well-known. Friedlaender was initially a supporter of Magnus Hirschfeld and his Scientific-Humanitarian Committee (Wissenschaftlich-humanitäres Komitee), an early German society that studied sexuality. However, in 1903 he broke away from Hirschfeld to found the organisation Gemeinschaft der Eigenen (Society of the Self-Determined),

along with fellow campaigner for homosexuality, Adolf Brand (see 3 Mar) and others.

While Hirschfeld believed queer people (predominantly gay men) had different experiences and feelings to everyone else, Friedlaender suggested that same-sex attractions were a natural part of all human life, particularly between a man and a younger boy.

In 1907, Friedlaender set up yet another group away from Hirschfeld, called The League for Manly Culture, which advocated that homosexual activity was a manly activity, helped the structure of society and could be practised by married men. The group disbanded soon after Friedlaender died by suicide on this date in 1908.

IVOR CUMMINGS

1913–1992

Ivor Cummings, a civil servant in the Colonial Office, was one of the first people to welcome those aboard HMT *Empire Windrush* when it docked at Tilbury on this date in 1948. The people aboard were coming to help rebuild war-torn Britain and Cummings was assigned to assist them in their resettlement. He went above and beyond his duties, helping arrivals find places to stay and jobs, even coming up with the idea to house those with no pre-arranged accommodation in a former air-raid shelter beneath Clapham Common. He is thought to have worked with Countess Edwina Mountbatten on national efforts to quash racism, courting the favour of King George VI, who abhorred discrimination. Born in England to a white English nurse and a Black Sierra Leonean doctor, Cummings was openly gay at a time when it was illegal. He is said to have chained-smoked using a long cigarette holder, addressing new arrivals as 'dear boy'.

Cummings was awarded an OBE for his services, but in an article published in the *Independent* newspaper in 2019, it was pointed out that he was largely absent from accounts of Black British History, perhaps owing to his queerness. The same article calls us to celebrate him now and names him the gay father of the *Windrush* generation.

AMROU AL-KADHI

B. 1990

British-Iraqi writer, actor and drag performer Amrou Al-Kadhi said they'd been asked to audition to play terrorists in TV and film more than 30 times before the age of 27. They sarcastically pointed out that 'since 9/11, there are genuinely more roles for Arab actors than ever before. Hurrah!'

Al-Kadhi, born on this date in 1990, has starred in films such as Steven Spielberg's *Munich* and *Venom: Let There Be Carnage*. Al-Kadhi's other work, which includes writing for books, TV and stage, as well as directing, performing in drag and journalism, often reflects their experiences as a Muslim, queer person. *Unicorn: The Memoir of a Muslim Drag Queen* (2020), by Al-Kadhi was heralded as 'A masterpiece of psychology, a major study of Islam and a definitive study of drag' by TV writer Russell T Davies (see 23 Feb), and won the Polari First Book Prize in 2020.

In drag, Al-Kadhi goes by the name Glamrou and began performing as a student. In a 2019 interview with the *Guardian* newspaper, they discussed how often their joy of drag was counteracted by family disapproval. Al-Kadhi recalls being told not to bring up 'this gay stuff' by their father. Despite this, Al-Kadhi spoke of loving the outfits that 'remind me of my mum the most'.

SYLVIA RIVERA

1951–2002

In 1950s New York City, Sylvia Rivera was born of Puerto Rican and Venezuelan descent and assigned male at birth. Orphaned early and an outcast because of her identity, she lived her early life on the streets, occasionally taken in by Greenwich Village drag queens.

Always a revolutionary, Rivera was involved in the Black Liberation Movement, the peace movement, the Stonewall riots and, with her close friend Marsha P. Johnson (see 24 Aug), she set up Street Transvestite Action Revolutionaries (STAR). The organisation, often funded by Rivera's and Johnson's sex work, took in homeless queer kids.

Rivera's activism was often at odds with other gay rights activists, particularly those focused on the assimilation of gays and lesbians into 'straight' society, and who sought to distance themselves from 'drag queens'. On this date in 1973, she took to the stage at Gay Pride to remind the crowd of the many STAR people in jail who didn't fit into their 'White middle-class club' for gays and needed help. 'I have been beaten. I have had my nose broken. I have been thrown in jail. I have lost my job. I have lost my apartment for gay liberation and you all treat me this way?'

Always fighting for the most marginalised queer people, Rivera is often credited with making sure that the T was firmly part of today's LGBTQ+ acronym.

GILBERT BAKER

1951–2017

Gilbert Baker was an American artist and an activist who made banners and flags for parades and marches. Harvey Milk (see 9 Jan), the openly gay San Francisco politician, and his team asked Baker to create a new symbol for the gay and lesbian political movement; something that could be used at the San Francisco Gay Freedom Day Parade that year. Baker came up with a rainbow flag made up of eight colours, which he and volunteers hand-dyed. The first rainbow flags, recognised as the symbol of LGBTQ+ people, were flown at the parade on this date in 1978.

Over time the rainbow flag has changed, dropping from eight to six colours: pink flag fabric was expensive and the turquoise and blue stripes simply became royal blue. Later versions, such as the Progress Pride flag, include a chevron along the hoist, featuring black and brown for people of colour, and the colours of the trans flag.

Remembering the flag being unveiled, Baker said, 'I knew instantly when I saw the reaction that it was going to be something. I didn't know what or how — but I knew.'

EDITH WINDSOR

1929–2017

'Few were as small in stature as Edie Windsor – and few made as big a difference to America,' said former US President Barack Obama, speaking after the death of the 5-foot woman who took the US federal government to court over the Defense of Marriage Act. This Act denied Windsor the same spousal rights as married heterosexual couples were afforded and meant that the IRS instructed her to pay hundreds of thousands of dollars in tax on her inheritance when her wife of two years (and partner of 40 years), Thea Spyer, died.

Windsor felt this was a terrible injustice and so decided to mount a legal fight, claiming the law was unconstitutional because of the 'differential treatment' it afforded to same-sex couples – and she won. While Windsor's original result, decided on this date in 2013, was limited to 13 states and the District of Columbia, her work paved the way for the eventual legalisation of same-sex marriage in the US in 2015, which provided same-sex couples with the same legal protections as heterosexual couples.

Days after her victory in the Supreme Court, Edith Windsor was Grand Marshal for the New York City's Gay Pride.

RUDOLF BRAZDA

1913–2011

During the Holocaust, gay men who had been incarcerated in concentration camps were made to wear a pink triangle on their clothes to identify their 'crime'. When Klaus Wowereit, the openly gay mayor of Berlin, prepared to unveil the city's memorial to gay and lesbian victims of persecution in Nazi Germany in May 2008, a television feature covering the event reported that the last-known surviving wearer of the pink triangle had died.

Rudolf Brazda was watching the television report at home in France and quickly notified German authorities that they were wrong, because he was a gay man who had been held in the Buchenwald concentration camp. Having been repeatedly persecuted under Paragraph 175, the German criminal legislation that outlawed male homosexual acts, Brazda had been sent to the Buchenwald concentration camp in 1942. After liberation, Brazda settled in France, where he met his life partner Edouard Meyer. The pair stayed together for more than 50 years until Meyer's death in 2003.

He was seemingly now the last of the 'pink triangle' survivors, and on this date in 2008, a few weeks after the official unveiling of the Berlin memorial, 95-year-old Brazda visited the site, where he was greeted by Mayor Wowereit.

STORMÉ DELARVERIE

1920–2014

On this date in 1969 the course of LGBTQ+ rights changed forever. The Stonewall Inn, frequented by the queer underclass of Lower Manhattan, was raided by the police. Because the bar was illegally trading without a liquor licence and was a meeting place for the queer community, the police intended to close down the bar. They expected the patrons to line up outside, take a beating and that some would go to jail. Things did not go as planned.

At a time when queer people were persecuted in all aspects of their lives, the patrons in the bar were used to such raids and police abuse. However, this time they fought back. Some attribute the uprising to Stormé DeLarverie, a singer and drag king of colour, who turned to the crowd after being beaten by police and shouted, 'WHY DON'T YOU DO SOMETHING?!' Do something they did. They retaliated, throwing coins and bottles, setting fires and eventually forcing the police to barricade themselves into the bar until back up came. The fightback grew into a three-day protest that became a revolution for LGBTQ+ rights.

In 2000, DeLarverie received the Gay Lifetime Achievement Award from Senior Action in Gay Environment, an organisation dedicated to improving the lives of LGBTQ+ elders.

BETTE MIDLER

B. 1945

Bette Midler's seven-decade career in the entertainment industry spans theatre, music, television and film. After starting out in Off-Broadway productions in the 1960s, she took to the stage at the infamous New York gay sauna, Continental Baths, in 1970 to establish herself as a singer. Almost 50 years later, on this date in 2019, she was the opening act at World Pride, held in New York City. Midler wears her LGBTQ+ ally badge proudly, saying, 'I really feel like I was at the forefront of the gay liberation movement, and I hope I did my element to assist it go forward.'

After Sylvia Rivera (see 24 Jun) upset revellers with her impassioned speech at the New York Pride Gala in June 1973 and Jean O'Leary (see 11 Oct) further angered the crowd with her thoughts on drag queens, Midler was brought on stage to calm the attendees down and re-unify them.

Midler is politically vocal on Twitter and uses her platform to call out homophobia, misogyny and other injustices. Almost 50 years to the day after she sang at the 1973 Pride march, Midler encapsulated the fears of queer people across America after Roe vs Wade was overturned, by tweeting 'GET READY, GAYS. YOU'RE NEXT.'

PROUD ALLY

HANNAH HÖCH

1889-1978

Hannah Höch was one of the few female artists welcomed into the Berlin Dada movement's inner circle. In 1917, she had met (and later began a relationship with) artist Raoul Hausmann who introduced her to the group. Dadaism was developed as a reaction to the folly of World War One and was critical of materialism, capitalism, the bourgeoisie and the Weimar Republic.

Höch's work primarily consisted of political collages and photomontages (a form she helped pioneer), in which she spliced together imagery cut from magazines, journals and fashion periodicals. Her work explored gender and identity and mocked the concept of the 'New Woman' in Weimar Germany – she did not shy away from criticising men and society's attitude towards women. In her short story/essay, 'The Painter', published in 1920, Höch mocked gender roles in relationships, writing a thinly veiled attack on her partner, Hausmann. After the pair separated, Höch had a nine-year relationship with Dutch writer Mathilda (Til) Brugman.

On this date in 1920, Höch exhibited a large photomontage named *Cut with the Kitchen Knife Through the Last Weimar Beer-Belly Cultural Epoch in Germany*, in the First International Dada Fair in Berlin. Typical of Höch's work, it was one of the most well-received pieces at the show.

TED BROWN

B. 1950

In the summer of 1972, Ted Brown was one of the activists gathered in the basement of the London School of Economics. It was here that the London arm of the Gay Liberation Front (GLF, originally founded after NYC's Stonewall riots) organised the city's first official Pride rally, which took place on this date in 1972. The rally culminated in a mass kiss-in in Trafalgar Square, at a time when this would have been cited as 'gross indecency', and thus against the law.

Ted Brown was an American immigrant born to Jamaican parents and he'd felt immediately at home when he attended an early GLF meeting: 'I'd never been in a room with other homosexuals who were angry about the way that we were being treated, and wanting to fight back about it.'

Brown has spent the subsequent decades campaigning against discrimination. He set up Black Lesbians and Gays Against Media Homophobia, motivated by a memory of an article entitled 'How To Spot A Possible Homo' in the *Sunday Mirror* in the 1960s.

Without people like Brown taking these brave steps, young queers wouldn't be safe to kiss each other in the street in daylight, just as he had done at the mass kiss-in, in Trafalgar Square, at London's first Pride rally.

HARRY HAY

1912–2002

Sometimes referred to as the original radical fairy, on account of being a gay activist as well as a hippy and communist, Harry Hay co-founded one of the US's earliest gay rights organisations, the Mattachine Foundation (originally called Society of Fools and later the Mattachine Society) in 1950.

The group was troubled from the outset, however, with disagreement on whether their cause should go down the route of assimilation into heterosexual society or whether gay people should acknowledge their differences and present themselves as an oppressed cultural minority, as Hay proposed.

Internal squabbles aside, when fellow founding member Dale Jennings was arrested for cruising in Los Angeles, Hay saw an opportunity to fight back and expose police entrapment. After collecting funds from gay people to pay for an attorney, Hay encouraged Jennings to admit to being a homosexual in court but deny making advances to the cop. Jennings was one of the first gay men to contest charges like this, as many often pleaded guilty to avoid public scrutiny. On this date in 1952 the jury's verdict was for acquittal, citing police intimidation, harassment and entrapment of homosexuals. This was a resounding win for the Mattachine Foundation, as well as a key moment for the Gay Rights Movement.

ELISA SÁNCHEZ LORIGA & MARCELA GRACIA IBEAS

1862–1909; c. 1867–UNKNOWN

The remarkable love story of Elisa Sánchez Loriga and Marcela Gracia Ibeas, which was chronicled in the 2019 Spanish film, *Elisa & Marcela*, is the tale of how two women were legally married in Spain in 1901, more than a century before same-sex marriage was legalised in the country on this date in 2005. The pair tricked a Catholic priest into marrying them, with Sánchez Loriga presenting as a man and calling herself Mario.

Despite initial attempts by Ibeas' family to keep the pair apart, the couple, both schoolteachers, ended up living near each other in rural Galicia and continued their relationship. After they married, a picture of their special day made its way to newspapers across Europe, and even into Argentina, and the couple were forced to flee.

They initially went to Portugal where Ibeas gave birth to a daughter, with an unknown father, and then onto Buenos Aires, where Sánchez Loriga married an older man. Ibeas and her daughter moved in with the couple under the guise of the pair being sisters but their relationship was soon exposed and Sánchez Loriga's new husband took her to court. Little is known about the end of their lives.

JOHN WATERS

B. 1946

When a movie's tagline is 'An exercise in poor taste' and its lead character declares herself 'the filthiest person alive', the audience is unlikely to expect a light romcom. But equally, they may not have been prepared for *Pink Flamingos*, the low-budget film written, directed, produced and edited by the American filmmaker and self-proclaimed Pope of Trash, John Waters. The movie stars drag queen, Divine, a larger-than-life performer with a ridiculous wig and make-up. While its release on this date in 1972 inspired a mixed reception, it remains a cult classic to this day.

A teenaged Waters made his first film in 1964, when his grandmother gave him an 8mm movie camera. His early films were largely low-budget, low-quality exploitation films, and it was only much later in his career that he received commercial success with *Hairspray*, again starring Divine, but also introducing Ricki Lake. *Hairspray* was later made into a Broadway musical and remade for cinema in 2007.

When speaking about his movies, Waters cites *Serial Mom* (1994) as his best: 'It's the only one we actually had enough money to make,' while declaring that *Pink Flamingos* was 'so badly done... it looked like a snuff film'.

LIL NAS X

B. 1999

After seeing the pain and bullying suffered by classmates who chose to come out at school, American teenager Montero Lamar Hill hid his sexuality. However, since becoming rapper Lil Nas X, the star found confidence and in 2019 he alluded to his sexuality in a tweet during Pride Month, while his hit 'Old Town Road' was at the top of the US Billboard Hot 100 chart. Appearing on BBC breakfast a few days later, on this date, he confirmed he was gay, saying he hoped he was 'opening doors' by being open himself.

In 2021, his performance of 'Montero (Call Me By Your Name)' at the BET Awards in LA ended with him kissing one of his male dancers. 'I feel like it's what needed to be done,' the artist said when asked about the kiss. 'It's easy to just hug a guy, but I feel like if you kiss the guy, you get straight to the point.'

Following his performance at the BET awards and the release of his music video for 'Industry Baby' (in which he dances naked in prison with other inmates) he responded to a barrage of homophobia online with calm wit and decorum, and debunked claims he was pushing the gay agenda. Lil Nas X has since won multiple awards.

MARTHA MAY ELIOT & ETHEL COLLINS DUNHAM

1891–1978; 1883–1969

Martha May Eliot and Ethel Collins Dunham met at college in 1910, and would become life partners in both work and love.

After studying medicine together at Johns Hopkins University, the pair became the first women in the medical school faculty at Yale, and went on to serve on the Children's Bureau (a national agency to improve the health of American children). Eliot worked with others on a landmark study of rickets, which established effective preventive measures for the condition across the US. Similarly, Dunham's book, *Premature Infants: A Manual for Physicians* (1948), set national standards for the care of newborns.

The pair were open about their relationship, which appears to have been generally accepted in their circles, and their love remained strong until the end of their lives.

Through their research and advocacy work, the pair improved medical care for countless women and their babies. Eliot was a US delegate to the first-ever World Health Assembly which took place 19 June–22 July 1946, and the only woman to sign the founding document. They were the first two women to be awarded the John Howland Award – the American Pediatric Society's highest honour, Dunham in 1958 and Eliot in 1967.

BARNEY FRANK

B. 1940

Barney Frank was elected to state legislature in Massachusetts in 1972. He turned the district from Republican to Democrat with his win, and the first bill he proposed attempted to introduce legal protection for gay people in matters of employment and housing — the first bill of its kind to be filed in the state of Massachusetts.

In 1987, Frank came out as gay — the first member of Congress to voluntarily do so. Two years later, he was involved in a minor scandal with a male escort, but following a reprimand from the House, he continued to serve and was later re-elected.

During his time in the US House of Representatives, Frank sponsored bills primarily involving finance, business and trade. In 2009, after the housing market collapsed, Frank and Senator Chris Dodd introduced landmark legislation to protect consumers in the future.

Frank made history again when, on this date in 2012, he married his partner Jim Ready, becoming the first sitting US representative to enter into a same-sex marriage. In a 2020 interview, Frank admitted he probably 'should have come out a little earlier', and said he was hopeful that one day an LGBTQ+ president could occupy the White House.

TONY WARREN

1936–2016

In December 1960, Manchester-based Granada Television aired a 13-part series about a working-class street in Salford. *Coronation Street* was an instant hit and more than 60 years later has become the world's longest-running television soap opera. The creator was Tony Warren, then an openly gay 24-year-old from Lancashire, born on this date in 1936. Originally a staff scriptwriter, he dreamed of writing about 'real people', and badgered his bosses to give his idea a chance.

Warren, out at a time before homosexual acts were decriminalised, experienced constant workplace homophobia. Of colleagues, years later he said, 'They ganged up… there was a terrible morning when there was story conference, and I sat there and I listened… and I said, "Gentlemen, I have sat here and listened to two poof jokes, to an actor referred to as a poof, to a line dismissed because it's poofy, and I would remind you that without a poof, none of you would be in work this morning."'

While *Coronation Street* seemed to lag behind its contemporaries in introducing a gay character (Todd Grimshaw in 2003), it was the first British soap to have a regular transsexual character. Hayley Cropper (introduced in 1998) became one of the show's most loved characters.

ROBERT RAUSCHENBERG

1925–2008

When Robert Rauschenberg died, his obituary in the *New York Times* summed up the breadth of his work and talents perfectly: 'A painter, photographer, printmaker, choreographer, onstage performer, set designer and, in later years, even a composer, Mr. Rauschenberg defied the traditional idea that an artist stick to one medium or style.'

Rauschenberg was one of a cohort of artists, including John Cage (see 16 Jan) and Jasper Johns, who signified a new era of experimentation in American culture with their work. In 2004, the Bob Rauschenberg Gallery in Florida became the first institutional facility to be named after the artist. Its inaugural exhibition, *Rauschenberg: Scenarios*, ran from 4 June to 11 July.

When Rauschenberg died, his sexuality was omitted from many of his obituaries. The *New York Times* skirted around the issue, saying he was survived by 'his companion, Darryl Pottorf'. These omissions have been widely criticised, for example by the *Guardian* newspaper which likened them to being 'as absurd as a James Brown obituary that omits to mention he's Black'. What should be remembered is the impact Rauschenberg's romantic relationships with artists such as Cy Twombly and Jasper Johns had on his work.

BLAIR IMANI

B. 1993

Blair Imani, a Black bisexual Muslim woman born and raised in Los Angeles, California, plays an active role in the Black Lives Matter movement, as well as highlighting other injustices she sees within her communities. On this date in 2016, she was arrested at a protest over police brutality, sparked by the death of Alton Sterling, a 37-year-old Black man, at the hands of law enforcement.

In October 2018, Imani released her first book, *Modern Herstory*, a celebration of 70 women, girls and non-binary people who have changed – and are still changing – the world. It was described by Sarah Kate Ellis, CEO of GLAAD, as 'an important step to inspiring the next generation of people to aim high and be proud'.

Imani came out during an interview with Fox News in June 2017, when the presenter chastised her by saying she wasn't a representative for Black people nor for LGBTQ people. 'I actually am a Black, queer woman in addition to being a Muslim,' she said.

The activist, educator and writer, whose TEDx talk on being queer and Muslim has almost 400,000 views on YouTube, has spoken about how the queer Canadian rock singers Tegan and Sara (see 24 Sep), and their song 'Closer', which acknowledged queer relationships, made her feel like she could be herself.

MURRAY BARTLETT

B. 1971

Australian actor Murray Bartlett has spent a large portion of his career starring in soap operas. He appeared in the Australian soaps *Neighbours* and *Home and Away*, and when he moved to the US, he worked on *All My Children* and *Guiding Light*, after landing a small role in *Sex and the City*.

His career blossomed further when he took on a number of queer roles in dramas by HBO and Netflix. First came *Looking* (2014) in which he played Dom, one of three lead queer, male parts, whose characters were living and loving in San Francisco. Then he successfully took up the role of Michael 'Mouse' Tolliver in the Netflix reboot of *Tales of the City*. He said 'being a gay man, I have a vested interest in wanting good queer stories to be told'.

On this date in 2021, *The White Lotus*, a dark comedy–drama about a luxury hotel and its guests, premiered on HBO with Bartlett playing the gay recovering drug addict hotel manager. The show won critical acclaim and brought Bartlett to a new audience. Referring to a rimming scene in the show, Bartlett said he was happy 'to show intimacy, especially between men, in a way that feels authentic… we don't see enough'.

RENÉE CAFIERO

B. 1943

On 19 September 1964, Renée Cafiero and her girlfriend Nancy Garden, both members of the Mattachine Society and the Daughters of Bilitis, took part in what is thought to be the very first public demonstration for gay rights in the US. The pair, along with the co-founder of the Daughters of Bilitis, Barbara Gittings (see 15 Dec) and Randy Wicker (see 19 Sep) of the Homosexual League of New York, led a picket outside the US Army Building in Manhattan, New York. They were there to protest the army's discrimination against gay people and its practice of disclosing draft records to employers.

The group handed out leaflets and carried picket signs proclaiming 'The Army Invades Sexual Privacy'. While the picket went unreported in the media and had little impact, Cafiero and the others had laid the groundwork for other such LGBTQ+ protests to take place and went on to organise others, including the annual Reminder Day protests that took place at Independence Hall, between 1965 and 1969.

Cafiero became one of the first openly lesbian delegates at the Democratic Convention, held 10–13 July 1972, and continues to be active in politics and LGBTQ+ rights. She was also an important member of the United Auto Workers labour union.

JAYNE COUNTY

B. 1947

Performing in New York and London in Andy Warhol's (see 3 Jun) play *Pork*, inspiring David Bowie (see 19 Feb), recording a live performance and album with a major record label who then refused to release it for 20 years, having Pete Burns of Dead or Alive as an avid fan and releasing two biographies are all things that Jayne County, the world's first transgender rock'n'roller, can lay claim to.

Born on this date in 1947, County, who was assigned the male sex at birth, grew up in Dallas, before moving to Atlanta and later settling in New York City. There she became a regular at the Stonewall Inn and took part in the famous riots in the summer of 1969.

Wearing make-up and dressing androgynously from an early age, County says she was happiest 'being in between or being neither'. When she moved to Berlin in 1979, she began to publicly identify as a woman and her stage name became Jayne County.

County performed as part of the proto-punk band Queen Elizabeth, fronted Wayne County & the Backstreet Boys, and was the lead singer of Wayne County & the Electric Chairs. Although she never broke into the mainstream, her back catalogue is extensive and her influence on punk rock is undeniable.

GEORGE WASHINGTON CARVER

1864–1943

When the George Washington Carver National Monument in Missouri, USA was officially opened on this date in 1953, it became the first national monument dedicated to an African American and the first to honour someone other than a president.

Born into slavery, kidnapped by slave raiders and then fostered by multiple families, Carver had an unsettled childhood. He became the first African American to earn a Bachelor of Science degree, when he earned one from Iowa State Agricultural School. He completed a master's degree in agricultural science and was invited by the speaker, author and presidential advisor, Booker T. Washington (whose name he later adopted into his own) to join the

Tuskegee Institute (now Tuskegee University) in Alabama. This was the first institution of higher learning for African Americans.

Carver never married, nor had children. The consensus among historians and his biographer seems to be that Carver was bisexual. Some speculate that in later life he had a relationship with the male lab assistant to whom he left his royalty earnings.

Carver became known as the peanut man, after he encouraged southern farmers to rotate their cotton crops with peanuts to improve soil quality. To help the farmers find a use for their new crops, Carver invented hundreds of peanut-based products, such as cooking oils, cosmetics and soaps.

LYDIA FOY

B. 1947

On this date in 2015, the Gender Recognition Act was passed in Ireland, meaning that trans people could now apply to have their preferred gender legally recognised by the state. The fight for this legislation was a long and complicated one, led primarily by Lydia Foy, a trans woman who applied to have her birth certificate legally changed in 1993. Foy was refused and so began a 20-year battle.

After the refusal, Foy began High Court proceedings with the help of FLAC (Free Legal Advice Centre). Her case was heard first in October 2000 by Mr Justice Liam McKechnie, who rejected her claim due to a lack of legislation on the matter and urged the Irish government to address the issue. When the case was heard again 10 years later in April 2007, McKechnie expressed frustration at the lack of progress. In May 2010, the government finally set up the Gender Recognition Advisory Group (GRAG), which ultimately led to the formation of the Gender Recognition Bill in 2014.

Foy's perseverance led to the change in the law, allowing those who come after her the recognition they deserve. Foy said that despite being exhausted as her fight went on, she continued the battle for 'everyone who was being bashed'.

BARBARA VICK

ACTIVE 1980S

In 1983, in a move brought in to try to prevent the spread of HIV through blood transfusions, men who had sex with men (MSM) were prohibited from giving blood in the US (this rule still applies in many countries around the world today). At a time when the queer community was in desperate need of donated blood, lesbians, many of whom had become caregivers to HIV/AIDS patients, stepped in to assist.

San Diego residents Barbara Vick and her partner held their first blood drive on this date in 1983, hoping that around 50 or so women would turn up to donate. In fact, there was a queue around the block when close to 200 women arrived to give blood.

Later known as The Blood Sisters, they organised regular drives and Vick set up an account with a private San Diego blood bank that allowed donors to specify that their blood was given to HIV patients in the gay community. She said, 'At that time, I don't think that women economically had as much to give as men. But this was something that they could do, the giving of themselves – and heart blood is such a basic thing.'

MARC ALMOND

B. 1957

Marc Almond rose to fame as half of the synth–pop duo Soft Cell in the 1980s. He met David Ball, the other half, at Leeds College of Art, and the pair created three studio albums together, from 1981 to 1984.

'Tainted Love', Soft Cell's debut single, released on this date in 1981, was a success on both sides of the Atlantic, hitting number one in the UK charts after a performance on *Top of the Pops* and spending nine months in the US Billboard Hot 100. Almond has spoken of the fame and success of that time as being like all hell breaking loose and the following years being thrilling, intoxicating and sleazy. In recent years he has spoken of yearning for what he sees as a now-disappeared gay community, eroded by the division of 'LGBT': 'I hate the way the LGBT thing has emerged. It separates.'

Soft Cell split in 1984 but Almond continued to make music, releasing singles such as 'Something's Gotten Hold of My Heart' (1989) with Gene Pitney, and 'Jacky' (1991). Even after a near fatal motorcycle accident in 2003, he continued to write and perform, saying, 'I have never stopped working. I'm a great believer in getting on with things.'

SAPPHO

610-570 BC

Born on the island of Lesbos, in the Aegean Sea, Sappho was one of the most admired poets in ancient Greece. Many believe her work spoke of the love between women, and the English word 'lesbian', the Greek word 'lesvia' and the Japanese 'rezubian' all derive from the name of her birthplace.

While there is still much discussion among historians as to whether Sappho was indeed a lesbian, the poet and her work have in any case become synonymous with lesbian culture. The word 'sapphic', derived from her name, is commonly defined as 'relating to lesbians or lesbianism', and the island of Lesbos is now a tourist destination for lesbians from all over the world. Women visit the village of Eressos, which is thought to be the birthplace of the poet in the 7th century BC.

In 2008, a small number of islanders from Lesbos went to court to try and ban the use of the word lesbian to describe gay women, claiming it was an insult to their identity. The court dismissed the request on this date in 2008, saying the word did not define the identity of the island residents and could be used by gay groups in Greece and abroad.

TAMARA DE LEMPICKA

1898-1980

The Polish artist, Tamara de Lempicka, rose to fame in Paris between the world wars, and a musical based on her life, *Lempicka*, opened in Massachusetts on this date in 2018.

Although she liked to keep an air of mystery about herself, it is generally accepted that she was bisexual and that she had a long relationship with Rafaela Fano, the subject of many of her paintings. Lempicka is also thought to have had a relationship with French singer and actress, Suzy Solidor – often referred to as 'the most painted woman in the world' on account of her sitting for, as well as Lempicka and many others, Francis Bacon, Man Ray and Pablo Picasso.

Lempicka's Art Deco-style work now sells for more than $20 million at auction. Famous collectors include Madonna, who has used Lempicka's work in numerous music videos, as well as on stage. Lempicka, reported to paint in nine-hour sittings, was a bold and empowering female painter for her time, once defined by the German magazine *Die Dame*, as 'a symbol of women's liberation'. She and her husband Baron Kuffner fled for America in 1939, where she continued painting and lived out the rest of her life.

ALEXANDER THE GREAT

356–323 BC

From the moment he ascended the throne aged 20, through to his thirtieth birthday, Alexander III of Macedon, thought to be born on this date, created one of the largest empires in history. This legacy, which invited the name Alexander the Great, is undisputed. His sexuality, however, has long been a matter of debate.

Despite him being married three times and spawning two sons, many cite his friendship with his lifelong friend Hephaestion as proof that he was gay, or bisexual. It is believed that Hephaestion's death hit the ruler so hard that he never fully recovered emotionally and mentally. Hephaestion was afforded an expensive funeral, so elaborate that Alexander tore down walls to create the funeral pyre.

More plausible evidence exists that Alexander had a long and sexual relationship with a eunuch named Bagoas, who had once been a lover of Great King Darius III. Some point to evidence that during a celebratory dance, whereby Bagoas won a dancing competition, the eunuch was congratulated by Alexander with a kiss given in front of his army.

So influential was Alexander's empire, it ushered in significant societal changes across the lands he conquered from Asia and Africa, although those he conquered also condemned him for the widespread destruction wrought by his invasions. Historians credit him with spreading the Greek culture of Hellenism far and wide, which led to advances in natural sciences, art and architecture across the world.

LOU SULLIVAN

1951–1991

Like many people included in this book, Lou Sullivan struggled to find a place for himself in the world. He was not only a transgender man, but also gay; a combination that medical and psychological professionals did not understand.

In his early twenties, Milwaukee born Sullivan moved away from his religious family and arrived in San Francisco, the city he would call home until the end of his life, on this date in 1975. Sullivan was a pioneer in the modern understanding of female to male (FTM) transgenderism. He found that FTM theory and advice was often just an afterthought to the more well-discussed male-to-female subject. Therefore, he made it his mission

to ensure those coming after him could find such information on the shelves of bookshops and libraries, publishing *Information For the Female-to-Male Crossdresser and Transsexual* in 1985, as well as a biography of Jack Bee Garland, another gay trans man with a similar story to his own, in 1990.

As well as writing the *Gateway*, a newsletter for trans people, between 1979 and 1980, Sullivan also lobbied for the American Psychiatric Association and the World Professional Association for Transgender Health to recognise gay trans men. It is largely due to his activism and writings that sexual orientation and gender identity are now seen as separate, unrelated concepts.

MARC JACOBS

B. 1963

At the height of his career, American fashion designer Marc Jacobs headed up his own fashion label, had 200 retail stores in 80 countries and was creative director of Louis Vuitton.

Jacobs has used his label for both charitable and political causes. He designed T-shirts with images of naked celebrities to raise awareness for skin cancer and, on this date in 2009, he released his 'I pay my taxes, I want my RIGHTS!' T-shirts, which were designed to raise awareness of and funds for legalising gay marriage in the US.

Jacobs attributes some of his early creativity to his well-travelled and educated grandma,

with whom he lived in Manhattan when he was a teenager. Speaking about her love and encouragement, Jacobs said, 'No one ever told me anything was wrong. Never. No one ever said, "You can't be a fashion designer". No one ever said, "You're a boy and you can't take tap-dancing lessons."... No one said it was wrong to be gay or right to be straight.'

After proposing to his partner, model-turned-candle-designer Charly Defrancesco, with a flashmob in a Chipotle restaurant in 2018, the pair married and moved to Rye, New York to make the Max Hoffman House, built by Frank Lloyd Wright, their home.

RUTH ELLIS

1899–2000

In 1915, when Ruth Ellis, born on this date in 1899, came out as a lesbian in Illinois, USA, aged just 16, it was a brave and momentous thing to do. Yet speaking about it 85 years later, she sounded unphased: 'I never thought about hiding who I was … I guess I didn't go around telling everybody I was a lesbian, but I wasn't lying about it either. If anyone asked me, I'd tell them the truth…'

When Ellis and her partner of 34 years, Ceciline 'Babe' Franklin, moved to Detroit in the 1930s, the pair started the Ellis and Franklin Printing Company from their home. That home later became known as the 'Gay Spot', a hangout for the Black gay community when Ellis and Franklin opened it up to those who were not welcome at white gay bars or Black straight clubs.

Ellis dedicated her life to helping Black LGBTQ+ people, particularly youths in need of shelter and support after being rejected by their families. In 1999, when Ellis was 100 years old, the Ruth Ellis Center was founded in her name in Detroit. The centre offers health and social support, advice, housing and many other services for LGBTQ+ youth with an emphasis on young people of colour.

RABBI SHARON KLEINBAUM

B. 1959

When the state of New York ruled in favour of gay marriage on this date in 2011, Rabbi Sharon Kleinbaum set up a Rainbow Chuppah outside the City Clerk Building to offer couples the chance for a religious marriage ceremony.

The liberal lesbian has served Congregation Beit Simchat Torah, the world's largest LGBT-focused synagogue, located in Manhattan, since 1992 when she became its first full-time rabbi. Taking this role on at the height of the AIDS epidemic, she offered support and care for those with the disease in a community where many members of her congregation were dying.

In 2010, Kleinbaum was part of Mayor Bloomberg's Commission on LGBTQ Runaway and Homeless Youth in New York, helping to put together an extensive report on improving the lives of this vulnerable group of young people in the city.

In 2021, Rabbi Kleinbaum was also chosen by President Joe Biden to join the US Commission on International Religious Freedom, which monitors religious freedom around the world. Recognising the often-difficult relationship between religion and LGBTQ+ rights, Kleinbaum aims to ensure religion is an instrument for freedom, not repression. She says, 'I wanted to be part of a future that would see Jewish values as a source of liberation.'

ROCK HUDSON

1925–1985

Rock Hudson was the archetypal all-American leading man: white, attractive and clean-cut. Even though he was sometimes linked romantically to Doris Day, he was plagued by rumours of his sexuality throughout his career, but he always denied being gay. With the help of his agent, Henry Willson, along with a 1955 marriage to aspiring actress Phyllis Gates, he managed to avoid an exposé being published. However, on this date in 1985 Hudson's publicist confirmed that he had AIDS.

Ronald Reagan's Republican government had completely ignored the HIV/AIDS epidemic for years, and many believe that Hudson's admission of his illness helped to change public perception of it, putting pressure on the government to respond. Shortly after Hudson's announcement, President Reagan publicity acknowledged AIDS for the first time when prompted by a reporter. He said it was a 'top priority' and referred to the millions of dollars his government had allocated towards developing a cure for HIV.

Just before Hudson's death the Hollywood film industry held an AIDS gala and raised more than $1 million for the cause. Burt Reynolds read a note from Hudson: 'I am not happy that I have AIDS… But if that is helping others, I can, at least, know that my own misfortune has had some positive worth.'

TOM DALEY

B. 1994

Tom Daley and his diving partner, Matty Lee, won their first Olympic gold medal in Tokyo's synchronised 10m platform diving event on this date in 2021. Daley had competed in four Olympics over 13 years, previously winning three bronze medals.

Daley came out as gay in a YouTube video in December 2013, where he spoke about meeting someone who changed his world, saying simply 'that someone is a guy'. The guy was Dustin Lance Black, American screenwriter, director and film and TV-maker, to whom Daley is now married and with whom he shares a son.

Daley is an avid knitter and crocheter with an Instagram account dedicated to showcasing the items he makes. Images of him knitting while spectating various 2021 Olympic events went viral and became some of the most recognisable images from the tournament of the diver off the boards.

In response to homophobic comments made during Russian State TV coverage of the Tokyo Olympics, Daley pointed out that there were 10 countries competing where being LGBTQ+ was punishable by death. When the 2022 Commonwealth Games came around, Daley led a successful crusade to have a group of queer people from Commonwealth countries with anti-LGBTQ+ laws enter the arena holding Progress Pride flags during the Opening Ceremony.

GORONWY REES

1909-1979

Born in Aberystwyth, home of the University College of Wales where he would later become principal, Goronwy Rees studied at New College, Oxford before becoming a journalist. He also served as a major in the army and later worked for MI6.

As principal of Aberystwyth University, Rees joined the government's committee on Homosexual Offences and Prostitution in 1954. He argued that the Committee should hear testimonies directly from homosexual men, as well as so-called experts, which in turn played an important part in the resulting Wolfenden Report. At the time, gay people were viewed as perverts and criminals, so Rees's stance on including them was revolutionary.

The report, which was highly controversial, laid the foundations for the later 1967 Sexual Offences Act, that partially decriminalised male homosexuality for the first time in England and Wales. Rees was described as 'by far the most lateral thinking and perceptive member of the committee' for his ideas. The act received royal assent and became law on this date in 1967.

Despite playing this huge part in the reform of homosexual laws, Rees was discredited later in life when, motivated by his Marxist and anti-fascist views, he began passing information to the Soviets and became involved with the spy collective known as the Cambridge Five.

PROUD ALLY

LEONARD BERNSTEIN

1918–1990

American composer Leonard Bernstein wrote music for ballet, theatre, opera and film, as well as choral works, chamber music, symphonies and orchestral music. However, his most famous work is the musical, *West Side Story*, with lyrics by Stephen Sondheim (see 4 Dec). The hit show has been nominated for 15 Tony Awards, and won two, in its various incarnations on Broadway spanning 60 years.

Bernstein's other works include the original score for the film *On the Waterfront*, starring Marlon Brando, which was released on this date in 1954, and the music for Broadway hit *On The Town* (1944).

Bernstein had love affairs with both men and women. He married a Chilean actress named Felicia Montealegre, who knew of his bisexuality, and the pair had three children together.

At the height of his career, Bernstein was one of the most popular and influential figures in 20th-century music. Unusually for a composer, he maintained and courted an active public persona, regularly appearing on TV. His performances as a conductor were also notable for his fastidious and often erotically charged full body movements that saw his arms and hips express the music.

ERIC ROFES

1954–2006

Educator and author Eric Rofes worked with multiple organisations across the US, aimed at improving the lives of gay people and those living with HIV and AIDS. In the 1980s, he was director of the Los Angeles Gay and Lesbian Community Services Center, and created one of the nation's earliest HIV prevention programmes, as well as setting up a shelter for homeless queer youth.

Rofes was an advocate of sexual freedom and expression, and in his controversial 1988 book, *Dry Bones Breathe: Gay Men Creating Post-AIDS Identities and Cultures*, he argued that the AIDS emergency had passed, and the gay community should now cast aside their crisis mentality. This ideology met with strong opposition from other gay activists at the time, criticised for being irresponsible and limited to the experiences of white middle-class gay men.

Rofes wanted a broader range of sexual health issues confronting gay men to be discussed. On this date in 1999 he delivered the opening address to over 300 people at the first Boulder Summit, a conference on gay men's health which he had helped to organise. In 2009, The Eric Rofes Multicultural Queer Resource Center was set up in Arcata, California. Its mission is to shift public opinion of the queer community on campus and in the local area from tolerance to acceptance.

DAVID KATO

1964–2011

At York Pride, held on this date in 2011, rainbow-coloured balloons were released into the sky to honour the memory of murdered Ugandan gay activist, David Kato, who had attended the University of York between 2009 and 2010. In 2021, the university announced that it would be naming its newest college on campus after Kato.

In Uganda, homosexual acts are illegal and carry punishments of many years in prison. When the Ugandan newspaper, *Rolling Stone*, outed Kato and other suspected homosexuals by printing their pictures in the paper (Kato's on the front page) and declaring 'Hang Them', Kato took the tabloid to court and won. A judge told

the paper to stop printing such photographs, declaring it a breach of privacy. Sadly, just weeks later, Kato was murdered.

Kato was originally a schoolteacher and after spending time in South Africa, he returned home to Uganda determined to make a change for LGBTQ+ people in his home country. When Ugandan MP David Bahati introduced an anti-homosexuality bill in 2009, Kato openly spoke out against it, and was labelled Uganda's first out gay man. He also worked with organisations such as Sexual Minorities Uganda (SMUG) and was a founding member of Integrity Uganda, a faith-based LGBT organisation.

ALICE OSEMAN

B. 1994

If you head to Alice Oseman's author page on the Amazon website, you can't help but be impressed. You'll discover that the British writer has released either a novel or a volume of her queer young adult graphic novel, *Heartstopper*, every year since 2014. You'll be further impressed when you learn that she signed her first book deal as a teenager, won the YA Book Prize in 2021 for her novel *Loveless* and, in 2022, turned *Heartstopper* into a major series for Netflix.

Oseman, who describes herself as aromantic and asexual, put an asexual relationship at the heart of her novel, *Radio Silence*, in 2016, saying, 'it was very important to me to show that asexuality is a real, valid identity, and that it can be a great struggle to share that even with those closest to you'.

Her debut novel, *Solitaire*, which was published on this date in 2014, deals with eating disorders, teenage mental health and LGBTQ+ relationships, and was called '*The Catcher in the Rye* for the digital age' by the *Times*.

When *Heartstopper* premiered on Netflix in 2022, it received rave reviews, a 100 per cent rating on Rotten Tomatoes and was called 'possibly the loveliest show on TV' by the *Guardian* newspaper.

BO LAURENT

B. 1956

American activist Bo Laurent was born with what doctors described as ambiguous genitalia, and was assigned male at birth. When Bo was two, exploratory surgery found she had a uterus and ovotestes (gonads with both ovarian and testicular tissue). Laurent's parents were advised to bring her up as female, to change her first name and not to inform her about her medical history. Doctors performed a clitoridectomy on her, entirely removing her clitoris, after which Bo (then known as Bonnie) stopped speaking for six months.

Fast forward to the 1990s after Laurent had quizzed her mother about her medical history,

and she put out an appeal to find other intersex people, setting up the Intersex Society of North America (ISNA). Laurent (using the name Cheryl Chase until 2008) made it her mission to change medical practice for intersex infants, arguing that surgery should not be performed on children but that intersex people should decide for themselves whether surgery was right, later in life. In 2000, ISNA was awarded the Felipa de Souza Human Rights Award.

On this date in 2006, Laurent was a key contributor to a letter on the management of intersex disorders published in *Pediatrics* journal, signed by 50 international experts.

LAUREL HUBBARD

B. 1978

In April 2018, New Zealand weightlifter Laurel Hubbard suffered what she thought would be a career-ending arm injury while competing in the Commonwealth Games in Australia. The transgender athlete who had previously competed at national level in the men's categories, was humbled by a public outpouring of support and said the 'Australian crowd was magnificent'.

Fast-forward three years to a mid-pandemic Tokyo on this date in 2021, and Hubbard became the first openly transgender athlete to compete at the Olympic Games. At 43 she was also the oldest weightlifter at the event. While concerns were raised about Laurel competing, the lifter received bountiful support from her home country and the International Olympic Committee (IOC). Kereyn Smith, New Zealand Olympic Committee chief executive, said, 'As the New Zealand Team, we have a strong culture of *manaaki* [caring] and inclusion and respect for all.'

Hubbard sadly failed her three attempts. In her press statement after the competition, the mild-mannered athlete thanked the IOC for having the courage and 'the moral leadership' to make sport open to all people. She also said she hoped that her being there could provide 'some sense of encouragement' and show 'there are opportunities to live authentically and as we are'.

GEORGE MONTAGUE

1923–2022

Regular attendees of Brighton Pride from the early 2000s on, would immediately recognise the man in the parade on a rainbow-decorated mobility scooter, yielding the sign, 'I'm the oldest gay in the village'. The sign (and scooter) belonged to George Montague, a gay rights activist, who served as one of the first-ever four Pride Ambassadors in Brighton & Hove, UK on this date in 2013.

Montague lived much of his life in the closet. He married and had three children with his wife Vera. They divorced amicably, after which he met his life companion Somchai Phukkhlai. The pair entered into a civil partnership in 2006 and later married at Brighton Town Hall in 2015.

In 1974, Montague had been convicted of gross indecency with a man. The law designating this an offence was repealed in May 2004, and in 2016 the UK government issued pardons to the gay and bisexual men convicted of such abolished sexual offences. Montague, however, was not satisfied with a pardon and went on to campaign for an additional apology. In April 2017, aged 93, Montague finally received a letter from the Home Office containing a full apology.

HÖRÐUR TORFASON

B. 1945

When Icelandic actor and musician Hörður Torfason came out publicly in a magazine interview on this date in 1975, he lost work and recalls that 'People spat on me in the street and I feared being attacked.' He had thoughts of suicide and fled to Denmark, before returning to Iceland determined to make a change for other queer people in his home country.

He founded the organisation Samtökin '78, in 1978 (hence the name), setting it up from his flat in Reykjavík. He aimed to make LGBTQ+ people more visible in society and provide social activities and services such as counselling, education and support for other queer people in Iceland. The association also runs successful youth clubs for young LGBTQ+ people and their allies.

Torfason continued to make music, putting out albums and touring regularly. On visiting new towns and cities he would always walk around them, determined to gain visibility for gay people. In 1993, Torfason left Samtökin '78 and in 1995 developed a successful online chat room enabling gay men to connect with each other. In 2018, as Samtökin '78 celebrated its 40th anniversary, Torfason said, 'I'm very happy that "my" organisation is still fighting for human rights. That was what I wanted from the start.'

RUTH COKER BURKS

B. 1959

'I never thought of myself as an activist, I just thought I was doing what I was supposed to do,' Ruth Coker Burks told the *Guardian* newspaper ahead of the UK paperback release of her book, *All the Young Men*, on this date in 2021. The book tells the story of how Burks took care of gay men dying from AIDS in Arkansas in the mid-1980s. These were men whose families had disowned them and whose friends were dying around them. The first time she helped a patient in hospital she spoke to the nurses about calling his mother, but their response was, 'Honey, his mama's not coming. No one's coming.'

From then on, Burks became the go-to AIDS carer in Arkansas. Nurses and church officials would call her when they had a lone patient who needed support, assistance or just a friendly face. She was a single parent, so would often take her daughter along to the hospitals with her.

In 2017, a short film by Rose McGowan, entitled *Ruth,* was released, telling the story of Burks' first encounter with an AIDS patient.

PROUD ALLY

SIR IAN MCKELLEN

B. 1939

On this date in 1970, just three years after the Sexual Offences Act legalised homosexual acts in England and Wales, the first gay kiss on British TV was beamed into millions of living rooms. The show was a BBC/Prospect production of the play *Edward II*, and the kiss was between Ian McKellen and James Laurenson. Recalling the kiss, McKellen said, 'I've met many Americans who said [our] performance was crucial in their lives when it aired on PBS. But the situation we were placed in was obscene! I mean we were breaking the law in Scotland at this point!'

McKellen is undoubtedly best known for his roles with the Royal Shakespeare Company, playing Gandalf in the *Lord of the Rings* movies (2001–03) and his numerous TV appearances. What some may not know is that he has long been a gay rights activist, protesting Section 28, the legislation brought in by Thatcher's government that banned the 'promotion' of homosexuality in state-funded UK schools, as well as lobbying for an equal age of consent.

Along with Peter Ashman, Michael Cashman (see 24 Jan), Pam St Clement, Lisa Power (see 12 Nov) and others, McKellen is a founding member of the LGBTQ+ political lobbying organisation Stonewall, and he continues to be an active supporter.

ALEXANDER MCQUEEN

1969–2010

Alexander McQueen, the openly queer designer from south London, once claimed he knew he was gay aged six. He began his career in tailoring on Savile Row as a teenager, before moving to theatrical costume producer Angels and Bermans. This move would underpin his future signature collections and iconic style.

His graduate collection from Central Saint Martins in 1992 was inspired by Jack the Ripper and was famously purchased in its entirety by stylist Isabella Blow — the start of a longstanding friendship. McQueen's iconic catwalk shows provoked and pushed the boundaries of how fashion was perceived. Alongside the clothes and models, an amalgamation of art, history, politics, technology and theatrics went down the runway — all equally important for the designer's end vision. His art sometimes courted controversy, such as his 1995 show 'The Highland Rape', featuring bedraggled models in see-though, ripped clothing. Accused of misogyny, the designer explained that he was in fact depicting the 'rape' of Scotland by England.

McQueen became Head Designer at Givenchy, won British Designer of the Year four times and, in 2011, a year after his untimely suicide, was posthumously honoured with an exhibition of his work called *Savage Beauty* at the Metropolitan Museum of Art, New York. Closing on this date after a three-month run, it attracted a record attendance to the museum.

GREG LOUGANIS

B. 1960

Considered by many to be the greatest diver in history, American Greg Louganis won his first gold medal on this date in 1984. He is the only male to win gold medals on both the 3-metre springboard and the 10-metre platform at consecutive Olympic Games (1984 and 1988).

During a dive in the 1988 Olympics in Seoul, six months after being diagnosed as HIV positive, Louganis made contact with the board and cut his head, bleeding into the pool. He had not disclosed his HIV status to Olympic officials from fear of causing a media storm and being denied the right to compete. He didn't admit this to anyone until years later, saying he was 'paralyzed with fear' at the time. 'I imagine some people will think I was irresponsible, and others may think I was heroic,' he writes. 'All I know is, at times of crisis like that, you just do what you think is best.'

Louganis credits his dogs for being a comfort to him through his tough HIV treatments, and he celebrated his longtime love for dogs by competing in agility competitions later in life, as well as working with Pets Are Wonderful Support (PAWS), an organisation that helps people with HIV care for their pets.

TOVE JANSSON

1914–2001

Despite homosexuality being illegal in Finland for most of her life, Tove Jansson, the author and artist behind the universe of the Moomins, still found ways to celebrate her queerness in Moominvalley.

The Swedish-speaking Finnish writer/illustrator, born on this date in 1914, published her first Moomin book in 1945 with little initial success. The Moomins were a family of troll-like creatures, white and wide-eyed in appearance with an affinity to nature, who featured in Jansson's stories of friendship and acceptance. As the author wrote more books, their popularity grew significantly.

Only recently recognised as a queer icon, it is thought that Jansson included some of her own love stories in the Moomin tales. In her thirties, Jansson had a relationship with married theatre director Vivica Bandler, which is thought to have inspired the characters Thingumy and Bob (Tofslan and Vifslan in Swedish, after Tove and Vivica). The two are depicted often holding hands and carrying a suitcase containing secret treasure, a charming metaphor for the pair's hidden love.

Tuulikki Pietilä, an American-born graphic artist who became Jansson's life partner, also appears in the Moomin books, as an androgynous character named Too-Ticky. Jansson and Pietilä lived out most of their relationship in a cabin they built on the island of Pellinki, Finland.

TROYE SIVAN

B. 1995

For someone so young, Troye Sivan has already played many different fiddles in the entertainment world. Born in South Africa but brought up in Perth, Australia, he made it to the finals of Australian talent competition *StarSearch* in 2007. He sings, writes music, is a successful YouTuber and acts on both stage and screen. His wide-ranging performances include playing a young James Howlett in *X-Men Origins: Wolverine*, and Oliver Twist and 'Boy' in Samuel Beckett's play *Waiting for Godot* on stage.

After coming out to his army of YouTube fans aged 18, Sivan did not shy away from his queerness, with gay love depicted in his videos and song lyrics that were about losing his virginity. On this date in 2014 Sivan won a Teen Choice Award for his YouTube video 'The Boyfriend Tag' with fellow YouTuber Tyler Oakley.

Sivan later admitted to changing the music video for 'My My My!', as he didn't want the male dancers to touch: 'I wanted to be as gay as possible while not allowing anyone to be like, "That's too gay,"' he said. In a world where queer artists still feel the need to self-censor, Sivan's continued success and millions of YouTube subscribers prove he's striking the right balance.

HANNAH GADSBY

B. 1978

'Hannah Gadsby beats Beyoncé to Emmy', read the *Guardian* headline in 2019, when the comedian received the award for best writing for a variety special for *Nanette*, her stand-up show that was recorded for Netflix earlier that year. The show deals with homophobia, sexism and sexual violence. She had first debuted it live in Australia in 2017, moving on to show it throughout August at the Edinburgh Festival Fringe, where she jointly won the coveted Best Show award.

The Tasmanian comedian, who is a lesbian and married to producer Jenney Shamash, has said that Nanette was made partly in response to Australia's virulent debate on same-sex marriage. When Gadsby introduced her wife to the world by way of an Instagram post, she wrote, 'My heartfelt thanks to everybody who voted for marriage equality.'

Gadsby was diagnosed with autism in 2017 and created her 2020 show, *Douglas*, around this subject. In 2022, Gadsby released her biography, *Ten Steps to Nanette: A Memoir Situation*, in which she described her neurobiological functioning as being like 'an alien who has been abandoned on Earth and left to muddle my way through life, without a reason, a mission, or any memory of home'.

JOE MEEK

1929–1967

Along the way to becoming a pioneering sound engineer, Joe Meek built circuits and deconstructed radios in his parents' shed as a child, was a radar technician in the Royal Air Force, then had a stint at the Midlands Electricity Board.

Finally, Meek set up a studio and production company named RGM Sound Ltd in his Islington flat. There, he experimented with techniques including compression, sound separation, spring reverb, tape loops and sampling. He wrote and produced many successful records, including the 1962 hit, 'Telstar', performed and released by The Tornados, which topped the UK Singles Chart and became the first British song to reach number one on the Billboard Hot 100, in the US.

Meek struggled with his mental health, and his homosexuality, for which he was once prosecuted, was a further cause of stress for him. Despite this, he included a remarkable queer soundbite on the B-side of The Tornado's record, 'Do You Come Here Often?' (released on this date in 1966), of two British gay men talking, partly in the secret gay language, Polari, about fashion and other men. The fact that Meek released this on a major label at a time when homosexuality was illegal in the UK, is both brilliant and bizarre.

GLADYS BENTLEY

1907–1960

Gladys Bentley was one of the most prolific Black entertainers in the US during the Harlem Renaissance, yet you've probably never heard of her. Dressed in a top hat and tuxedo, singing the blues, playing the piano and flirting with female members of the audience, Bentley was a gender-bending success story.

She rose to fame performing at gay speakeasy, The Clam House, in Harlem, New York in the 1920s. 'Even though they knew me as a male impersonator, they still could appreciate my artistry as a performer,' said the singer, acknowledging her popularity. During this period, she told reporters she had married a white woman and she was often billed as a male-impersonator, seemingly out and proud as a queer, Black woman.

After touring America, Bentley moved to California, where she performed in more high-class establishments, 'toning down' her queerness and even wearing skirts on stage. In an interview with *Ebony* magazine in August 1952, she claimed to have married two men and to have received medical treatments that enabled her to reclaim her 'womanliness'. As society grew more conservative and homosexuality was seen as a threat to America, Bentley's 'heterosexual reinvention' was perhaps primarily for self-preservation, to enable her to continue the performing she loved.

MA RAINEY

1886–1939

The fact that American blues singer Ma Rainey sang the line, 'Went out last night with a crowd of my friends… They must've been women, 'cause I don't like no men,' from her 1928 hit 'Prove It On Me Blues', is scarcely proof that she was a lesbian. However, her singing about women wearing men's clothes in 'Shave 'Em Dry Blues', recorded in August 1924, and her close relationship with bisexual singer Bessie Smith is evidence enough for some.

Gertrude 'Ma' Rainey, who got the 'Ma' part of her name when she married Will 'Pa' Rainey, began performing as part of a travelling minstrel show, before turning her rough and powerful voice to singing the blues. She became known as the Mother of the Blues and was signed to Paramount Records in 1923. She recorded more than 90 records with them, appealing to both Black and white audiences and touring the country.

In 1984, *Ma Rainey's Black Bottom*, a play by August Wilson focusing on a recording session of the singer, premiered on Broadway in New York. It had numerous revivals, including one with Whoopi Goldberg playing the lead, and in 2020 the film of the play aired on Netflix. It won a Golden Globe, BAFTAs and two Academy Awards.

CÉLINE SCIAMMA

B. 1978

As a child in France, Céline Sciamma was introduced to the world of film by her grandmother, a fan of classic Hollywood movies. She visited her local cinema up to three times a week as a teenager and went on to study at the French Film school, La Fémis. While there she wrote the script for her first feature film, *Water Lilies*, a love triangle involving three adolescent girls who meet at a swimming pool. Released on this date in 2007, it was shown at Cannes Film Festival and won numerous festival awards.

The films of Sciamma, who identifies as a lesbian, focus on female experiences, particularly the relationships women and girls have with each other. The filmmaker also examines the cinematic convention of the 'male gaze' in her work, challenging the objectification of women in cinema as seen through men's eyes. She champions the 'female gaze', saying, 'It's about do you share the experience of the woman you're looking at? ... are you *with her* or are you *looking at her*?'

Sciamma's 2011 film, *Tomboy*, tells the story of a gender non-conforming child and their experience of making new friends upon moving to a new neighbourhood. It won numerous accolades, including the Jury Award at the 2011 Teddy Awards at the Berlin Film Festival.

LOTA DE MACEDO SOARES

1910–1967

When landscape architect Maria Carlota 'Lota' Costallat de Macedo Soares joined Conservative politician Carlos Lacerda's administration in the Guanabara state in Brazil in 1960, she is said to have pointed to some rubble directly in front of his apartment and said, 'Give me this fill, this *aterro* (landfill). I'll make it into a Central Park.' With her vision, that land eventually became the 269-acre Parque do Flamengo (Flamengo Park) in the city of Rio de Janeiro. The sprawling park was modern in design, comprised more than 11,000 trees and incorporated a modern art gallery and an airport.

Macedo Soares, who had no formal training in her field, spent the last 16 years of her life in a relationship with the American poet Elizabeth Bishop.

The pair lived in a splendid modernist house in Rio de Janeiro, which Macedo Soares had designed. Sadly, Macedo Soares suffered with her health, contracting typhoid and then having a nervous breakdown, which led to her committing suicide at just 57 years old. On this date in 2013, *Reaching for the Moon*, a film depicting the couple's relationship, was released. The title refers to the soaring lampposts that illuminate the Parque do Flamengo by night, creating a false moonlight.

TERRENCE HIGGINS

1945-1982

Welsh-born Terrence Higgins (Terry) moved to London as a teenager. He became a reporter for the House of Commons' official record, *Hansard*, alongside working as a barman and DJ in gay nightspots. In the 1970s he would often travel to New York but in 1980 he was forced to return home because of unexplained illnesses. Higgins' health quickly worsened as he developed what we now know to be AIDS and, tragically, he died on 4 July 1982. He was one of the first men in Britain known to die of an AIDS-related illness.

After Higgins' death, his friends wanted to do something to help raise awareness and funds for research about GRID (Gay-Related Immune Deficiency) as it was initially called, and in 1983 decided to set up an organisation in his name. The blue plaque now on the outside wall of an east London pub on Old Street states, 'The first meeting of the Terrence Higgins Trust was held here on 17 August 1983'.

The charity was the first of its kind to be set up in the UK, responding to the HIV epidemic by offering support and raising awareness as well as funds. It has continued to fight HIV/AIDS for 40 years.

JOHN CURRY

1949-1994

In 1976, figure skater John Curry was the first man to take the European and World Figure Skating Championships medals and win gold at the Olympics in one season.

As a child, Curry had a passion for ballet, but his parents steered him towards skating. At 16, he moved from Birmingham to London and trained under Arnold Gerschwiler. He later emigrated to the US, where the skating facilities were better. Curry incorporated his ballet skills into his skating, which enabled him to stand out among his competitors. At the 1976 Winter Olympic Games in Innsbruck, he performed three perfect triple jumps in his routine, deliberately including 'masculine' jumps to satisfy some judges who previously thought his style was 'too feminine'.

Curry was publicly outed as gay by German tabloid newspaper *Bild-Zeitung*, an act viewed by some as part of a smear campaign by officials opposed to his style of skating. However, Curry remained popular and was voted BBC Sports Personality of the Year in 1976.

In 1987, while running his own skating school in New York, Curry discovered he was HIV positive. He returned to the UK to spend his remaining time with his family and died seven years later. Billingham International Folklore Festival of World Dance's 2019 event, taking place 10–18 August, paid tribute to Curry with an entire programme dedicated to him.

MONICA HELMS

B. 1951

'I was five years old, growing up in Arizona, and I prayed to God to turn me into a girl. You can't tell me that this is a choice,' said navy veteran and transgender rights activist, Monica Helms, in an interview with *Atlanta Magazine* in 2020, when discussing her creation of the Transgender Pride flag.

Helms, who served aboard the submarines USS *Francis Scott Key* and USS *Flasher* on deployments of up to 70 days each, created the flag in 1999 after encouragement from Mike Page, the creator of the Bisexual Pride flag. She describes the flag as 'the traditional color, light blue, for boys, pink for girls,

and a single white stripe for those who are transitioning, gender neutral, or intersex'. The Trans Pride flag's first public outing was at Arizona Pride in 2000, when Helms waved it as she marched. On this date in 2014, Helms donated her original flag to the Smithsonian Museum for all to see.

Helms, who now lives with her wife in Cobb County, Georgia, also created the Transgender American Veterans Association in 2003, to provide a supportive community for veterans who identify under the transgender umbrella. The association is still active today.

MOHSIN ZAIDI

B. 1985

When barrister, Mohsin Zaidi, released his powerful coming-of-age memoir, *A Dutiful Boy*, about growing up queer in a strict Muslim household in east London, on this date in 2020, it was named Book of the Year by the *Guardian*, GQ and *New Statesman*. It went on to win the Polari First Book Prize and the prestigious Lambda Literary Award.

Zaidi, a barrister who studied at the University of Oxford, was involved in the high-profile case whereby a pair of Christian hotel owners refused a double-bedded room to a same-sex couple in 2010. He has also been a General Counsel/Legal Director of Pride in London.

The author struggled to align his identity and sexuality with his Muslim upbringing when he was younger, later explaining in a newspaper interview, 'For gays, I was too Muslim. For Muslims, I was too gay. For whites, I was too Brown, and for my family, I was too white.' The author and barrister is now an advocate for LGBTQ+ rights and BAME representation, and sits on the board of Stonewall, the UK's largest LGBTQ+ rights charity and lobbying group.

VITO RUSSO

1946-1990

On this date in 2013, the Gay and Lesbian Alliance Against Defamation (GLAAD), America's lesbian, gay, bisexual and transgender media advocacy organisation, introduced the 'Studio Responsibility Index' – a report that analyses the quantity, quality and diversity of images of LGBTQ+ people in films from major Hollywood studios. Part of that report included the 'Vito Russo test', whereby a film only passes if it includes an LGBTQ+ character who is not solely defined by their sexuality or gender identity and has a significant impact on the plot.

Russo became active in gay politics in the 1970s and it was his outrage at the media's scant and inaccurate coverage of the AIDS pandemic that led him to co-found GLAAD to monitor LGBTQ+ representation in the media.

Many would describe Russo as the inventor of queer film studies. His pioneering book, *The Celluloid Closet* (1981), originally based on lectures he gave at colleges, film festivals and museums around the world, was a thorough analysis of the portrayal of LGBTQ+ people in movies and became the leading reference on the subject. After his death in 1990, the go-ahead was given for his book to be made into a feature-length documentary and this was eventually released in 1996.

SIR MATTHEW BOURNE

B. 1960

British choreographer and dancer Matthew Bourne started dance classes at the age of 22, relatively late for someone so successful in the field. Bourne is most well-known for staging and recreating classic ballet in new, groundbreaking and, sometimes, controversial ways.

His 1995 version of *Swan Lake* featured bare-chested male dancers, and the lead prince fell in love with a male swan; a brave move for a 19th-century ballet in the conservative London dance world. While this homoerotic re-telling of the story was generally applauded due to Bourne's spectacular staging and choreography, it met with some homophobic criticism. One newspaper captioned a photograph of the male swans with the words 'Bum me up, Scotty'.

Nevertheless, the production won a Laurence Olivier Award, two Tony Awards and became the longest-running ballet in both London's West End and on Broadway.

Bourne and his company, New Adventures, have subsequently staged productions for, among others, *My Fair Lady* (2001), *Edward Scissorhands* (2005) and *The Red Shoes* (2016). His *Dorian Gray*, which debuted at the Edinbugh International Festival throughout August 2008, had record-breaking ticket sales.

Bourne was knighted in the Queen's New Year Honours list in 2016. He was also awarded the Queen Elizabeth II Coronation Award — one of the most revered honours in the world of dance.

JAMES BALDWIN

1924–1987

James Baldwin was an American novelist, essayist, playwright and activist. His work dealt with racial injustice, sexuality and was a tool for social change, and in the case of his 1956 novel *Giovanni's Room*, offered solace. Here, Baldwin openly and empathetically explored homosexuality through the same-sex relationships of an American man living in Paris (where Baldwin also lived for a time). The book was notable for being published in 1956, six years before any state in the US decriminalised homosexual acts between consenting adults (Illinois became the first to decriminalise consensual sodomy in 1962).

His sixth and final novel, *Just Above My Head*, was published in August 1979 and dealt with incest, war, poverty and the civil rights struggle. It received mixed reviews.

Baldwin's writings were highly influential in the civil rights movement of the 1960s. It was his aim to make white Americans more aware of the struggles of his Black brothers and sisters, and to this end he published essays such as 'Nobody Knows My Name: A letter from the South' in magazines like the *New Yorker*, *Partisan Review* and *New York Times Magazine*, reaching a mostly white audience.

While primarily resident in France, Baldwin travelled to the American South giving lectures on the country's racial divide, and by 1963 his influence on the movement and notoriety gained him the cover of *Time*.

MARSHA P. JOHNSON

1945-1992

Stories about trans rights activist Marsha P. Johnson abound, not all of them true. That she 'threw the first brick' at the Stonewall uprising, for example, was denied by Johnson herself, who said she only arrived at the Stonewall Inn when the revolt was already under way. Lesser-known but true is that she was part of a series of screen prints of drag queens and transgender club-goers that Andy Warhol (see 3 Jun) created in 1975, called 'Ladies and Gentlemen'.

Johnson was born on this date in New Jersey in 1945. By her early teens she found herself, often homeless, in Greenwich Village, New York. This is where Johnson was able to become herself. She dressed as she pleased and gave herself a new name: the P stood for 'Pay it no mind' and she claimed 'Johnson' from a Howard Johnson restaurant she frequented. 'I was no one, nobody, from Nowheresville, until I became a drag queen,' Johnson said.

In Greenwich Village she met her lifelong friend Sylvia Rivera (see 24 Jun) with whom she set up Street Transvestite Action Revolutionaries (STAR), a charity supporting homeless LGBTQ+ youth. Despite the fact the pair struggled with drug abuse and were often penniless themselves, they leased a property from the mafia (STAR House) to give shelter to the homeless queer kids of NYC.

ADRIAN

1903–1959

Adrian Adolph Greenburg is the gay man in Hollywood that hardly anyone has heard of, yet he is responsible for one of the most iconic items in queer film and culture. He designed the ruby slippers worn by Judy Garland, as Dorothy, in *The Wizard of Oz*, released on this date in 1939!

American film director and producer Cecil B. DeMille installed Adrian as head designer at MGM studios in 1928, giving him control over the wardrobes of some of the biggest stars of the day, such as Katharine Hepburn, Jean Harlow and Greta Garbo. He is credited with being responsible for Joan Crawford's padded, wide-shouldered look.

It's documented that Adrian was openly gay within the film community, however, in 1939, he married his film-star friend, Janet Gaynor, in what was thought to be a 'lavender marriage' – a marriage of convenience to mask the sexual orientation of one or both partners, which was not uncommon in Hollywood.

When Adrian left MGM in 1942, he created his own successful couture line, selling clothes across America and receiving a Coty Award for Fashion in 1944. However, Adrian missed out the biggest award in film – the Oscar – as the costume category was not introduced until after he did most of his work.

GAVIN GRIMM

B. 1999

While he always knew he felt at odds with the female body he was assigned at birth, American Gavin Grimm only found the language to understand and express it when he saw the anime cosplayer, Twinfools, transition from female to male. Grimm highlights the importance of the internet for trans people in allowing them to find others like themselves, and forge friendships and communities.

After a fairly uneventful coming out to friends and family, an anonymous complaint was sent to Grimm's school about his use of the boys' bathroom. This led the Gloucester County School Board to bar Grimm from the boys' facilities, forcing him to use a makeshift unisex bathroom, instead.

Grimm sued the school board and eventually won his case when the 4th US Circuit Court of Appeals ruled that he'd been discriminated against, stating, 'There is no question that the board's policy discriminates against transgender students on the basis of their gender nonconformity.' On this date in 2021, more than six years after the battle began, the board was ordered to pay Grimm's legal fees and in response the former student said, 'This outcome sends a strong message to other school systems that discrimination is an expensive, losing battle.'

JEANETTE WINTERSON

B. 1959

When writer and lecturer Jeanette Winterson lived in her car after leaving her parents' home as an adolescent, she saw it as her own private place. 'I had books and safety. I never felt safe at home.' She had been adopted after being born to a teenage girl in Manchester on this date in 1959, but said she never felt any attachment to her adoptive parents.

Winterson's first novel, *Oranges Are Not The Only Fruit*, was semi-autobiographical and dealt with lesbianism, family relationships and religion. It won critical acclaim, the Whitbread Award for a First Novel and in 1990 was made into a BBC television adaptation.

Winterson has written throughout her life and has more than 20 publications to her name. In 2019 she published *Frankissstein*, a love story about a young transgender doctor and a professor involved in AI. Sex dolls, gender and Mary Shelley all feature in the narrative, described in the *Guardian* as 'a work of both pleasure and profundity, robustly and skilfully structured'.

In the biography on her website, Winterson, an out lesbian who has been married, acknowledges that 'There's nothing here about relationships, I know. And that's because for women, relationships become the focus of everything, and it's boring, so I decided not to write anything at all…'

BAYARD RUSTIN

1912–1987

Mention the March on Washington for Jobs and Freedom that took place on this date in 1963, and many people will think of Martin Luther King and his 'I have a dream' speech. Fewer people will be familiar with Bayard Rustin, a key organiser of the march and a close advisor to Dr King, often referred to as 'Mr. March-on-Washington' by those in King's circle.

Rustin had spent time as part of Gandhi's movement in India, which helped cultivate his learning of nonviolent resistance. He shared this philosophy of pacifistic protest with Dr King and A. Philip Randolph, an African American labour-union president and socialist who headed up the march. Dr King said, 'We are thoroughly committed to the method of nonviolence in our struggle and we are convinced that Bayard's expertness and commitment in this area will be of inestimable value'.

Rustin had been arrested for homosexual acts in the 1950s, causing many people in and outside the civil rights movement to attack him and label him a pervert. This led him to being the behind the scenes advisor and rarely the spokesperson, until later in life when in the 1970s and 80s he spoke publicly about LGBTQ+ rights.

KARL HEINRICH ULRICHS

1825–1895

It was on this date in 1867 that lawyer and writer Karl Heinrich Ulrichs stood before the Congress of German Jurists in Munich asking for a repeal of anti-homosexual laws. His defence is often dubbed as the first public 'coming out' in modern society.

Ulrichs offered a new terminology that helped to birth the concept of sexuality and its innate nature: he coined the term *Urning* (men attracted to men, as he identified) and *Urningin* (women attracted to women) in a move away from terms like sodomite, which emphasised the act of homosexuality rather than the person. This was two years before the word 'homosexuality' was created.

Ulrichs was jeered, interrupted and shouted down during his speech, yet his lauded words would later inspire revolutions. Many LGBTQ+ activists, particularly German sexologist Magnus Hirschfeld, underline how indebted we are to his bravery.

Ulrichs' legacy was cemented in Berlin where a street has now been renamed after him. In sweet irony, Einemstraße was originally named after Karl von Einem, a Nazi sympathiser who supported homosexual persecution. You can find Ulrichs' name in many German street names today.

ANNE, QUEEN OF GREAT BRITAIN

1665–1714

Anne, Queen of Great Britain, had poor health throughout her life, and she and her husband, to whom she was reportedly devoted, suffered the loss of 17 children. Over time, a valid discussion surrounding the queen possibly being bisexual or a lesbian has come about.

Anne and Sarah Churchill, Duchess of Malborough, had been friends from childhood; their close relationship was evident in the affectionate letters they exchanged. During her reign, Anne appointed Churchill's cousin, Abigail Hill, to the royal household, causing rivalry between the cousins, as the queen seemingly transferred her affections to the new arrival.

The relationship between Anne and Hill became the subject of gossip, with political pamphlets claiming Hill performed 'dark deeds at night' for her Majesty. Were these circulated by Churchill in jealousy, or were they simply lies with a political agenda? Many historians argue this kind of impassioned friendship was commonplace between women at the time and did not necessarily indicate a romantic or sexual relationship.

On this date in 2018, *The Favourite*, a film about Anne's supposed love triangle, premiered at Venice International Film Festival. Olivia Coleman went on to win an Academy Award for Best Actress for her portrayal of Anne in it.

DIRK BOGARDE

1921–1999

British actor Dirk Bogarde shot to stardom in the 1954 comedy *Doctor in the House*. Several sequels later, this crowd-pleasing pin-up made the bold decision to take the lead in a controversial mystery-thriller about a (seemingly) secretly gay barrister who falls victim to blackmail for homosexuality. The role was offered to three other actors, all of whom either declined it or changed their minds. *Victim* was released on this date in 1961, six years before the UK's Sexual Offences Act decriminalised 'homosexual acts in private between consenting adults'.

Victim, thought to be the first English-language film to use the word 'homosexual' and sympathetically present the problems experienced by homosexuals at that time, was groundbreaking.

Michael Relph (producer) and Basil Dearden (director) created the film as an open protest against homophobic British laws. Many believe that *Victim* and Bogarde (a closeted gay man living with his partner Anthony 'Tote' Forwood) helped to improve attitudes towards gay men and ultimately played a part in the partial decriminalisation of homosexuality in England and Wales in 1967. The Act's legislator, Lord Arran, praised Bogarde for his courageous contribution, 'It is comforting to think that perhaps a million men are no longer living in fear.'

MUNROE BERGDORF

B. 1987

When British activist Munroe Bergdorf was hired to front a big campaign for the beauty brand L'Oréal in August 2017, she was thrilled to be given such a large platform as a mixed-race trans woman. Her joy was short-lived, as L'Oréal dropped her on this date in September 2017 when she called out white privilege on her private Facebook page and was accused of racism against white people. A press and social media storm ensued. After some public back-and-forth L'Oréal's management invited Bergdorf to settle their grievances, and in an unexpected move hired her to sit on their diversity and inclusion board.

Bergdorf continued to use her voice to discuss and expose systemic racism, transphobia, homophobia and misogyny in today's society. In 2018 she allowed cameras to follow her as she underwent facial surgery for a Channel 4 documentary called *What Makes A Woman?*

In February 2021, Bergdorf left Twitter, calling out the platform for failing to invest effectively in algorithms that identify transphobic speech or racism. Despite facing the threats of violence and abuse that she campaigns against daily, Bergdorf told friend Jameela Jamil, on her podcast in 2020, 'I love that I'm trans, I would never take it back. I love my trans sisters, I love my Black sisters, I love my queerness. I am so happy that I'm queer.'

KEITH HARING

1958–1990

Keith Haring believed that 'Art is for everybody.' He wrote that 'the public has a right to art' in a manifesto he produced when he arrived in New York in 1978. Haring 'drew' his bold, cartoon-style motifs on abandoned streets and all over the New York subway system – pops of bright art activism, as the city was pulling itself out of a bleak depression.

At the height of his fame Haring opened Pop Shop in SoHo, NYC, a store that sold affordable T-shirts, badges and other items emblazoned with Haring's colourful imagery and catchy slogans like 'Crack is Wack'.

Haring's art focused on politics and social injustice. AIDS, poverty, drugs, racism and homophobia were all running themes, and in the year before his death he set up the Keith Haring Foundation to help tackle such issues after he was gone. The foundation's two main focuses are still the education and prevention of AIDS and HIV and enriching the lives of underprivileged children.

On this date in 2014, Haring became one of the first honourees on San Francisco's Rainbow Honor Walk – a 'walk of fame' installation celebrating LGBTQ+ individuals.

JANE ADDAMS

1860-1935

Jane Addams was an activist, feminist and humanitarian who spent most of her life helping others. In September 1889, she co-founded Hull House, a settlement house in Chicago, with her long-term partner, Ellen Gates Starr. This was one of the first settlement houses in the US, providing free classes in literature, art and history to the poor, women and immigrants. The house, which promoted social and moral reform as well as race relations, was supported by upper- and middle-class benefactors, many of whom were wealthy women Addams recruited herself.

Addams was a co-founder of the American Civil Liberties Union, and in 1931 became the first American woman to receive the Nobel Peace Prize. While the work she did, including public health reform and advancing child and labour laws, has been well documented over the years, her sexuality was erased from the history books until recently.

Addams shared the later part of her life, and her home, with Mary Rozet Smith, a wealthy philanthropist who helped run Hull House. In recent years, the Jane Addams Hull-House Museum held an exhibition called 'Was Jane Addams a Lesbian?' and in 2008, she was inducted into the Chicago LGBT Hall of Fame.

JAZZ JENNINGS

B. 2000

Jazz Jennings is an American television and YouTube star, who was assigned male at birth but knew from an early age that she identified as a girl. With supportive parents who fought for her right to attend school as a girl, she used female pronouns and the bathroom of her choice from the age of about five.

In 2007, Jennings drew national attention when she was identified as one of the 'youngest known cases of an early transition from male to female', in a television interview on *ABC News* with Barbara Walters. Over the years, Jennings has used her platform to educate and raise awareness of the issues facing trans youth. The teenager spoke at the 2015 Human Rights Campaign Foundation's Time to Thrive Conference in Portland, Oregon, where she reminded the audience that 'Close to 50 per cent of trans youth will attempt suicide by the time they are 21.'

Jennings has featured on multiple TV shows, and her own reality show, *I am Jazz*, has run for seven seasons since 2015. Jennings is the co-author of a children's book based on her experience as a transgender child, also entitled *I Am Jazz*, which was released in the US on this date in 2014.

FRANCIS LEE

B. 1969

Francis Lee left his rural home in West Yorkshire for London when he was 20. He made his way as an actor for 20 years, appearing in popular British television shows, but in 2012 he moved behind the camera and began writing and directing films.

His breakout feature was *God's Own Country* (2017), a film which dealt with the blossoming gay relationship between a young farmer and a migrant worker. Filmed in Yorkshire, it took Lee back home (where he has since settled). The film won numerous awards, including the Männer Jury Award at the Berlin International Film Festival, Best Film at the Evening Standard British Film Awards and, on this date in 2017, Best International First Feature at the Galway Film Fleadh.

Lee's second film, *Ammonite*, about the 19th-century fossil hunter, Mary Anning (see 16 May), was released in 2020. It revolved around a relationship Anning had with another woman. While many historians believe Anning was queer, some challenge this, along with Lee's decision to depict her in a same-sex relationship. He said he wanted to elevate her as a working-class woman, 'I wanted to contextualise her in terms of a relationship. And because men had blocked and overlooked her… this relationship couldn't be with a man.'

SYLVESTER

1947-1988

Sylvester, born Sylvester James Jr in Los Angeles, California, on this date in 1947, was an androgynous, genderqueer, falsetto-voiced music artist whose disco hit, *You Make Me Feel (Mighty Real)*, made him a household name in 1978.

After graduating high school, Sylvester moved to San Francisco and joined the Cockettes, a gender-bending, hippy, LSD-infused group who performed across the bay area and eventually in New York City. After leaving the Cockettes, Sylvester had minor success fronting a band named *Sylvester And The Hot Band*, and later as a nightclub singer in the Castro district of San Francisco.

The singer's big break came when he teamed up with the visionary electronic music producer, Patrick Cowley, to create and release *You Make Me Feel (Mighty Real)*, written by James Wirrick. Taken from Sylvester's album, *Step 11*, the song became an international hit.

When Sylvester died of an AIDS-related illness in 1988, he'd sold more than 500,000 records and the *New York Times* declared that he'd 'delighted audiences of every race and sexual persuasion with his funky, spiritual style singing'. In his will, the artist stipulated that royalties from his music go to AIDS charities and activist organisations.

FLORA MURRAY

1869–1923

Flora Murray was a pioneering doctor from Scotland. Female doctors were not just uncommon when she began her medical training at the London School of Medicine for Women (the first medical school in Britain to train women), they were actively discouraged from the career.

After working at the Belgrave Hospital for Children and the Chelsea Hospital for Women, Murray co-founded the Women's Hospital for Children in London in 1912, along with Louisa Garrett Anderson. Murray and Garrett Anderson, now widely believed to have been life partners, were both members of the Women's Social and Political Union (WSPU) and staunch suffragettes. They cared for women who had gone on hunger strike for their cause and those who were force-fed in prison, as a result.

In September 1914, after the outbreak of World War One, Murray and Garrett Anderson set up a hospital in Hotel Claridge in Paris, treating injured soldiers. After hearing of its success, the British government asked the women to return to London to take charge of Endell Street Military Hospital in 1915, where approximately 26,000 patients were treated before it closed in 1919.

Murray published her experiences as a female doctor in *Women as Army Surgeons: Being the History of the Women's Hospital Corps in Paris* (1920), dedicating the book to Garrett Anderson, who she described as 'Bold, cautious, true and my loving companion.'

QUINN

B. 1995

Professional Canadian soccer player, Quinn, had already won a bronze medal at the 2016 Olympic games in Rio de Janeiro, Brazil, when they came out as trans on this date in 2020. Sharing their truth on Instagram, Quinn, who goes by one name only, encouraged cis people to share their pronouns on their social media profiles and to listen to other trans and non-binary voices.

In August 2021, Quinn made Olympic history when they became the first openly transgender athlete to ever win an Olympic medal. The gold medal was awarded to Quinn and the Canadian women's soccer team when they defeated Sweden 3-2 in Tokyo.

As a teenager, Quinn played in both the 2012 FIFA U-17 Women's World Cup and the 2014 FIFA U-20 Women's World Cup. Their stellar performance on the field continued and as an adult Quinn played in the final of the 2017 Algarve Cup in Portugal and the 2019 FIFA Women's World Cup.

When asked about the issues that trans people face in sport, Quinn said they felt optimistic for change: 'Change in legislature. Changes in rules, structures, and mindsets.' They were also pleased to report that their teammates had been supportive and 'embraced change'.

MARTINA NAVRATILOVA

B. 1956

Coming out voluntarily in 1981, at the height of her stardom, was a brave and unprecedented step for tennis champion, Martina Navratilova. After defecting from Czechoslovakia to the US in 1975, Navratilova enjoyed many years of success and by the time she originally retired from singles play in 1994, she had won 167 singles titles in total. Since the open era began, she has also won more overall Grand Slam tennis titles than anyone else in the world.

A long-time activist for queer rights, Navratilova took part in the March on Washington for Lesbian, Gay and Bi Equal Rights in 1993 and spoke at the subsequent rally. The star also campaigned against Amendment 2, which was designed to prevent sexual orientation being a protected class in law in Colorado.

In 2019, Navratilova was removed from the advisory board of LGBTQ+ sports advocacy group Athlete Ally, following disparaging comments she made about trans athletes. Athlete Ally viewed her comments as 'transphobic' and 'based on a false understanding of science and data'. In response, the tennis star co-founded Women's Sports Policy Working Group, aimed at finding a 'middle ground' for female trans athletes and non-trans athletes to compete under one umbrella.

On this date in 2006, Navratilova hung up her racket after winning the US Open mixed doubles, playing alongside Bob Bryan.

LIV LITTLE

B. 1994

Liv Little set up the gal–dem platform in 2015. It is a media company and British publication, primarily online but sometimes in print, which is run by and tells the stories of people of colour from marginalised genders. The gal–dem site states that the 'current journalistic landscape is 94 per cent white and 55 per cent male and gal–dem is actively trying to redress this imbalance in the media'.

Little, who identifies as part of the QTIPOC community, was raised in southeast London and studied at the University of Bristol, graduating in 2016. Her projects, which champion minority groups who are disadvantaged on the basis of disability, gender, race and sexuality, and alongside gal–dem, include activities with the Victoria and Albert Museum and the *Guardian* newspaper. In 2018, she worked with the vodka brand Absolut and Stonewall (the LGBTQ+ charity) on the Drop of Love campaign, which encouraged people to actively become allies to marginalised communities.

On this date in 2020, Little announced she was stepping down as CEO of gal–dem to become president of the board. The following year it was announced that her debut novel, *Rosewater*, had been snapped up by a publisher in a six-figure deal.

MARK BINGHAM

1970-2001

On this date in 2001, United Airlines Flight 93 crashed into a grassy, empty field in Somerset County, Pennsylvania. It had left Newark International Airport in New Jersey that morning, destined for San Francisco International Airport in California, but was hijacked by four terrorists who planned to crash the plane into the US Capitol building in Washington, D.C. Four passengers were able to take the plane from the terrorists and, sacrificing their own lives, diverted it off its collision course to save countless civilians. One of those passengers was 6-foot 4-inch gay rugby player and PR exec, Mark Bingham.

Bingham and the other passengers who helped thwart the terrorists have become heroes since the tragedy. Bingham's mother, Alice Hoagland, a former United Airlines flight attendant, made sure her son's name was remembered, championing LGBTQ+ rights and campaigning for airline safety after her son's death.

In 2002, a biennial international rugby union competition predominantly for gay and bisexual men, called the Bingham Cup, was established in Mark's memory. Bingham's name appears on both the Flight 93 National Memorial in Pennsylvania and on the National September 11 Memorial's South Pool in New York.

STEVE OSTROW

B. 1932

The Continental Baths in the basement of the Ansonia Hotel in New York City brought together sex, socialising and entertainment. Steve Ostrow was the man behind the baths, which opened on this date in 1968.

In the early days, it was often raided by police as homosexuality was illegal in New York, and entrapment of patrons by undercover police was common. After around 200 raids, Ostrow gathered approximately 250,000 signatures protesting the harassment, and along with other members of the LGBTQ+ community, took these to City Hall. He believes this contributed to having 'the laws changed so that homosexuality in private among consenting adults was not illegal'.

The baths grew in size, opulence and attendance: a dance floor and entertainment space were added, which opened up to the public for cabaret and music events. The dance floor was often full of people dancing in towels, bathing suits, clothes or nude, as legendary New York DJs Larry Levan (see 21 Oct) and Frankie Knuckles (see 26 Feb) spun their tunes. The venue, which boasted Bette Midler (see 29 Jun) and Barry Manilow among its performers, closed in 1976.

Ostrow later moved to Australia, where he set up Mature Age Gays, a group committed to helping older queer people suffering from isolation, loneliness and loss.

WILLI NINJA

1961-2006

If Madonna is the first name that comes to mind when someone mentions 'Voguing', then the second name to pop into your head should be Willi Ninja. In fact, Ninja is often wrongly credited with inventing the Vogue style of dance, which was actually popularised at the drag balls of Harlem, New York in the 1980s and 90s. Ninja did, however, teach, help popularise and simply embody Voguing.

Ninja was the 'mother' of his own dance troupe, the House of Ninja, with a group of adopted gay and trans children under his wing. During this period, the Harlem drag ball scene was a place where queer African American and Latino youth were able to come together and express themselves through fashion and dance.

Ninja rose to fame as one of the central figures featured in *Paris is Burning*, an award-winning documentary about the Harlem ball scene, released on this date in 1990. After starting out Voguing in the park, he moved on to balls, then music videos and then taught it. He later walked the runway for Jean Paul Gaultier (see 13 Apr) and even taught millionaire socialite, Paris Hilton, how to sashay down the red carpet.

IFTI NASIM

1946–2011

When poet and writer Ifti Nasim died aged 64 in his adopted city of Chicago, the *Chicago Tribune* called him 'one of the most famous Chicagoans most Chicagoans have never heard of'. It also reported that around a thousand people packed into the city's Muslim Community Center to pray over his body.

Nasim, born on this date in 1946, emigrated from Pakistan to the United States at the age of 21 to flee persecution as a gay man in his home country. Speaking about bringing shame on his family, he once said, 'In Islam, you can never be a homosexual. You might as well be a dead person.'

Once settled in Chicago, he sold luxury cars for Loeber Motors and began writing poetry in Urdu, Punjabi and English alongside this full-time job. Deemed controversial due to its theme of gay love written in Urdu, Nasim's collection of poetry, *Narman* (meaning 'half-man, half-woman' in Persian), was published in 1994 and brought the writer much acclaim.

In 1986, Nasim founded Sangat/Chicago, an organisation supporting the South Asian LGBTQ+ community in the city. Nasim was recognised for his activism, as well as his writing, when he was inducted into the Chicago LGBT Hall of Fame in 1996.

ANTHONY PERKINS

1932–1992

When Alfred Hitchcock's thriller, *Psycho*, was released in September 1960, first in the US and then a few weeks later on this date in the UK, Anthony Perkins' life changed forever. The actor played Norman Bates, the murderous lead character. Perkins was praised for his performance, and Norman Bates became one of the most iconic characters in film history.

While the performance brought Perkins widespread fame, it became somewhat of a curse as people couldn't see him in any other role. Signed to Paramount Studios, Perkins was initially billed as a teen idol in romantic roles (he had previously released

pop music), but this path closed abruptly after *Psycho* was released.

Perkins struggled with his sexuality. Despite Paramount's objections, he led a gay lifestyle in the early part of his life. He was unhappy, however, and underwent gay conversion therapy to 'cure him' of his homosexuality. In 1973, aged 41, Perkins married model and photographer Berry Berenson and the pair went on to have two children. While many were dubious about the relationship, former partner Tab Hunter said 'Who am I to decide – to even discuss – what was right for him? That was his own choice... and for him it was the right decision.'

BRIAN PADDICK

B. 1958

During his time serving in the Metropolitan Police in London, Brian Paddick became the most senior gay police officer in the country, rising to deputy assistant commissioner. After his retirement from the force, he ran for the role of mayor of London in 2008, and in 2012 as a Liberal Democrat candidate, but was unsuccessful both times.

As police commander of the south London borough of Lambeth, Paddick controversially introduced a scheme whereby officers would only caution people caught with cannabis for personal use, instead of arresting them. This was intended to create better relations in the community and free up time for the police.

While some claimed Paddick was going soft on drugs, others praised his actions.

In 2018, Paddick spoke publicly about the dangers of chemsex (sex under the influence of stimulant drugs), after the death of an old boyfriend who overdosed on the drug GHB while at a party. He highlighted the fact that GHB was listed as a class C drug, classified as lower than cannabis. In 2022, the UK government reclassified it as a class B substance.

On this date in 2013, Paddick was appointed to the House of Lords where his areas of focus include crime, civil law, justice and rights, and housing and planning.

JACQUELINE WILSON

B. 1945

Children's author and former Children's Laureate Jacqueline Wilson was 74 before she spoke publicly about her same-sex relationship with partner Trish. The author, who had previously been married to a man, said she'd 'never really been in any kind of closet' and that it was 'old news for anybody that has ever known anything much about [me]'. She chose to speak publicly about her relationship in a *Guardian* interview in 2020, a few months before her 111th book, *Love Frankie*, was published on this date. The main character, Frankie, is a tomboy who falls for a fellow female classmate.

Wilson, who started out as a journalist at the teen magazine *Jackie*, has had unprecedented success as a children's author. As well as selling more than 25 million books, she was the author most borrowed from public libraries in the UK between 2000 and 2010. Her literature focuses on issues experienced by young girls, with her series centred around the character Tracy Beaker, a girl in foster care, arguably her most well-known stories. These books were also made into a successful television series, which ran for five series in the 2000s.

In 2008, Wilson was appointed Dame Commander of the Order of the British Empire (DBE) in the New Year Honours list.

DEREK JARMAN

1942–1994

Derek Jarman, a maverick of British cinema, was making his own films using a Super 8mm camera and rejecting the regular script-driven narrative of popular filmmaking by 1975. His first film, *Sebastiane* (1976), celebrated the male body and homoeroticism and featured only Latin dialogue. In 2000, the Sebastiane Award (named after Jarman's film) was created. It is an LGBT film award given out in September every year at the San Sebastián International Film Festival in Spain.

As well as putting homosexuality at the forefront of his films, Jarman was also a gay rights activist and one of the first public figures in the UK to reveal he was HIV positive. He was arrested in 1992 when, alongside Peter Tatchell (see 12 Apr) and LGBT+ direct action group OutRage!, he marched on Parliament to demand the repeal of anti-gay laws. Jarman directed music videos, such as the provocative 'It's A Sin', for the Pet Shop Boys, and worked with musical greats including Bob Geldof, Marianne Faithfull, Marc Almond (see 17 Jul) and The Smiths.

Jarman died from an AIDS-related illness in 1994. In 2008, an award was created in his name: the Jarman Award offers financial assistance and support to artists working with moving images – in particular, those celebrating experimentation, imagination and innovation in UK film. In 2019, a blue plaque commemorating Jarman was unveiled in Shad Thames, southeast London where the filmmaker once lived and worked, reflecting his unique creative legacy.

RANDY WICKER

B. 1938

On this date in 1964, Randy Wicker, Craig Rodwell, Renée Cafiero (see 12 Jul) and a handful of others held a small protest outside the Whitehall US Army Induction Center, in New York City. They were protesting the army's failure to keep gay and bisexual men's draft records confidential and carried signs reading 'ARMY INVADES SEXUAL PRIVACY'. It is thought that this was the first public demonstration for gay rights in the US.

Wicker was part of the early gay rights group, the Mattachine Society, and participated in numerous activities with the organisation, despite being frustrated that their actions weren't more radical. Wicker took part in the Sip-in (see 21 Apr), a defiant act against the State Liquor Authority that took inspiration from the sit-ins of the civil rights movement. He was also one of, if not the, first person to publicly admit their homosexuality on radio.

Speaking in 1989, Wicker said he believed what he (and others) did in the early 1960s paved the way for the Stonewall riots: 'What my generation did, we built the ideology, you know.' Yet, despite this, when the 25th anniversary of Stonewall came around, Wicker, along with Larry Kramer (see 14 Mar) and Harry Hay (see 2 Jul) snubbed the main parade and took part in an alternative march, protesting the mainstreaming of Pride.

BILLIE JEAN KING

B. 1943

Billie Jean King has a lot of firsts to her name. She was the first woman to be chosen as *Sports Illustrated's* Sportsperson of the Year, she was the first female athlete to earn more than $100,000 in prize money in a single season, and in 1973, she became the first president of the Women's Tennis Association.

On this date in 1973 King won the famous 'Battle of the Sexes' tennis match, against Bobby Riggs. Riggs, a self-proclaimed male chauvinist, had previously goaded King, saying she wouldn't beat him because women were inferior and couldn't handle the pressure of the game. Their match was attended by 30,000 spectators at the Houston Astrodome and watched on TV by a staggering 90 million people worldwide. King beat Riggs in three sets: 6-4, 6-3, 6-3.

While King had preferred to keep her relationships and sexuality private, she was publicly outed in 1981 when her ex-partner took legal action against her, which resulted in their previous relationship becoming public knowledge. 'It was horrible,' King later said, but she decided to confirm her identity on the basis of her mother telling her 'To thine own self be true.' Years later when asked what she'd do differently, King said, 'I'd come out earlier.'

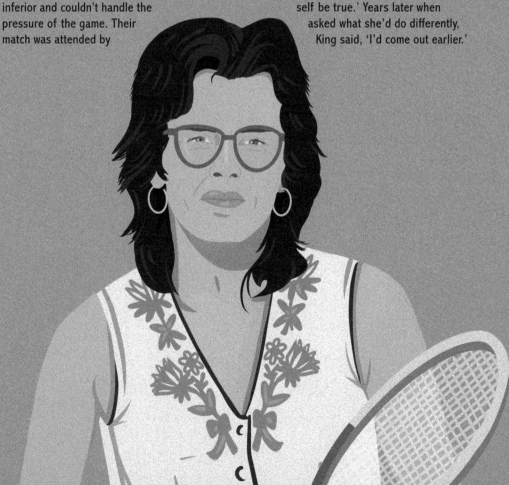

HIDA VILORIA

B. 1968

When in 2017, Hida Viloria became the second person in the US known to be issued with an intersex birth certificate, they said, 'After decades of working for intersex visibility, to see the word "intersex" on this government document, correctly acknowledging who I am, is monumental. I've always been proud to be intersex, and now I'm prouder than ever to be a New Yorker!'

Viloria, who is the founding executive director of the Intersex Campaign for Equality, the world's first international intersex organisation, has written the activist memoir, *Born Both: An intersex Life* (2017) and with Professor Maria Nieto a biology text,

The Spectrum of Sex: The Science of Male, Female, and Intersex (2020).

Viloria has campaigned tirelessly for an end to non-consensual, medically unnecessary surgeries on infants born with physical characteristics that don't fit the stereotypical definitions of male or female. Thankful that they weren't subjected to such surgeries, they argue against the medical term 'Disorders of Sex Development' and call for intersex people to be accepted and recognised as themselves, rather than as people needing to be 'corrected'. On this date in 2007, Viloria appeared on *The Oprah Winfrey Show* to discuss being intersex, describing the exposure to 20 million viewers as 'an activists' dream come true'.

DAN SAVAGE

B. 1964

Queer adults often tell struggling young LGBTQ+ kids that 'it gets better'. American writer and broadcaster Dan Savage amplified this message on this date in 2010, in response to a wave of teenage suicides sweeping the United States. Along with his husband, Terry Miller, he made a YouTube video telling tormented LGBTQ+ youths that life will get better as they grow older.

This video, which has had over two million views, led to the *It Gets Better Project*, which compiled thousands of similar messages of hope, including videos by Barack Obama, Anne Hathaway and Lady Gaga. The project reaches millions of young people each year through its media programme and educational resources.

Savage rose to fame with his tongue-in-cheek sex and relationship advice column, *Savage Love*, in the 1990s. Alongside a show on *MTV* and the role of editor-in-Chief of the *Stranger* alternative newspaper in Seattle, Savage is politically active. In 2003, after former US senator Rick Santorum compared homosexual sex to child rape and bestiality, Savage set up a website giving a rather explicit definition for a new word 'santorum'. It became a top result for any internet search on Santorum's name and the stunt (known as a 'Google bomb') still worked at time of writing.

DEMI LOVATO

B. 1992

'I've always known I was hella queer, but I have fully embraced it,' declared singer/ songwriter Demi Lovato in 2021, when she came out as pansexual in an interview on *The Joe Rogan Experience* podcast. The star, who had previously come out as queer, also came out as non-binary later that year, one of the first big-name music stars to do so. In 2022, she adopted she/her pronouns again, explaining 'I'm such a fluid person.'

The singer released her debut album, *Don't Forget*, on this date in 2008. She continued this success with follow-up albums and tours, amassing 24 million record sales, as well as being a judge on *The X Factor USA* and appearing on the TV show *Glee*.

Lovato is no stranger to media interest in her personal life, as her long-term struggles with drug and alcohol addiction, including a near-fatal overdose in June 2018, are well documented. Lovato has opened up about these issues in documentaries exploring addiction, eating disorders and mental health, raising awareness and campaigning for support.

The star, who was misdiagnosed with bipolar disorder, is an avid mental health activist, creating the Lovato Treatment Scholarship Program to help pay for the treatment of people suffering with mental illness. She also works with Substance Abuse and Mental Health Services and Save the Children.

TEGAN & SARA QUIN

B. 1980

Canadian identical twin sisters Tegan Rain and Sara Keirsten Quin are best known as queer indie pop duo, Tegan and Sara. The pair's first studio album, *Under Feet Like Ours*, came out in 1999 and since then they have released a further nine albums, including *Still Jealous* in 2022, which was a reimagining of their 2004 album, *So Jealous*. They have been nominated for a Grammy Award and three times for Outstanding Music Artist at the GLAAD Awards, winning twice.

On this date in 2019, the duo published *High School*, their popular coming-of-age memoir. In 2021 they announced that it would be made into a TV series for Amazon's streaming service.

In 2016, after touring North America, meeting fans and LGBTQ+ charities and organisations, the sisters set up the Tegan and Sara Foundation with a mission to improve the lives of LGBTQ+ women and girls. A key role of the foundation is to support grassroots organisations and activists that don't receive the funding they need. An open letter from the sisters on the foundation's website says it exists to help 'dismantle the systems of inequity that prevent LGBTQ girls and women from reaching their full potential. Together, we can make a difference.'

MARK ASHTON

1960–1987

The 2014 film *Pride* tells the story of Mark Ashton and his support for the mining communities in England and Wales in the 1980s. Along with his friend Mike Jackson, Ashton set up the Lesbians and Gays Support the Miners organisation, which held fundraisers and marches to support the families of striking miners. One of the group's most successful events was a fundraising concert at Camden's Electric Ballroom, named 'Pits and Perverts', appropriating a name given to them by a disparaging tabloid newspaper.

Described by his friend Chris Birch as 'an Irishman, a communist, an agitator', Ashton united the LGBTQ+ and mining communities against their joint enemy, the Thatcher government, proving they had more in common than differences dividing them.

Ashton died of AIDS-related complications at just 26, but his legacy endures. The 1980s pop duo, The Communards, wrote the song 'For a Friend' for Ashton, while a blue plaque honouring him was placed above Gay's The Word bookshop in London, and on this date in 2018, Paris officials named a park in the city after him in commemoration of those who have lost their lives to HIV. The Mark Ashton Garden sits near the Seine, in the heart of the historic Marais quarter.

CATHERINE OPIE

B. 1961

If you viewed two of Catherine Opie's most well-known photographs — *Self-Portrait/Pervert* (1994) and *Self Portrait/Nursing* (2004) — side-by-side, you would instantly recognise them as works by the same artist. Both feature the artist herself as the subject: the first shows her shirtless, wearing a gimp mask and with the word 'Pervert' freshly carved into her chest; the second shows her again shirtless, but this time breastfeeding her child, with the decade-old 'Pervert' scar visible across her chest.

Opie, whose retrospective at the Guggenheim Museum opened on this date in 2008, was born in Ohio, but now lives in California where she is Chair of the Department of Art at the University of California, Los Angeles. She has shot countless images of lesbians and queer people in the United States, many from the leather dyke and sadomasochistic communities of which she's been a part. Much of her other work consists of images of Los Angeles freeways without traffic and mini-malls not yet open to shoppers.

In 2011, the absence of one person in particular in a body of work became its most striking feature. She shot the inside of the Bel Air home of Elizabeth Taylor (see 27 Sep); yet, she never photographed Taylor herself and the actress died midway through the project.

ELIZABETH TAYLOR

1932–2011

As *Vanity Fair* magazine put it in a 1992 interview with the film star and activist, 'Elizabeth Taylor brought AIDS out of the closet and into the ballroom, where there was money — and consciousness — to be raised.' Taylor was one of the first Hollywood stars to speak out in support of people with HIV/AIDS when she agreed to become the chairperson of the Commitment to Life dinner in 1984, an AIDS benefit founded by seven gay men.

Taylor set up the American Foundation for AIDS Research (amfAR) with a group of physicians and scientists in 1985 and the Elizabeth Taylor AIDS Foundation (ETAF) in 1991. Both organisations aimed to raise funds, help research and raise awareness. When her good friend Rock Hudson died of AIDS in

1985, Taylor called on President Ronald Reagan to speak publicly about the disease. She also testified to Congress, advocating for additional HIV/AIDS funding and research in 1986, 1990 and 1992. For her AIDS research support, Taylor was awarded the Legion of Honor, France's highest civilian award.

Taylor was also Founding Chairperson of the Macy's Passport Fashion Show, which raises money and awareness for AIDS/HIV causes and takes place every September.

When Taylor died in 2011, the star's *New York Times* obituary stated that she raised over $100 million to fight AIDS, while the *LA Times* obituary claims the figure was $270 million! No matter which figure is correct, Taylor's work made a huge difference to the lives of thousands of people living with HIV.

PROUD ALLY

ARMISTEAD MAUPIN

B. 1944

One of the most famous fictional queer literary characters of the 20th century has to be Anna Madrigal, the marijuana-growing landlady who sprang from the mind of writer Armistead Maupin onto the pages of the *San Francisco Chronicle* in 1976 and then as part of his *Tales of the City* book series.

The series followed the lives of a group of San Francisco residents, with Maupin drawing many storylines from his own experiences as a gay man in the city. It had queerness at its heart, telling the stories of trans people, sex workers, gay men, lesbians and bisexuals with humour and warmth. These were stories not often told to a wide audience, yet Maupin was able to appeal to the more general reader by making them fall in love with characters who might normally be alien to them, over coffee and a newspaper in the morning.

Maupin wrote nine books in the series over the course of 35 years, and the early novels were adapted for a mini-series produced by the UK's Channel 4. These first aired on this date in 1993 and ran for three seasons. Netflix later picked up the series and *Armistead Maupin's Tales of the City* premiered on the streaming service in 2019.

W.H. AUDEN

1907–1973

Born in York, UK in 1907, Wystan Hugh Auden is considered one of the most skilled and creative poets of the mid-20th century. He collaborated with writers such as Christopher Isherwood (see 13 Feb), composer Igor Stravinsky and poets Louis MacNeice and Chester Kallman, his life partner.

In 1947, Auden published the book-length poem *The Age of Anxiety: A Baroque Eclogue*, which won the Pulitzer Prize for Poetry in 1948. Written in alliterative verse, it struck a chord with readers, capturing a cultural moment and the anxiety that Western society was feeling during World War Two.

In his early twenties Auden lived in Berlin, and along with his friend Isherwood, immersed himself in the decadent homosexual subculture of the Weimar Republic. He met rent boys and working-class patrons of the local gay bar, but it was the societal struggles and stories of the people he met that he was really interested in. He emigrated to America just ahead of the war in 1939, and there he met Kallman. The pair's early relationship was fraught, as Auden wanted monogamy while his lover favoured promiscuity. Eventually the pair settled into an agreed partnership that only ended when Auden died in Austria on this date in 1973.

ALISON BECHDEL

B. 1960

Alison Bechdel's comic strip, *Dykes To Watch Out For*, ran in various printed publications and online for twenty-five years, between 1983 and 2008. The strip featured a group of primarily lesbian characters making their way through life in a US city, with storylines often involving current political commentary.

It also introduced the concept of the Bechdel Test for movies to the world, assessing the representation of women in film, via its characters discussing watching films. To pass the test, a movie must have two female characters who have a conversation with each other about something other than a man.

In 2006, Bechdel published a 'tragicomic' graphic memoir about her childhood, focusing in particular on the suicide of her father, who killed himself shortly after she came out. The book, *Fun Home*, made the *New York Times* bestseller list and was later adapted into a musical for the stage, opening for previews on this date in 2013. When it transferred to Broadway a few years later, it won five Tony awards.

In 2021, Bechdel, who has a black belt in karate and a love for fitness, wrote *The Secret to Superhuman Strength*, a graphic novel about her relationship to the world through exercise.

AXEL & EIGIL AXGIL

1915–2011; 1922–1995

On this date in 1989, Danes Axel and Eigil Axgil became the first same-sex couple in the world to enter into a civil partnership. After decades of campaigning, the Axgils (who created their shared surname by merging their first names together) were able to help bring about the legislation that made Denmark the first country in the world to legalise same-sex partnerships.

In his thirties, Axel set up a group called *Kredsen af 1948* (Circle of 1948), Denmark's first gay rights organisation, which later became LGBT Danmark. This is where the pair met and is still Denmark's largest political organisation for LGBTQ+ people.

During their lifetimes, the Axgils produced a newspaper for gay people (illegal at the time), ran an LGBTQ+ bed and breakfast and were also imprisoned for pornography after publishing photos of naked men through their modelling agency.

When the pair finally entered into their civil partnership, Eigil urged, 'Be open. Come out. Keep fighting. This is the only way to move anything. If everyone comes out of the closet then this will happen everywhere.' The couple's tireless campaigning and resultant positive change in Denmark led the way for many other countries to also legalise same-sex partnerships in the years that followed.

NANCY CÁRDENAS

1934-1994

In 1973, Nancy Cárdenas became the first person in Mexico to come out as gay on live television, on a show called 24 *Horas*. Cárdenas was inspired by the gay liberation movements happening in Europe and the US, and wanted to improve the lives of LGBTQ+ people in her own country.

As well as being a staunch activist, Cárdenas was a journalist and writer who penned plays, poetry and fiction. She also worked as a theatre director and producer, and as her career progressed she included lesbian themes at the centre of her work, putting on queer theatre productions such as a 1985 stage adaptation of *The Well of Loneliness*, a novel by Radclyffe Hall (see 16 Nov).

Cárdenas founded the Frente de Liberación Homosexual (Homosexual Liberation Front), thought to be Mexico's first queer activist organisation and, after hosting a lesbian forum at the United Nations International Women's Year Conference in 1975, wrote a Mexican Lesbian Manifesto. Three years later, she headed the first gay Pride march in the Plaza de las Tres Culturas on this date in 1978.

Cárdenas' home was a meeting place for lesbians and feminists, with women often gathering there to discuss issues or simply socialise.

ORLANDO CRUZ

B. 1981

On this date in 2012, Orlando Cruz became the first boxer to come out as gay while still competing professionally. He told the world, 'I want to be true to myself. I want to try to be the best role model I can be for kids who might look into boxing as a sport and a professional career.'

In 2016, ahead of his fight against Terry Flanagan to become WBO lightweight World Champion, Cruz spoke openly about his dreams, 'I want to inspire the gay community by becoming a World Champion... Everyone has been very supportive since I came out three years ago. I have the support of my family, friends and fans.' While he didn't win this fight, Cruz's openness in such a hyper-masculine sporting competition makes him a champion to the LGBTQ+ community.

Cruz has spoken about the pain he felt when he was initially rejected by his father, after coming out to his parents aged 19. Over time Cruz's father accepted his sexuality and regretted his actions. Cruz married his long-time partner José Manuel Colón in 2013 in Central Park with both parents in attendance.

KENNY EVERETT

1944–1995

The legend goes that Kenny Everett, Freddie Mercury (see 20 Apr) and Cleo Rocos once took Diana, Princess of Wales (see 16 Feb), to a gay bar, the Royal Vauxhall Tavern, in drag disguise. Whether true or not, the story certainly aligns with Everett's notoriously mischievous and outlandish personality.

After making his name in pirate radio, the DJ moved to the newly created BBC Radio 1, where his first show, *Midday Spin*, aired on this date in 1967. He was fired shortly afterwards for making an 'indefensible' joke about the Transport Minister's wife. Over the next few years, he worked at Capital Radio before

returning to the BBC, crafting his distinctive style as a DJ, using sound equipment to create jingles and introducing his audience to his crazy comedic personas. His humour, along with characters such as Sid Snot, translated well to television and he had many successful shows, including *The Kenny Everett Video Show* (1978) and *Brainstorm* (1988).

Everett, who was married to the singer and psychic Audrey 'Lady Lee' Middleton for 10 years, struggled to accept his sexuality but came out publicly as bisexual later in life. He also bravely disclosed his status when diagnosed as HIV positive in 1987.

HUBERT DE GIVENCHY

1927–2018

Few Hollywood stars are instantly recognisable simply by the cut of their dress or their silhouette, but thanks to French fashion designer, Hubert de Givenchy, Audrey Hepburn was afforded this accolade.

The pair began a decades-long relationship, both personal and professional, when Hepburn turned up to a fitting at Givenchy for her movie, *Sabrina,* in 1954. The designer ended up making virtually all of the star's clothes for her subsequent films. Givenchy was responsible for the now-iconic little black dress (LBD) Hepburn wore for her role as Holly Golightly in *Breakfast at Tiffany's*, released on this date in 1961. Givenchy's

other lifelong relationship was the one he had with his life partner, Philippe Venet, a fellow fashion designer who as well as running a couture house, worked for Givenchy throughout his career.

Born into French aristocracy, Givenchy left home at 17 for an apprenticeship in Paris. He advanced quickly, founded his own fashion house in 1952 and became the first major fashion designer to create a luxury Ready to Wear collection, fulfilling the needs of the post-war middle class. He remained at Givenchy's helm until 1988, when he sold the company to French fashion conglomerate LVMH, and finally retired aged 68 in 1995.

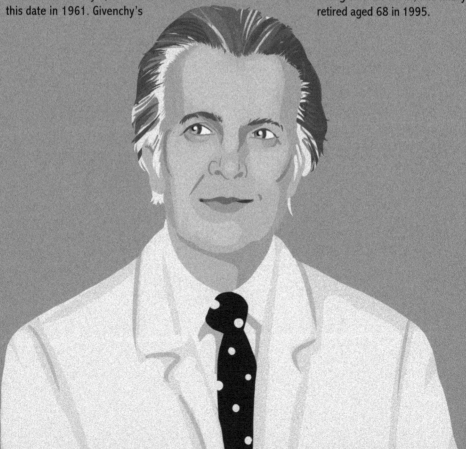

ARSHAM PARSI

B. 1980

Iranian human rights activist Arsham Parsi says his ultimate goal is to have homosexuality decriminalised in Iran, where it is currently punishable by death. Until then, he is dedicated to helping LGBTQ+ people seeking escape and refuge from their home countries where their sexuality endangers their life.

Parsi set up Rangin Kamin (Rainbow Group) in Iran in 2001, a mainly online group for LGBTQ+ Iranians, which evolved into the Iranian Queer Organization (IRQO). After fleeing Iran for Turkey and then Toronto in Canada, where he now lives, he founded the International Railroad for Queer Refugees (IRQR), to help at-risk queer people find safety through emergency relocation and other assistance. The organisation's website proudly states that it has a 93 per cent success rate helping LGBTQ+ individuals find safety since it was founded.

On this date in 2010, Parsi gave an emotional speech at the Lethbridge Community Celebrating Diversity Conference in Alberta, Canada. He said he had a dream that 'one day no one will be executed, tortured, arrested, imprisoned, isolated or disowned by their families and communities merely for the crime of being queer'. He requested that the date become a memorial day dedicated to all the Iranian queers who have died.

PUSSY RIOT

FORMED 2011

Outside Russia, the Russian feminist punk-rock band Pussy Riot is arguably better known for its protests than its music. The group has a fluctuating membership of female members, and its music and performances are primarily concerned with human and LGBTQ+ rights. Although many of the band remain mysterious, it was confirmed in a 2012 interview that at least one member was from a sexual minority. On this date, President Putin's birthday, in 2020, members of Pussy Riot hung Pride rainbow flags on government buildings in Moscow.

The group regularly holds unauthorised guerrilla gigs, where it criticises the Russian state. The band's most famous act of protest came when it performed Pussy Riot's 'Punk Prayer' at the Moscow Cathedral of Christ the Saviour in 2012 to protest the Orthodox Church leaders' support for Putin. Weeks later, three band members were arrested and sent to prison for 'hooliganism motivated by religious hatred'. Their conviction attracted global attention and Amnesty International condemned Russia, calling the women prisoners of conscience.

In March 2022, Nadya Tolokonnikova, one of the members sent to prison for the punk prayer protest, spoke about her latest project – a crypto fund called UnicornDAO – which aims to support the careers of female and LGBTQ+ artists by buying their artwork.

GEORGE HISLOP

1927–2005

Gay activist George Hislop is credited with helping to make Toronto in Canada a sanctuary for gay refugees. In 1977, he helped to convince the Department of Immigration to overturn a law barring LGBT people from settling in the country. Queer people looking to settle had previously been categorised alongside 'prostitutes… pimps or persons coming to Canada for these or any other immoral purposes'.

With his partner Ronnie Shearer's support, Hislop dedicated his life to human rights in Canada. He organised the first Canadian gay rights demonstration on Parliament Hill in 1971, was instrumental in keeping the gay bathhouses running when they were raided by police and campaigned against police entrapment of gay men in public toilets.

When Shearer died in 1986, Hislop applied for survivor partner benefits under the Canada Pension Plan (CPP) but his claim was denied as he was 'the wrong sex'. Hislop fought this decision, which eventually led the Supreme Court to rule that the word 'spouse' applied to gays and lesbians. From 2000, CPP survivor benefits were paid to those widowed after 1 January 1998. This date meant Hislop would miss out but, after further court battles, Hislop was eventually paid 14,000 Canadian dollars of partial arrears, just before he died on this date in 2005.

ANNA RÜLING

1880–1953

On this date in 1904, the German journalist, Anna Rüling, was invited to speak at the annual meeting of the Scientific-Humanitarian Committee. Founded by Magnus Hirschfeld in Berlin, this is the first known gay scientific-political organisation. The speech Rüling gave that day, the only one at the event to discuss lesbianism, is now heralded as the first ever public political speech to address issues faced by lesbians.

Rüling's ideology was that the fight for lesbian rights should be aligned with the fight for women's rights, and she argued that the women's movement should include it under their umbrella. Viewed today, Rüling's speech is problematic in that she argued that lesbians were more similar to heterosexual men as they were not ruled by emotions. She further claimed that: 'Without the power and cooperation of the "*Urninds*" [lesbians], the Women's Movement would not be successful today.'

Notwithstanding current changed attitudes, Rüling was extremely brave to speak in favour of such issues, and also courageous enough to come out herself. As a young woman she faced constant pressure from her family to marry a man and this led to her teachings that LGBTQ+ people should not marry as it would make them miserable.

LAXMI NARAYAN TRIPATHI

B. 1978

The Indian transgender activist Laxmi Narayan Tripathi has had a varied career, beginning her activism with protests against the closure of dance bars when she worked as a singer in Maharashtra. She went on to become a Hindi film actress, dancer, reality TV star, writer and president of the DAI Welfare Society, the first organisation for eunuchs in South Asia.

In 2011, Tripathi entered the Bigg Boss house to take part in the Big Brother-style reality show. When she was evicted after six weeks, the *Hindustan Times* declared her a strong, determined and opinionated person, and said that she proved 'transgenders are after all, the same humans as all!'

Tripathi also set up the Astitva Trust, which petitioned the Indian Supreme Court for transgender recognition in 2014. This led to a landmark ruling that recognised a third gender and granted all constitutional rights to transgender people in India. When Tripathi organised India's National Conclave of Transgenders in 2021, she applauded supportive parents of transgender children.

In 2020, Tripahi helped bring together a team of 25 transgender people from across India to climb Friendship Peak in the Himalayas, scaling the peak from 6 to 11 October. They hoped to overcome negative attitudes towards transgender community, with a visible display of triumph against adversity.

JEAN O'LEARY

1948-2005

It may come as a surprise that a lesbian nun would describe her time in a convent as '...one of the best experiences of my life', but that's exactly how Jean O'Leary felt. After years in the convent, where she said she had about eight relationships with women, O'Leary went to university in New York and became involved in the early gay rights movement.

She noticed that women were not given a voice in gay rights organisations such as the Gay Activists Alliance (GAA), and co-founded the Lesbian Feminist Liberation group. She also co-founded the National Gay and Lesbian Task Force and established the first National Coming Out Day, which takes place annually on this date and is intended for queer people to publicly declare their sexuality.

At the 1973 New York Pride rally, after Sylvia Rivera gave her famous speech (see 24 Jun), O'Leary gave her own speech. She said men had 'been telling us who we are all our lives' and by dressing up as women for profit, they were being exploitative. O'Leary later said she'd changed her view and expressed a desire that history view her comments in context.

O'Leary was involved in Democratic politics and with the help of Midge Costanza, a closeted lesbian on President Jimmy Carter's staff, she organised a landmark meeting between the president's senior staff and lesbian and gay rights activists in 1977.

EVELYN WAUGH

1903-1966

Evelyn Waugh is considered to be one Britain's most brilliant satirical novelists. His works include *Decline and Fall* (1928), *A Handful of Dust* (1934) and *Scoop* (1938). Waugh's own life experiences often inspired his novels, and they would usually be sharply written works of satire.

His first marriage ended when his wife had an affair, after which Waugh converted to Roman Catholicism, a subject that would inform much of his subsequent writing. In his 1945 novel, *Brideshead Revisited*, Waugh tells the story of Charles Ryder, a military captain who has survived World War One, and his relationship with Catholicism and an aristocratic family. Ryder meets the son of the family, Sebastian Flyte, at the University of Oxford and the pair develop a close friendship that borders on romance.

According to Waugh's biographer, Paula Byrne, who published the writer's life story in 2009, he had multiple gay love affairs while he studied at Oxford. She claims that diary entries and letters between Waugh and a fellow student prove these relationships happened.

Granada Television produced a TV adaptation of *Brideshead Revisited*, starring Jeremy Irons, that first aired on ITV on this date in 1981. The show won the BAFTA for Best Drama series that year and brought about a revival of interest in, and appreciation for, Waugh's work.

SIMON NKOLI

1957–1998

When South African activist Simon Nkoli came out to his family, aged 20, they took him to priests and psychiatrists to try and change his sexuality. Nkoli faced further struggles when he fell in love with a white man whose family did not accept their interracial relationship. Only when the pair made a tragic pact to commit suicide together rather than be kept apart, did Nkoli's family accept his relationship to some degree.

As secretary of the Congress of South African Students (COSAS) Nkoli faced issues due to his sexuality, and his later position in the Gay and Lesbian Association of South Africa (GASA) was also challenging because the group, which was mainly made up of white men, was strictly apolitical and opposed to his anti-apartheid activism.

Believing his fight as a gay man was intrinsically linked with his fight as a Black man, Nkoli founded the Gay and Lesbian Organization of the Witwatersrand (GLOW) in 1988. GLOW organised the first South African Pride, held on this date in 1990, and was instrumental in laying the groundwork for South Africa to become the first country in the world to ensure the protection of the rights of LGBTQ+ people was written into the constitution.

JODY DOBROWSKI

1981–2005

At around midnight on this date in 2005, Jody Dobrowski was brutally attacked by two men as he walked across Clapham Common in London. The men were heard shouting homophobic slurs as they kicked and punched Dobrowski and told one witness who tried to intervene, 'We don't like poofters here, and that's why we can kill him if we want.' Jody died of his injuries the next day.

The assailants were soon arrested and were sentenced, on 16 June 2006, to life imprisonment, with a minimum of 28 years to be served. There was widespread media coverage of the attack, which put homophobia in the spotlight, highlighting that

while it was legal to be gay in the UK, it wasn't wholly safe to be so. The sentencing was particularly significant at the time, as it's thought to be the first instance in which a judge used motivation based on sexual orientation as an aggravating feature when sentencing for murder.

Funds for a memorial were raised and a bench with Jody's name on it now sits on Clapham Common. During National Hate Crime Awareness Week in October 2020, police and LGBTQ+ advisors gathered to repaint and restore the bench to honour Jody and raise awareness of hate crime.

PAT PARKER

1944–1989

Poet Pat Parker wrote verse from an early age, but found her true voice when, with two failed marriages behind her, she began to identify as a lesbian.

Houston-born Parker moved to the San Francisco Bay Area in 1966. She became involved with the fight for improved women's health and safety after her sister was murdered by her husband, and after her own experience of domestic violence at the hands of her second husband, playwright and Black Panther Ed Bullins. Parker worked as the director of the Oakland Feminist Women's Health Center, was a member of the Black Women's Revolutionary Council and was involved in the early days of the Black Panther movement.

Parker's poetry addressed the issues she fought for head on, with her 1970s poem 'My Lover is a Woman' boldly discussing interracial, female love, 'Woman Slaughter' exposing the unjustness of domestic violence by men and 'Legacy (for Anastasia Jean)' critiquing homophobes who disagree with gay parenting. Parker's poetry enjoyed renewed interest when *The Complete Works of Pat Parker* was published on this date in 2016.

Parker sadly died from breast cancer aged just 45, but her legacy is honoured by the Pat Parker Poetry Award, awarded to Black, lesbian, feminist poets annually.

RUTH HUNT

B. 1980

Ruth Hunt was chief executive of Stonewall, the UK LGBT+ rights charity, from August 2014 to August 2019. During her time there, she was instrumental in cementing the charity's commitment to campaigning for trans equality – a decision that caused internal disagreement and outside criticism from some members and donors at the time. Hunt said, 'We had a moral responsibility... Our lack of trans inclusion was utterly baffling... It's all part of the same hatred – people do not differentiate.'

During Hunt's tenure, the charity expanded from 75 to 160 staff and grew its income from £5.4m to £8.7m. She led campaigns to tackle homophobic bullying in schools, working with and training teachers, as well as increasing Stonewall's engagement with groups from different ethnicities and religions. A lesbian and a practising Catholic, Hunt has said that Christianity taught her about 'love, equality and respect, which is at the heart of the work I do at Stonewall'.

Hunt, who is Welsh and has a degree in English Literature, was named Baroness Hunt of Bethnal Green, in the London Borough of Tower Hamlets, on this date in 2019, after being nominated in Prime Minister Theresa May's Resignation Honours list.

FRANK OCEAN

B. 1987

R&B artist Frank Ocean has a lot of awards to his name. His debut album, *Channel Orange*, won Best Urban Contemporary Album at the Grammys in 2013 and Ocean was named International Male Solo Artist at the BRITs in the same year. His videos have been nominated for numerous MTV Video Music Awards and NME named him International Male Artist in 2017.

Ocean's style of R&B is best described as alternative and experimental. Apple music called him 'the millennial J.D. Salinger' and described his second album, *Blonde*, as 'a daring set of ambient post-R&B that slips into your bloodstream'.

In 2014, when Ocean went public on his Tumblr blog about experiencing unrequited love for a man, he received an overwhelming amount of support from fellow R&B artists, including Beyoncé and Jay-Z.

On this date in 2018, Ocean held the first in a series of club nights in New York called PrEP+, which he intended as an homage to a 1980s NYC club experience that never happened due to the HIV/AIDS epidemic. The nights were designed to be an 80s clubbing experience if the drug PrEP had been invented in that era.

CASTER SEMENYA

B. 1991

When South African Olympian athlete, Caster Semenya, was asked in 2019 if she would ever take testosterone-suppressing medication to enable her to keep racing, her response was 'Hell no.' Days earlier, Semenya, who has a medical condition known as DSD (differences of sex development), lost a legal battle challenging the International Amateur Athletics Federation's rule regulating testosterone levels for women. DSD results in levels of natural testosterone that exceed those of most women. This has dogged Semenya's career, as many argue that her biological traits give her an unfair advantage.

Semenya has achieved 35 first places in competitions throughout her career. Her success earned her the South African Sportswoman of the Year Award in 2012, and on this date in 2016 she was one of the women's nominees for the IAAF's 2016 World Athlete of the Year. In 2019, *Time* magazine named her one of their 100 Most Influential People of the Year.

Semenya did not compete in the 2021 Tokyo Olympics, due to new rules that bar female athletes from competing in races from 400 metres to 1 mile if they refuse to lower their naturally high testosterone levels. Semenya vows to continue fighting the rulings by World Athletics, saying the battle is not just about her but also future athletes who may face similar discrimination.

ALAN HOLLINGHURST

B. 1954

'The search for love, sex and beauty is rarely this exquisitely done,' said the United Kingdom's first openly gay cabinet minister, Chris Smith (see 30 Jan), about Alan Hollinghurst's novel, *The Line of Beauty*. The book, set in Thatcherite Britain in the 1980s, won the Booker Prize for fiction on this date in 2004 and was the first gay novel to do so in the 35-year history of the prize.

Hollinghurst's other novels include *The Swimming-Pool Library*, which won the Somerset Maugham Award in 1989. It was published while Margaret Thatcher's anti-gay Conservative government was in power in the UK and the AIDS epidemic was tearing through the queer community. The sexual adventures of the novel's promiscuous young narrator were refreshing and written with 'stylistic prowess and attentive rigor that made previous writers of sexually explicit fiction, gay and straight alike, look squeamish and incurious by comparison', said the *New York Times*.

Hollinghurst believes the timing of his early novels was fortunate, saying he was '...coming along just as gay lit as a genre was really coming into its own, and finding there was this whole fascinating, unexplored world to write about'.

ANNIE LEIBOVITZ

B. 1949

Photographer Annie Leibovitz has shot countless celebrities throughout her career. She was chief photographer at *Rolling Stone* magazine until 1983 and later worked for *Vanity Fair*, *Vogue*, the *New York Times Magazine*, *Life* and *Time*. In 1991, she became the first woman and only the second living photographer to exhibit at the National Portrait Gallery in Washington, D.C. She took the last photograph of John Lennon just hours before he was shot in 1980. The iconic image graced the cover of the *Rolling Stone* magazine's commemorative issue for Lennon.

Leibovitz had a 15-year-long relationship with writer and philosopher Susan Sontag (see 24 Nov), yet the pair never lived together and rarely spoke publicly about it.

When Sontag died in 2004, Leibovitz was the benefactor in her will and had to pay a huge amount of inheritance tax, because with no equal marriage laws then in place, gay couples were not exempt.

A major retrospective of her work, *Annie Leibovitz: A Photographer's Life, 1990–2005*, debuted at the Brooklyn Museum on this date in 2006, featuring both professional and personal photographs, including those of her family and Sontag.

Leibovitz has been named a Living Legend by the Library of Congress and in 2009, she received the Lifetime Achievement Award from the International Centre of Photography.

LARRY LEVAN

1954–1992

Described as 'the first superstar DJ', Larry Levan was the resident DJ at New York's Paradise Garage for a decade from 1977. Throughout those years, Levan presided over a 'Saturday Mass' congregation of devoted dancers who worshipped him like a messiah.

It was as a teenager in New York that Levan began his DJ career, playing at the Gallery club and also at Continental Baths, the legendary gay bathhouse where Bette Midler (see 29 Jun) got her break. Here, he also worked with (and influenced) House Music DJ, Frankie Knuckles (see 26 Feb).

As well as in the DJ booth, Levan also spent time in the studio, recording remixes and dance versions of songs for labels including Prelude and West End. He worked on dance music for Skyy, the Peech Boys and Loleatta Holloway, but his career was sadly cut short when he died of heart failure aged just 38. *Larry's Garage*, a documentary about Levan's life and work, was released on this date in 2020.

Throughout his career Levan was a fan of drag queens. Perhaps as a byproduct of surrounding himself with them, he was known to be a bit of a diva himself sometimes, but he continued to be loved both in and out of the DJ booth.

JUSTIN FASHANU

1961–1998

Justin Fashanu was the world's first professional footballer to come out publicly. '£1m soccer star: I am GAY', ran the headline of the *Sun* newspaper on this date in 1990.

Fashanu, who rose to stardom aged 18 and won the Match of the Day Goal of the Season Award in February 1980, played for 22 different clubs during his 19-year career. After coming out, he was harassed by the media, and endured endless racist and homophobic abuse from the terraces and off the pitch. But, perhaps most damaging of all, his brother, fellow footballer John Fashanu, disowned him and gave an interview to Black community newspaper the

Voice, with the headline, 'My Brother is an Outcast'. At this time, many British tabloids were steeped in anti-gay rhetoric, running pieces like 'AIDS is the wrath of God, says vicar'.

Despite the abuse, Fashanu said he didn't regret coming out. He did it in response to a teenage friend committing suicide after being shunned by homophobic parents, saying he 'wanted to do something positive to stop such deaths'. Sadly, Fashanu also took his own life in May 1998, but his niece Amal has ensured he has a positive legacy. She set up the Justin Fashanu Foundation, which aims to promote mental health and fight discrimination in football.

KENZO TAKADA

1939-2020

Kenzo Takada studied at the Bunka Fashion College in Tokyo, and had moved to Paris and launched his first fashion collection in his own shop by the age of 31, despite once being told 'that it was impossible for a Japanese man to work in the fashion industry in Paris'.

Initially, Takada's label was named Jungle Jap, and quickly graced the cover of *Elle* magazine, but to avoid the derogatory connotations of the word 'Jap', the designer rebranded as Kenzo. In October 1976, he opened his flagship store, Kenzo, in the Place des Victoires. The designer enjoyed the theatrical, once holding a show in a circus tent and arriving on the back of an elephant.

The brand became internationally successful and in August 1993 luxury-products maker LVMH acquired the Kenzo company for approximately $80 million. Kenzo had lost his partner, French architect Xavier de Castella, to an AIDS-related illness a few years earlier and by 1999 he stepped back from the fashion business to concentrate on his other love: art, returning to his love of drawing.

Takada received a lifetime achievement award at the 55th Fashion Editors' Club of Japan Awards ceremony in 2017, and sadly died of Covid-19 complications in 2020.

JUNO DAWSON

B. 1981

In November 2015, *This Book is Gay* by British transgender activist Juno Dawson, intended to help young adult queer people on their journey, gained unwanted media attention when its place in the library in Wasilla, Alaska was challenged. A parent claimed that placing it in the juvenile section was 'straight-up paedophile kind of behaviour'.

Dawson, who had been crowned The Queen of Teen the previous year (an award for young adult fiction writers), responded by putting her trust in the librarians. She said, 'The goal of the book is to make young LGBT+ people feel less isolated and alone… I would imagine that in Alaska there are numerous young people who keenly feel that solitude.'

Born in West Yorkshire, Dawson had already released a string of bestselling YA books before coming out as trans in a BuzzFeed interview on this date in 2015. In the interview Dawson discussed why they were still using he/him pronouns, suggesting, 'You wouldn't call a butterfly a butterfly until it had hatched.'

As well as writing novels, Dawson is a journalist, an actress and a school role model for the LGBTQ+ charity Stonewall.

CHELLA MAN

B. 1998

In 2019, Chella Man was voted tenth in the *Dazed* 100 list, a global celebration of next-gen names leading change across their fields. By then, aged just 22, the self-described 'deaf, Jewish, genderqueer, trans masculine, Chinese, person of colour' was signed to IMG Models, had his own successful YouTube channel and had given a TEDx talk about his transition.

Later that year, Man joined the cast of DC Universe's live-action superhero series *Titans*, and on this date in 2019, the episode named after his character, Jericho, aired. Discussing the debut of the character, who is also deaf and uses sign language, Man said, 'I RARELY saw sign authentically represented growing up, so this opportunity made my heart soar. I hope to make you all proud!'

Man, who is based in New York City and also credits himself as an artist, director and author, later became the first trans masculine face of YSL Beauty as the brand launched their Nu Collection campaign in 2021. He also created a range of jewellery called the Beauty of Being Deaf collection, consisting of gold earpieces that fit over hearing aids and cochlear implants, created to amplify and celebrate a person's Deaf identity without overshadowing it.

STEPHANIE HIRST

B. 1975

Radio DJ Stephanie Hirst, who was assigned male at birth, started her career aged 12 making tea for DJs at 96.3 Radio Aire, in Leeds, UK. She went on to work at radio stations across Yorkshire, including Capital FM Yorkshire, where she co-hosted the breakfast show, *Hirsty's Daily Dose* for 11 years. She was also a presenter on the Channel 4 Top 40 chart show, *Hit40UK*.

Soon after abruptly leaving the airwaves, Hirst came out as trans in 2014, undergoing surgery that she says saved her life. Years later she explained that she had surgery privately 'because I could, and that [it] would free up

another place in the system... for someone who is less fortunate than myself'. Hirst also revealed she'd been bullied at school for being effeminate and that at the age of 17 was told not to pursue transitioning by a doctor, who said, 'you won't have a successful life, you will lose friends and family'.

Hirst returned to radio with shows such as *Stephanie Hirst's Vinyl Revival* and *Stephanie Hirst's Belters*, one of the most streamed shows on the Hits Radio app. On this date in 2016 she was awarded a 'Fellowship' at the Radio Festival recognising her outstanding contribution to the field.

JOSH CAVALLO

B. 1999

'I'm a footballer and I'm gay' are words rarely heard when it comes to the world of top-tier, male, professional football. Yet on this date in 2021, this is what Adelaide United player, Josh Cavallo, told the world via Twitter. This made him the only openly gay, top-flight footballer on the planet at the time. In May 2022, 17-year-old Jake Daniels, who plays for Blackpool FC, also came out, making him the UK's first active male professional footballer to do so.

Cavallo, who was born in Victoria, Australia, has played for Western United and Adelaide United, and won Adelaide United's A-League Rising Star award in June 2021. He said he went home and cried after winning the award because he felt he was living a double life 'stuck in this shadow... not being my authentic self'. After coming out, his teammates, management and a host of queer celebrities all supported and congratulated him.

Since he came out he has joined other sportspeople such as Tom Daley (see 26 Jul) in highlighting the homophobia prevalent in many competitors' home countries, and has voiced a desire for sport to help improve the discrimination experienced by LGBTQ+ people in these countries.

ROSE ROBERTSON

1916-2011

At the outbreak of World War Two, Rose Robertson, a secretary from south London who was born this day in 1916, was enlisted in the Special Operations Executive and was sent to France in 1941. Here, as she spied on German troops, she met two male French resistance agents who would send her down a path she never dreamed of.

While lodging together, Robertson walked in on the young men as they embraced. Curious, and with no understanding of homosexuality, she asked them to explain. The story the young men told touched her. They spoke of their relationship, but also of the rejection they'd received from their families because of

it. Years later, married with children, Roberston took in two young gay lovers with a similar story as lodgers.

This prompted her to set up 'Parents Enquiry', the first helpline in the UK to support parents and their LGB children. Through it, Robertson offered help and advice and acted as a mediator to thousands of parents and their children. The helpline became so successful that local authorities and the police often sent people her way.

Robertson went on to found FFLAG (Families and Friends of Lesbians and Gays), an organisation still dedicated to supporting parents and families and their LGBT+ members.

PROUD ALLY

MATTHEW SHEPARD

1976-1998

Matthew Shepard was a 21-year-old student at the University of Wyoming who fell victim to one of America's most harrowing hate crimes. On 7 October 1998, he was taken by two young men to a rural area in Laramie and pistol whipped, tortured and tied to a barbed wire fence, where he was left to die. Shepard died five days later in hospital, surrounded by his family.

The brutal events that lead to Shephard's death garnered huge media attention and began a nationwide fight against bigotry and hate in the US. His parents, Judy and Dennis Shepard, set up the Matthew Shepard Foundation to inspire individuals, organisations and communities to embrace the dignity and equality of all people.

They fought tirelessly to introduce legislation that would prevent this kind of tragedy happening to parents of other queer kids. On this date in 2009, then-US President Barack Obama signed into law the Matthew Shepard and James Byrd, Jr. Hate Crimes Prevention Act, which added 'sexual orientation' to hate crime legislation.

The Matthew Shepard Foundation speaks to the legacy of his life. Channelled into its work is Shephard's belief in equality and a heartfelt mission: to eradicate hate in favour of 'understanding, compassion, and acceptance'.

IAN ALEXANDER

B. 2001

People might recognise Ian Alexander primarily as the first transgender, non-binary character in *Star Trek* history, playing Gray in the third season of *Star Trek: Discovery*, from November 2020. However, Alexander had already broken new ground years earlier when, appearing as Buck in the Netflix show *The OA*, aged just 14, they were the first out trans Asian American actor on television. Following on from their success in *The OA*, it was announced on this date in 2017, that Alexander would voice the transgender character of Lev in the game *The Last of Us Part II*.

When Alexander and co-star Blu del Barrio were cast as the first recurring gender non-conforming, transgender or non-binary characters in the *Star Trek* franchise, the actor said 'trans people exist everywhere… So, of course, they would exist in space.'

Utah-born Alexander originally came out as trans male at the age of 14 but later decided to identify as trans masculine, saying they shifted 'more [to] the genderless realm of things'. Along with co-star del Barrio, Alexander is providing an important positive representation of trans and non-binary people to the world and across the galaxy, boldly going where no non-binary actors have gone before.

LEE BREWSTER

1943–2000

Lee's Mardi Gras Boutique 'will turn you into the girl you've always wanted to be.' according to *New York* magazine in 1999. The Manhattan boutique run by Lee Brewster catered to an array of customers looking for larger-sized dresses and shoes — primarily crossdressers, drag queens and trans women. Brewster, a drag queen and 'crossdresser activist' who preferred the pronouns he/him, provided a safe space for his varied customers, including many straight men who weren't able to 'present' publicly. Despite moving the store numerous times, he always made sure it had a discreet entrance, never on the ground floor.

Brewster took part in early queer activism with gay rights organisation the Mattachine Society, helping to organise their fundraising drag balls, which he later staged himself at the Hotel Diplomat. At one of these balls, on this date in 1969, he announced the birth of his clothing store.

Brewster founded the Queens Liberation Front in 1969 and successfully fought the legal discriminations against drag queens and crossdressers in New York. 'We legalized the wearing of "drag" in New York City bars and cabarets. No longer could a club be closed, or patrons arrested just because there was a crossdresser present,' said Brewster.

FRIDA KAHLO

1907–1954

Mexican artist Frida Kahlo had polio as a child and was plagued with health problems throughout her life. At 18 she was in a near-fatal bus accident, and this had the biggest impact on her life. Bedridden for months, she began painting on a specially constructed easel that enabled her to do so lying down.

Kahlo was openly bisexual and courted Hollywood starlet Dolores del Rio in the late 1930s, and she was also in love with American painter Georgia O'Keeffe. Kahlo is thought to have had multiple lovers of both sexes, but it is her husband Diego Rivera, whom she divorced and remarried, who was most prevalent in her life and work.

The pair travelled the US together and Rivera constantly encouraged Kahlo to paint. Her first solo exhibition began on this date in 1938 at the Julian Levy Gallery in New York City and was a great success. She exhibited again in Paris the following year and sold a painting to the Louvre, the first 20th-century Mexican artist to do so.

Kahlo painted herself into much of her work and has been described as both Surrealist and Magical Realist. Her art grew in popularity after her death, particularly in the 1970s, and is now praised for its depiction of Mexican culture.

MAHMUD OF GHAZNI

971–1030

The Kingdom of Ghazna was made up of what is now Afghanistan, Pakistan, northwestern India and most of Iran. The empire was presided over and expanded by Mahmud of Ghazni, a ruler of the Turkic Ghaznavid dynasty, who led his army into many battles and expeditions, most notably (and continually) against the Punjab and northeastern India. Here, he defeated Jaipal, the ruler of the Punjab, with 15,000 troops on horseback, despite the Indian army comprising almost triple this number and 300 elephants!

Some historic accounts of his life suggest that Mahmud of Ghazni had a romantic relationship with his male slave, Malik Ayaz, who he later appointed to the position of general in the army. While homosexuality is viewed as immoral and sometimes even criminal in this part of the world today, much Persian poetry uses homoerotic language and plenty of stories of love affairs between men and boys exist.

Mahmud of Ghazni is thought to have been a great orator, bringing art and culture to his empire and providing beautiful gardens and mosques for his people. He is thought to have been born on this date.

PABLLO VITTAR

B. 1993

With an openly homophobic president, Jair Bolsanaro, in office from 2019 to 2022, Brazil has not been the easiest place to be queer in recent times. But singer, songwriter, actor and drag queen, Pabllo Vittar is a beacon of hope for the country's LGBTQ+ community.

Vittar began drag aged 17 and rose to fame when she performed an exceptional version of Whitney Houston's 'I Have Nothing' on Brazilian TV in 2014. Fast forward to 2018, and Vittar became the first drag queen to be nominated for a Grammy, in the Best Urban Fusion/Performance category for 'Sua Cara'. One year later, on this date in 2019, the star became the first drag queen to win a statuette at the MTV Europe Music Awards, also opening the show performing her hit 'Flash Pose'. On winning the award, Vittar said she'd imagined herself performing there one day and told people not to give up on their dreams.

The star, who boasts millions of Instagram followers – around three times as many as RuPaul – uses her voice for the community, saying, 'My career isn't just about singing and being famous, it's about fighting over and over until we get our rights… we deserve to be respected.' During the Covid-19 pandemic Vittar organised a fund-raising live-streamed Pride event called 'Pride with Pabllo and Friends'.

NICOLA ADAMS

B. 1982

2012 was a big year for British boxer, Nicola Adams. Not only did she come second in the IBA Women's World Boxing Championships in China, she also won Gold at the London 2012 Summer Olympics. Adams was nominated for BBC Sports Personality of the Year, and on this date in 2012, she was listed at number one in the *Independent on Sunday's* Pink List, a tally of 101 of the most influential LGBT figures in Britain. By the end of the year it had also been announced that West Yorkshire-born Adams would be appointed Member of the Order of the British Empire (MBE) in the 2013 New Year Honours list.

In 2020, Adams became the first celebrity to be paired with a same-sex partner on the UK dance competition show, *Strictly Come Dancing*. The decision to feature same-sex couples was much debated, with ballroom purists arguing against it. Adams said '...professional dancers dance with people of the same sex all the time; you dance in a nightclub with your friends. I just wanted to break down the thing of it being a big deal when it's not.'

Adams and her partner Ella Baig welcomed their son into the world in July 2022.

ESSEX HEMPHILL

1957-1995

Chicago-born Essex Hemphill began writing poetry as a teenager and was soon performing in coffee houses, educational institutes and theatres to packed crowds. Much of Hemphill's work centred around the experience of the African American gay community, and during a reading at Howard University in 1980 Hemphill publicly proclaimed his homosexuality.

His poetry was political, addressing issues of race, sexuality, HIV/AIDS and the family. Hemphill often signed off letters and other prose with his warm, friendly signature, 'Take care of your blessings', and in November 2010, the New York Public Library held an exhibition under the name 'Take Care of

Your Blessings', which showcased rare and unpublished manuscripts of Hemphill's, as well as photographs, fliers, posters and programmes.

Hemphill self-published his early works *Earth Life* (1985) and *Conditions* (1986), both of which addressed the impact of AIDS on the Black community and the gay community as a whole. After gaining national recognition for his anthology, *In the Life* (1986), he went on to win a Lambda Literary Award in 1991 for editing the anthology *Brother to Brother: New Writing by Black Gay Men*, and then won the National Library Association's Gay, Lesbian, and Bisexual New Author Award for his own collection *Ceremonies: Prose and Poetry* (1992).

TAMMY BALDWIN

B. 1962

When Tammy Baldwin was elected to the US Senate on this date in 2012, she not only made history as the first Wisconsin woman to do so, but she was also the first openly gay politician to achieve this. She first ran for the Dane County Board of Supervisors in 1986 and often points to the two gay people elected to the board before her as paving the way. 'While the "firsts" represent history, the "nexts" represent real progress,' she says.

Speaking about why it's important for LGBTQ+ people to be elected to government, Baldwin said, '…when you are not in the room, the conversation is about you. But when you are in the room, the conversation is with you. That changes everything.' A progressive Democrat, she introduced the Equality Act of 2021, which would provide full protections for LGBTQ+ Americans against discrimination. The bill was passed by the House of Representatives and at the time of writing awaits its hearing in the Senate.

Along with fellow Democrat, Barney Frank (see 7 Jul), Baldwin formed the Congressional LGBTQ+ Equality Caucus in June 2008, with a mission to promote LGBTQ+ issues at federal level, lobbying for equal rights and the repeal of discriminatory laws.

ELEANOR ROOSEVELT

1884–1962

Before she married the soon-to-be president, Franklin Roosevelt (a distant relation, hence the same surname), Eleanor Roosevelt worked as a volunteer teacher for the New York poor and joined the fight to reform bad industrial working conditions. Once married, she continued her humanitarian work, volunteering for the Red Cross and helping in hospitals during World War One.

She was active in Democratic Party politics, campaigning on behalf of women, the poor and championing the civil rights movement for African Americans. As First Lady, she not only supported her husband's efforts, but excelled at her own, creating a blueprint for a more engaged role in the White House administration for the women who came after her. One of her biggest achievements came when she served as a US delegate to the United Nations, where she oversaw the passage of the Universal Declaration of Human Rights.

In the years since her death on this date in 1962, Roosevelt's sexuality has been a point of discussion, with many citing her close relationship with journalist Lorena Hickok as proof of her bisexuality. When not together the pair exchanged intimate letters over many years; in one, Roosevelt writes, 'I ache to hold you close...'

GEORGE TAKEI

B. 1937

After the outbreak of World War Two, California-born George Takei spent much of his childhood in internment camps in Arkansas and California, along with his family and 120,000 other Japanese Americans. Takei, who became an actor and starred as Mr Sulu in the long-running *Star Trek* series, later developed a Broadway musical called *Allegiance*, based on his childhood experiences.

Allegiance premiered at the Old Globe Theatre in San Diego in 2012 and set an all-time box-office record for the 80-year-old playhouse. On this date in 2015, *Allegiance* began its Broadway run with Takei, once again, taking the lead.

As Mr Sulu in *Star Trek*, Takei became recognisable across the world, appearing not only in the show but also in multiple films of the franchise and on the sci-fi convention circuit. Takei has a partner of over 35 years but despite being vocal on politics and human rights, had never spoken about being gay until 2005, believing it would affect his career: 'The one cause that was the most personal to me, I had to stay quiet on because I wanted my career.'

Takei and Brad Altman were married in 2008, becoming the first same-sex couple to apply for a marriage licence in West Hollywood.

BRIAN EPSTEIN

1934–1967

On this date in 1961, music manager Brian Epstein is credited with discovering The Beatles; years later Paul McCartney would refer to him as 'the Fifth Beatle', which is quite the accolade.

When Epstein saw the Fab Four at the Cavern Club in Liverpool, he was immediately impressed by their music and charm, but felt that for success, their image needed work. Moving their style away from leather jackets and jeans towards black suits and mop haircuts, he also fired their drummer, Pete Best, and replaced him with Ringo Starr. The rest, as they say, is history.

As a gay man living at a time when homosexuality was illegal in the UK, Epstein felt the full weight of the law on numerous occasions. In his early twenties, he was charged with 'persistently importuning various men for immoral purposes' and, while serving in the Royal Army Service Corps, was arrested for wearing army uniform at a gay nightclub. Forced to undergo psychiatric treatment, he came out to his psychiatrist and was discharged from the army.

Like many in the 1960s, Epstein experimented with drugs and sadly died of an accidental overdose at the age of 33. In 2020, a movie biopic on Epstein's life was announced, called *Midas Man*, celebrating his incredibly influential role in the 1960s music scene.

JÓHANNA SIGURÐARDÓTTIR

B. 1942

Jóhanna Sigurðardóttir was elected as an MP in Iceland's Social Democratic Party in 1978 — incidentally the same year that the National Organisation of Lesbians and Gay Men in Iceland was formed, named Samtökin 78. In 2009, Sigurðardóttir became not only the first female prime minister of her country, but also the first openly LGBTQ+ prime minister anywhere in the world.

She had previously married and had two sons with her husband before they divorced in 1987. After an early career as a flight attendant, Sigurðardóttir entered politics and in 1994 ran for, but lost, the leadership of her party.

She began a same-sex relationship with Jónína Leósdóttir, and the pair entered into a civil partnership. During her time in office as prime minister, Iceland passed a marriage equality law in 2010, which Sigurðardóttir and Leósdóttir quickly took advantage of.

Multiple bankers and politicians who were associated with Iceland's financial collapse in 2008 were brought to justice by Sigurðardóttir's government and the economy somewhat improved.

On this date in 2021, Sigurðardóttir was awarded the Women Political Leaders Trailblazer Award at the Reykjavík Global Forum.

MICHAEL DILLON

1915–1962

Assigned female at birth, Michael Dillon studied at St Anne's women's college, Oxford. At the outbreak of World War Two, he moved to Bristol and started taking testosterone. He later underwent surgery with Sir Harold Gilles, a plastic surgery expert who more usually worked on injured soldiers, who pioneered the operation that gave Dillon his penis.

He legally became Laurence Michael Dillon around 1944, and went on to study medicine at Trinity College Dublin. In 1946 he wrote *Self: A Study in Ethics and Endocrinology*. It was one of the first works to separate transgenderism from homosexuality. After reading his book, Roberta Cowell (see 15 May), the first known British trans woman to undergo reassignment surgery, tracked down Dillon and the pair forged a close friendship. Dillon would later perform an illegal orchidectomy (removal of testicles) on Cowell.

Years after his death, Dillon's autobiography, *Out of the Ordinary*, was published around this date in November 2016. In it he describes realising the world did not see him as he saw himself, when a male friend opened a gate and stood aside to let Dillon through: 'Suddenly I was struck with an awful thought… "He thinks I'm a woman." …I had never thought of myself as such despite being technically a girl.'

LISA POWER

B. 1954

Lisa Power has been called the Matriarch of British LGBTQ+ activism. She charts coming out in Wales in the 1970s as both dramatic and, at the same time, unremarkable. She was snapped unknowingly while at a protest about unfair dismissal of queers sparked by the firing of a gay man from the department store British Home Stores (BHS), and appeared in the local press with a placard saying 'BHS unfair to gays'. She said, 'Before I knew where I was, I was a double-denim-wearing, badge-wearing, placard-carrying lesbian.'

After moving to London at the end of the 70s, Power began volunteering at the Lesbian and Gay Switchboard and a life of LGBTQ+ activism began. She went on to co-found LGBTQ+ rights lobbying group, Stonewall, and also co-founded the *Pink Paper*, a fortnightly printed publication in the UK covering gay and lesbian issues. The paper ran in print from this date in 1987 until 2009. It then went online until 2012 when it ceased permanently.

As Secretary-General of the International Lesbian and Gay Association, Power was the first out LGBTQ+ person to speak at the UN in New York. She has also been the Policy Director for the Terrence Higgins Trust, the UK's leading HIV and sexual health charity, and is now an organiser for Pride History Month at Pride Cymru, as well as a trustee at the Queer Britain Museum in London.

MARLOW MOSS

1889-1958

An online search for Marlow Moss's art yields numerous articles and discussions comparing her work to that of the Dutch painter Piet Mondrian. The pair knew each other, and their work undeniably shares striking similarities, both concerned with black lines, white space and blocks of primary colour. The ongoing debate around the two is 'who influenced whom?'

When Moss's work was featured in a solo show at Tate Britain in 2014, *AnOther Magazine* wrote, 'Like so many women, Moss has been written out of art history,' and heralded her as 'one of Britain's most important Constructivist artists... a radical lesbian and Drag King'.

Born in London, Moss adopted an androgynous persona throughout her life. She studied in Paris under the French painter Fernand Léger and was a founding member of Abstraction-Création — a group of non-figurative artists that included Barbara Hepworth and Auguste Herbin.

Despite a move towards sculpture in later life and the loss of some of her earlier paintings during World War Two, enough of her art has survived for Moss's legacy to remain. On this date in 2019, drag queen Sasha Velour picked Moss's 'Composition in Yellow, Black and White' for their artwork of choice as part of the LGBTQ+ Icons at Tate Britain series.

KIM PETRAS

B. 1992

Ahead of the MTV Europe Music Awards (EMAs), held in Budapest, Hungary, on this date in 2021, Kim Petras said it was 'a dream come true' to be the first-ever transgender performer at the event.

Referencing Hungary's poor track record on LGBTQ+ legislation, Petras also said, 'I just hope that it can bring joy to people watching… make people feel like they're not alone because, with the censorship of LGBTQ media in Hungary, I think it's so powerful that I get to perform and that I get to show who I am and that I don't get censored.'

Assigned male at birth, Petras had reassignment surgery aged 16 following evaluation by the head of the psychiatric unit at Frankfurt Hospital. At the time, the media reported that Petras was the youngest person in the world to undergo this surgery.

Petras achieved phenomenal success releasing music under her own imprint, BunHead Records, before being signed to a major label in 2021. Paris Hilton appeared in the video for her debut single, 'I Don't Want It All', she got her first Top 40 hit with 'Heart to Break' in 2018 and released a full Halloween-themed album, featuring Elvira, Mistress of the Dark, in October 2019.

DAVID HOCKNEY

B. 1937

David Hockney painted his lover, Peter Schlesinger, into his work many times. As early as 1963, the painting *Domestic Scene* featured one of the pair showering while the other washed his back. This was a bold depiction of homosexuality in the same year the Sexual Offences Act was passed in the UK, which decriminalised private homosexual acts between men aged over 21.

Hockney was born in Yorkshire, UK, studied at the Royal College of Art in London and was influential in the British Pop Art movement. He headed to Los Angeles in the 1960s, where the Californian lifestyle can be seen in many of his paintings. A number of his works also depict people he knows: his parents, friends and lovers past and present.

One of Hockney's most well-known works, *Portrait of an Artist (Pool with Two Figures)* (1972), shows Peter Schlesinger submerged in a swimming pool, while Hockney stands overlooking him, the rolling landscape of Southern France in the distance. On this date in 2018, the painting set a record for the most expensive artwork sold by a living artist when was sold to an unknown buyer for $90.3 million in New York.

RADCLYFFE HALL

1880–1943

When the writer Radclyffe Hall and her book, *The Well of Loneliness*, were put on trial in Bow Street Magistrates Court in London, the magistrate's judgement, given on this date in 1928, declared it obscene, saying, 'It would tend to corrupt those in whose hands it should fall.' He went on to say that it was an offence against public decency and ordered it to be destroyed.

The Well of Loneliness had no obscenities and was well-written; Hall's only perceived crime was to portray lesbian relationships as natural. Following the verdict, copies were destroyed, and the book was banned in England until 1959, when the Obscene Publications Act was altered. the *New Stateman* called the book 'One of the first and most influential contributions of gay and lesbian literature.'

The book tells the story of tomboyish Stephen, a female who hunts, wears trousers, cuts her hair short and comes to realise that she is attracted to women. The character bears resemblance to the author herself, who had cropped hair, wore a monocle and bow tie, and liked to go by the name John. Hall and her long-term partner, sculptor Una Troubridge, were regular attendees at the Parisian lesbian salons held by American writer Natalie Barney, which were also attended by the portrait painter Romaine Brooks (see 2 May).

MICHELLE VISAGE

B. 1968

Michelle Visage joined *Ru Paul's Drag Race* as a judge in 2011, having been friends with RuPaul since they met on the New York club scene in the 1980s. She had previously been part of the queer ballroom drag 'house' Magnifique when she moved from New Jersey to New York, so the pair moved in the same circles.

In 2021, Visage took part in the BBC show *Strictly Come Dancing*, and chose Voguing for her Couple's Choice dance, seeking to bring gay culture to national TV. On this date in 2021, after being eliminated from the competition, she posted a heartfelt dedication to the LGBTQ+ community, referencing the Voguing dance, on Instagram.

Despite sleeping with both men and women when she was younger, Visage prefers to be labelled an ally rather than as bisexual, saying, 'I don't want to take anything away from somebody who's truly living a bisexual lifestyle.' Visage won the Attitude Ally Award in 2020 and said at the time, 'being an ally is as important as being a mother to me' (she has a gay daughter). In 2022, Visage recorded a video on how to be a good ally, including advice such as not putting words in the mouths of queer people when defending them, and welcoming queer family members.

PROUD ALLY

GLUCK

1895–1978

The 20th-century artist, Gluck (born Hannah Gluckstein), rejected prefixes and suffixes such as Miss, Ms or Mrs for themself. The artist's work, always exhibited in solo shows by their own instruction, featured landscapes, portraits and flora and fauna, including arrangements by famed florist Constance Spry, who was a lover of Gluck's.

Gluck's 1937 painting *Medallion (YouWe)* is a dual portrait depicting the artist and their lover, American socialite Nesta Obermer. It was later used on the cover of Radclyffe Hall's (see 16 Nov) 1928 novel, *The Well of Loneliness*, one of the earliest published works of lesbian fiction.

Gluck left a legacy for British oil painters when, in the 1950s, they successfully campaigned to the British Standards Institution for oil paints to be of a better quality.

On this date in 2017, an exhibition of Gluck's work opened at the Brighton Museum and Art Gallery, where they had donated much of their work and possessions in the 1970s. The Royal Academy review at the time said *Medallion (YouWe)* had 'become an iconic image of same-sex desire. The questions it codes of identity, sexual orientation, same-sex union and equal marriage rights are very much to the fore.'

SUE HYDE

B. 1937

American activist Sue Hyde has been at the forefront of the fight for LGBTQ+ rights for many years. She pushed for the repeal of US sodomy laws and led a campaign to defend LGBTQ+ families in Massachusetts when state lawmakers banned the placement of foster children with lesbian and gay parents. She also worked to help preserve marriage rights for same-sex couples and fought to end the military's ban on openly gay service members.

Hyde joined the National Gay and Lesbian Task Force in 1986 and co-founded what became their premier annual event, the Creating Change Conference, the first of which was held on 18–20 November 1988. One of Hyde's intentions behind starting the conference was to help 'break the isolation that organizers and activists said they felt often being the only or one of the few people in their own city or community doing the work'.

As a writer, Hyde was news editor at *Gay Community News* in Boston from 1983 to 1985, and her book, *Come Out and Win*, was published in 2007. It discusses the challenges faced by homeless gay teens and what can be done to help them.

In 2018, Hyde became executive director of the Wild Geese Foundation, an advocacy group that directs resources to small non-profits focusing on LGBTQ+ people, youth, women, BIPOC, reproductive justice, food and water access.

ZINAIDA GIPPIUS

1869-1945

Often mentioned alongside her husband, the Russian novelist and religious thinker Dmitry Merezhkovsky, Zinaida Gippius made her own place in history as a writer. She penned plays, poetry, novels and critical essays. The pair were both influential in the burgeoning Symbolist movement.

Born on this date in 1869, Gippius began writing poetry at the age of seven and was already published by the time she married at 19. The nature of the couple's relationship has often been questioned, with suggestions that they were asexual. It is thought that she had various romantic (not sexual) relationships with women and, perhaps most surprisingly, she and her husband entered into something of a throuple with friend and writer Dmitry Filosofov. The trio campaigned to bring Russia's revolutionary thinkers and religious leaders together under a 'New Church', until Gippius and her husband fled the country after the 1917 October Revolution.

Gippius purposefully switched between masculine and feminine gendering in her poetry and even seemed to advocate queerness and bisexuality, writing, 'It is equally good and natural for any person to love any other person.' Gippius' prose, such as, 'I do not desire exclusive femininity, just as I do not desire exclusive masculinity,' has also brought about modern discussions as to whether the writer was non-binary.

THE LADY CHABLIS

1957–2016

Nightclub performer The Lady Chablis (whose name genuinely included 'The' after she legally changed it to reflect her stage name) started out working in Club One, Savannah, Georgia in 1988, entertaining audiences as a drag star. However, as a trans woman, she later expressed regret that she 'had to wear that label "drag queen". I've never been comfortable with that label.'

The Lady Chablis first garnered public attention when she featured in John Berendt's book *Midnight in the Garden of Good and Evil*, which was based on a true crime story. When the book was later made into a film, released on this date in 1997 and directed by Clint Eastwood, Chablis played herself and became even more famous as one of the first transgender performers in mainstream film.

After the book was released, Chablis made regular appearances on television, continued to perform at Club One and used her fame to raise money for diabetes and LGBTQ+ charities. When the star died aged 59 in 2016, Club One wrote on its Facebook page that she paved the way for female impersonation in Savannah, but that 'No one, however, could outshine the Grand Empress herself.'

ANDRÉ GIDE

1869-1951

André Gide, a French writer and humanist, won the Nobel Prize for Literature in 1947 – the first openly gay man to do so. Born on this date in 1869, he wrote more than 50 books, both fiction and autobiographical.

Gide, a sickly child, had a strict Protestant upbringing, and after writing his first autobiographical piece entitled *Les Cahiers d'André Walter* (*The Notebooks of André Walter*) in 1891, he travelled to North Africa where he was able to loosen the shackles of Victorian societal and sexual constraint. There he spent time with Oscar Wilde (see 26 Apr) and Lord Alfred Douglas, who encouraged a nervous Gide to act on his feelings for young men. It is thought that the trio participated in what may now be viewed as some questionable sex tourism.

Gide, who was a communist, spent his life travelling and writing. His literary works were often controversial, whether they championed the joys of being gay in *Corydon* (1920), or shared stories of mutual masturbation and interracial lovemaking in his autobiographical work, *If It Die* (1920).

As well as a daughter and an extensive collection of literature, Gide left behind his often-quoted mantra: 'It is better to be hated for what you are, than to be loved for something you are not.'

ALLEN GINSBERG

1926-1997

When Beat Generation poet Allen Ginsberg died in 1997, his *New York Times* obituary described him as having 'a sort of teddy-bear quality that deflected much of the indignation he inspired'. His prose featuring drugs and sex could be shocking, but in line with his hippy ideology, it sought to demystify drug use and promote peace and love.

Ginsberg's poem, 'Howl', published in November 1956, discussed homosexual sex at a time when it was illegal, and became a manifesto of sexual revolution for the youth of the day. The poem became the subject of an obscenity trial when the San Francisco City Lights bookshop was prosecuted for selling it. However, when a California state court later ruled in favour of free speech, it became a landmark case in the historical battle against literary censorship.

Along with fellow queer Beat poets, William S. Burroughs and Jack Kerouac, Ginsberg helped to define 1960s counterculture, inspiring (and singing with) Bob Dylan, championing the anti-Vietnam war movement and spreading a Buddhist message through his prose. He received many awards and was often celebrated by the institutions he seemingly opposed, receiving the National Arts Club gold medal and being inducted into the American Academy and Institute of Arts and Letters.

SUSAN SONTAG

1933–2004

Susan Sontag is perhaps most well-known for her essay 'Notes on "Camp"' in which she breaks down the boundaries between 'high' and 'low' culture and discusses what exactly is and isn't 'camp'. Her other works include *On Photography* – six essays investigating power dynamics between photographer and subject, described by the *New Yorker* as 'The most original and illuminating study of the subject.'

As well as being a philosophical writer, Sontag also made films and wrote plays, short stories and novels. On this date in 1986, the *New Yorker* published her short story *The Way We Live Now,* in which a group of friends based in New York experience the early days of the AIDS epidemic.

Sontag reluctantly identified herself as bisexual as a teenager and subsequently married sociologist Philip Rieff, with whom she had a son. Following her divorce, Sontag had companions of both sexes, although only addressed the subject of her sexuality in 2000 when a forthcoming unauthorised biography threatened to out her.

Sontag had an on-off 10-year relationship with photographer Annie Leibovitz (see 20 Oct), yet neither admitted they were lovers in Sontag's lifetime. It was only after her death that Leibovitz told a journalist to call them 'lovers' in their interview.

CONNIE NORMAN

1949–1996

Connie Norman described herself as 'an ex-drag queen, ex-hooker, ex-IV drug user, ex-high-risk youth, and current post-operative transsexual woman who is HIV positive'. She was also an AIDS activist and the host of the first daily commercial talk radio show about queer issues, in Los Angeles.

The Connie Norman Show first aired on this date in 1991 and ran every weekday evening. As well as dealing with topics affecting the LGBTQ+ community, Norman's pioneering radio show also featured guests and reserved a weekly slot for queer comedians.

Norman, who was diagnosed with HIV in the 1980s, was part of ACT UP, the AIDS activist group, and worked with the AIDS

Healthcare Foundation. She fought for better healthcare for people living with HIV/AIDS, and for wider access to HIV testing. Norman was well-known for being able to speak openly and honestly with everyone. Michael Weinstein, the president and co-founder of the AIDS Healthcare Foundation said, 'Her outspokenness frequently made people uncomfortable, but she said things that needed to be said.'

In 2021, Norman and her incredible achievements were brought back into the spotlight through a documentary film about her life's work, *AIDS Diva: The Legend of Connie Norman.*

SUNIL GUPTA

B. 1953

Indian–Canadian photographer, Sunil Gupta, moved from New Delhi to Montreal, Canada with his family as a teenager and took up photography in New York in the 1970s. His photographs have been exhibited around the world.

On this date in 1982, the *Guardian* newspaper ran a piece by Gupta entitled 'They Dare Not Speak its Name in Delhi… the Secret Suffering of India's Homosexual Community'. At a time when being gay in India was still illegal (it was decriminalised in 2018), Gupta staged photographs that obscured subjects' faces as they stood near historical monuments that doubled as cruising grounds. He noted that

queer people in India were required to present 'a conventional puritanical public image'.

Some of Gupta's most recognisable queer photographic work comes from his black-and-white portrait series, *Lovers: Ten Years On*, taken between 1984 and 1986 in the UK. After coming out of a 10-year relationship, Gupta set about shooting portraits of gay couples in long-term relationships as social commentary. With HIV/AIDS turning public opinion against the acceptance of homosexuality, and the media portraying LGBTQ+ people as sick and/or deviant, the couples in *Lovers: Ten Years On* are shown as ordinary, often white, middle-class professionals in long-term relationships.

GEORGINA BEYER

B. 1957

When Georgina Beyer was elected to the New Zealand Parliament on this date in 1999, she became the world's first transgender Member of Parliament. Standing with the Labour Party, she won the traditionally conservative, safe blue seat of Wairarapa. Prior to this, Beyer, a former sex worker who underwent gender reassignment surgery in 1984, was elected as the mayor of Carterton in 1995, making her the world's first trans mayor, too!

In 2004, the Labour government passed the Foreshore and Seabed Act, which granted ownership of beaches and waterway areas to the state, effectively removing Māori claims to the land. Beyer, who is Māori spoke about the personal struggle this presented her at the time, explaining that she felt divided by her heritage and her party, calling it 'an absolute nightmare'.

Beyer, who was raised by her grandparents for a time when her father was sent to jail, also worked in radio broadcasting and as an actress, receiving a NZ Guild of Film and Television Award in 1987. She has been a trustee of the NZ AIDS Foundation and a Justice of the Peace as well as being awarded the Lifetime Achievement Award at the 2005 Glammies.

QUEEN LATIFAH

B. 1970

In June 2021, when the American musician and actress Queen Latifah, who is notoriously quiet about her private life, accepted her Lifetime Achievement Award at the BET Awards, she effectively ended years of speculation surrounding her sexuality. 'Eboni, my love. Rebel, my love. Peace. Happy Pride!' she declared, referring publicly for the first time to her partner Eboni Nichols and their son.

Latifah began her hip-hop career with her debut album, *All Hail The Queen*, released on this date in 1989. In 1993, the single 'U.N.I.T.Y' from her album, *Black Reign*, secured her the Grammy Award for Best Rap Solo Performance.

Latifah has addressed male chauvinism and the sexist treatment of women in her music, and has spoken out about the shame and stigma attached to women described as 'big girls'.

The star has also had a successful film career, in front of and behind the camera, starring in movies such as *Hairspray* and *Chicago*, which garnered her a Best Supporting Actress nomination at the 2003 Academy Awards. She has also produced numerous films, which consciously place Black actors in leading roles. In 2021, Latifah starred in and became an executive producer of the new CBS crime drama, *The Equalizer*.

PAMELA LYNDON TRAVERS

1899-1996

On this date in 2013, *Saving Mr Banks*, starring Emma Thompson and Tom Hanks, was first released in cinemas in the UK. It recounted writer Pamela Lyndon Travers' relationship with Walt Disney during the making of *Mary Poppins*, the film based on the English nanny character in Travers' books. While the film was fictionalised, its portrait of Travers as grumpy and difficult was by all accounts true, as was her dislike of the finished film, which starred Julie Andrews in the title role.

Born in Queensland, Australia to a drunken English bank manager father, Travers began her career as an actress before turning to writing poetry, fiction and journalism. When she moved to London, Travers continued to write for Australian newspapers as well as writing drama, films and literary criticism, but it was her second novel, *Mary Poppins* (1934), that made her truly successful. She continued writing the Mary Poppins series of books for the next 40 years.

It is thought that Travers had relationships with both men and women, but understandably due to societal opinions at the time, kept this private. Evidence of this is particularly strong in Travers' own writing, when she spoke of a tumultuous relationship she had with bookshop owner Jessie Orage. The writer never married and had an adopted son.

HAL CALL

1917–2000

Hal Call was one of the first people to talk about homosexuality in a positive way on television. *The Rejected*, the first gay-themed documentary on US TV, aired on San Francisco's KQED network on 11 September 1961.

Call was one of the first members of the Mattachine Society, an early US gay rights group. He was also a businessman and the founder of Pan-Graphic Press, a gay printing press, and later the Adonis Bookstore. His empire expanded when he added peep shows into the mix and began operating the Circle J Club. The Circle J kept going for five years after

Call's death, but eventually closed its doors for the final time on this date in 2005.

Call advocated that homosexuals should be assimilated into wider heterosexual society, that gay men are fundamentally the same as everyone else. In 1964, he presented his argument to the American public when he assisted with a 14-page report on homosexuality for *LIFE* magazine. While much of the article painted gay men as sad and sordid, many saw this stepping out of the closet and into public consciousness as a positive step for the gay community.

CHRISTINE JORGENSEN

1926-1989

A new kind of American celebrity was born thanks to a story that ran in the *New York Daily News* on this date in 1952. Emblazoned across its front page were the words 'Ex-GI Becomes Blonde Beauty'. It introduced Christine Jorgensen and her 'sex-change' to the world, claiming she was the first patient to receive this kind of treatment (she wasn't). She did, however, become the first person in the US to gain fame and notoriety for such surgery, and she went on to use her profile for good, educating others on gender identity by lecturing at universities.

Unusually for LGBTQ+ people at the time, Jorgensen was embraced by the curious American public and courted by the press, who focused on her GI status and war effort before her transition, celebrating her as both a hero and now a beauty.

Jorgensen said that she had no idea her transition 'was going to affect the rest of the world'. She went on to become an entertainer, performing in nightclubs, later wrote her autobiography and was the subject of a 1970 Hollywood film, *The Christine Jorgensen Story*. When speaking about her journey, Jorgensen said, 'We didn't start the sexual revolution but I think we gave it a good kick in the pants!'

JANET MOCK

B. 1983

Janet Mock's debut book, *Redefining Realness*, (2014) was the first book written by a trans person who transitioned as a youngster. It was released in paperback on this date, after the hardback made it onto the *New York Times* bestseller list earlier that year. Three years later, in 2017, Mock published her second memoir, *Surpassing Certainty*, which chronicled her life in New York as a trans woman of colour in the world of magazine publishing.

In 2018, Mock made a successful move into television when she became a writer, producer and director on Ryan Murphy's HBO TV show *Pose*, which centred around a group of trans women and queer people on the ballroom scene in New York in the 1980s and 1990s. The show was notable for the fact that it cast trans actors in trans roles. Mock made history working on the show's episode entitled, 'Love Is the Message', becoming the first transgender woman of colour to write and direct an episode on television ever.

During the season three premiere event, Mock gave a 15-minute speech in which she called out unequal pay for women and the discrimination suffered by transgender women in the industry. 'Fuck Hollywood,' she said. 'This makes you uncomfortable? It should.'

LESLIE CHEUNG

1956–2003

Leslie Cheung was one of Hong Kong's biggest music stars during the golden era of Cantopop in the 1980s. His song, 'Monica', released in 1984, topped the charts and became the bestselling single in Hong Kong history. He also had a successful film career, taking multiple lead roles in director Wong Kar-Wai's films, including *Days of Being Wild*, which was released in December 1990 and *Happy Together*, which was nominated for the Palme d'Or at the Cannes Film Festival in 1997.

Cheung played with gender identity in his appearance, often presenting androgynously, which prompted the media to question his sexuality. He publicly came out as bisexual and introduced his long-term partner, Daffy Tong Hok-tak, to his audience. His coming out was not particularly well received, and the media often ignored his own admission of bisexuality, instead reporting him as gay. Some homophobic elements of the press also claimed he was 'haunted by a female ghost' or used other such slurs.

Tragically, Cheung took his own life in 2003 after a long battle with depression. Despite societal pressures, Cheung's family allowed his partner Daffy to take the role traditionally reserved for a person's spouse in mourning and at the funeral.

STEPHEN SONDHEIM

1930-2021

American composer and lyricist Stephen Sondheim enjoyed a long and successful career in musical theatre. His work was unconventional; he himself said he didn't fit into the corporate, cookie-cutter style that often led to box-office success.

Partnerships between lyricists and composers such as Rogers and Hammerstein (*South Pacific*), Rice and Lloyd Webber (*Joseph and the Amazon Technicolour Dreamcoat*) and Lerner and Loewe (*My Fair Lady*) have always been common in musical theatre. Yet, Sondheim preferred to write both the music and the lyrics in productions he worked on. One of his most famous works,

Into The Woods, premiered at the Old Globe Theatre in San Diego, California on this date in 1986. Sondheim also wrote music and lyrics for *Sweeney Todd* (1979) and *Merrily We Roll Along* (1981), as well as the lyrics for *West Side Story* (1957) and *Gypsy* (1959).

Sondheim came out as gay relatively late in his life and described it as both difficult and joyful. He eventually married, as an octogenarian, in 2017. When he died in 2021, Barbra Streisand said on Twitter, 'Thank the Lord that Sondheim lived to be 91 years old so he had the time to write such wonderful music and GREAT lyrics!'

ELLIOT PAGE

B. 1987

A Hollywood star from an early age, Elliot Page's journey has been played out in the public eye. Assigned female at birth, Page publicly came out as a trans man via Instagram and Twitter posts in December 2020, aged 33. The posts began: 'Hi friends, I want to share with you that I am trans, my pronouns are he/they and my name is Elliot.'

Two years after playing a teenage vigilante in the movie *Hard Candy* in 2005, Page played the titular role in the coming-of-age movie *Juno*, released on this date in 2007. For this performance, Page was nominated for an Academy Award. Page's many major Hollywood films and television series include Christopher Nolan's 2010 science-fiction thriller *Inception* and the Netflix reboot of Armistead Maupin's *Tales of the City*. For season three of the *Umbrella Academy*, creator Steve Blackman rewrote scripts to incorporate a story for Page's character to transition on the show too, saying 'it's a credit to Elliot'.

Around the time Page came out, a wave of anti-trans state legislation was proposed in the US, aiming to limit health care and take away the rights of trans people. Page spoke out, appealing to people to educate themselves on the 'misinformation and lies'. He has also worked with transathlete.com to help protect trans children.

KIM FRIELE

1935–2021

'Norway became a better, more free and more diverse land to live in,' said Norway's prime minister at the state funeral of human and gay rights activist, Kim Friele (Karen-Christine Friele), on this date in 2021. One of the first people to publicly acknowledge her sexuality in Norway in the 1960s, Friele became part of, and soon ran, the gay organisation The Norwegian Association of 1948 (Det Norske Forbundet av 1948).

During her time as an activist, Friele led a campaign for the repeal of section 213 of the Penal Code, the Norwegian law that criminalised homosexuality, and in 1977 she was part of a group that won a battle to prevent homosexuality being classified as a psychiatric diagnosis.

In 1995, Friele and her partner Wenche Lowzow, who was the country's first openly gay Member of Parliament, became the first couple to enter into a legal same-sex partnership in Norway.

Soon after her death, calls began for a permanent memorial for Friele; the municipality of Bergen wants to name an urban space after the activist. While there is usually a waiting period of five years in such cases, Thor Haakon Bakke of the council's urban development agency suggested this should be waived, as 'Friele was very important to many.'

MAKI MURAKI

B. 1974

On this date in 2016, Maki Muraki became the first out lesbian to receive the Women of the Year award from *Nikkei Woman*, a Japanese magazine that describes itself as being 'for working women in their 20s and 30s who yearn to work and live by their own values'. The award recognised the work that Muraki had done for women and LGBTQ+ people in the workplace, helping to improve their conditions. Japan lags behind other G7 countries when it comes to LGTBQ+ rights. It has yet to legalise gay marriage and has no protection for its citizens against employment discrimination, making Muraki's work all the more important.

Muraki, who is a graduate of Kyoto University, is the head of the Osaka-based Japanese LGBTQ+ rights organisation, Nijiiro ('Rainbow') Diversity. The Japanese activist delivered countless lectures and worked with a number of companies to implement policies to help eradicate discrimination based on sexual orientation and gender identity. Speaking about her hopes for the future at the awards ceremony in 2016, Muraki said, 'I hope many more LGBT-friendly measures will be taken and those who are struggling with their sexual orientation and gender identity will be saved in the future.'

PENNY WONG

B. 1968

A senator for South Australia since 2001, Penny Wong was the first openly lesbian woman in Australian parliament. She was born in Malaysia to an Australian mother and Malaysian father, and moved to Adelaide aged eight. Here she obtained a Bachelor of Arts in Jurisprudence, a Bachelor of Laws with Honours and subsequently completed a Graduate Diploma of Legal Practice at the University of South Australia.

Wong served as Climate Change and Water Minister for the Australian Labor Party in 2007–10, expanding the Renewable Energy Target, and then as Minister for Finance and Deregulation, working on budgets and women's employment issues. In 2013, after a change in government, she became Leader of the Opposition in the Senate – the first woman to occupy the role.

Wong's position in parliament is particularly important representationally, as a disproportionate percentage of ministers and senators of English, Scottish, Welsh or Irish origin rule a more racially mixed population. In 2017, she campaigned for same-sex marriage in Australia and 62 per cent of the country favoured the change in the law to allow it. It received royal assent from the Governor-General on this date in 2017 and became legal the next day. Wong lives with her partner, Sophie Allouache, and their two children in Adelaide.

ISAAC JULIEN

B. 1960

Even before graduating from London's Central Saint Martins School of Art in 1984, Isaac Julien had already set up Sankofa Film and Video Collective with a group of fellow aspiring filmmakers. The collective, supported by the Greater London Council and Channel 4, was dedicated to developing independent Black film culture in the areas of production, exhibition and audience.

Julien is an installation artist who primarily works in film, exploring sexuality, race and queer history. His 1998 black-and-white film *Looking for Langston*, is an exploration of the American poet and leader of the Harlem renaissance, Langston Hughes. It features imagined, fictional scenes interspersed with archival footage and presents the daily dangers faced by queer people of colour. It's thought to have been the inspiration for David Fincher's music video for Madonna's 'Vogue'.

Julien's 1999 work, *The Long Road to Mazatlán*, was exhibited in San Antonio from this date in 1999 and was shortlisted for the 2001 Turner Prize. Playing out across three screens, it focuses on two cowboys and reflects upon the construction of masculinity. Inspirations for the work included James Dean (see 9 Mar) in the 1956 film *Giant* and the 1968 film *Lonesome Cowboys* by Andy Warhol (see 3 Jun).

BRIAN GRADEN

B. 1963

As his own website boasts, Brian Graden 'is one of the most successful executives in the history of television'. His meteoric rise began when he commissioned two young talents named Trey Parker and Matt Stone to produce a video Christmas card; this card turned into the animated TV show *South Park*. With Graden as co-developer and producer, *South Park* became one of US television's biggest successes of all time, winning Emmys in 2005, 2007, 2008 and 2009.

Graden was president of entertainment for MTV network's music channels for 13 years, responsible for moving it away from its music roots towards reality-based programming; he launched reality TV shows such as *The Osbournes*, *Jackass* and *Punk'd*. Graden was also president of Logo TV, the LGBTQ+ network that launched the formidable reality show, *RuPaul's Drag Race*.

At MTV, Graden oversaw a campaign called Fight for Your Rights: Take a Stand against Discrimination. As part of the campaign on this date in 2001, the channel screened an original docudrama about the homophobic killing of Matthew Shepard, a gay college student from Wyoming (see 29 Oct). The movie aired without adverts, and it was followed by a continuous scroll of the names of hate-crime victims along the bottom of the screen for seventeen hours with no other programming.

TOM FORD

B. 1961

When Tom Ford became creative director at Gucci in 1994, the brand was considered unfashionable and was almost bankrupt. Ford turned the label around, bringing in photographer Mario Testino and stylist Carine Roitfeld to create a new, modern image for Gucci's advertising campaigns. He was credited with bringing sex appeal back to the label, and 10 years after Ford started at the label, Gucci was valued at over $10 billion.

Ford lived in both the US and UK with his long-term partner, former fashion editor Richard Buckley and their son until Buckley died in 2021. Ford, known for provocative comments and toying with the press, once told *Advocate* magazine, 'I don't think of myself as gay. That doesn't mean that I'm not gay. I just don't define myself by my sexuality.'

In 2009, Ford directed his first film, *A Single Man*, based on a novel by Christopher Isherwood (see 13 Feb) and starring Colin Firth. It depicts a few days in the life of a grief-stricken college professor as he contemplates suicide, following the recent death of his boyfriend. The highly stylised feature premiered in the US on this date and won Ford and his team critical acclaim and many award nominations.

STEPHANIE BEATRIZ

B. 1981

When the character of Detective Rosa Diaz came out as bisexual to her family during the 100th episode of comedy show *Brooklyn Nine-Nine*, which aired on this date in 2017, it was art imitating life for the actor who played her. Stephanie Beatriz is herself bisexual and came out publicly on Twitter in 2016. When one of the show's writers called her to discuss the idea of making her character bisexual, she said 'Absolutely. Yes. I'm so excited! Yes! Yes! Yes!'

The portrayal of a regular bisexual character on such a light-hearted comedy show was seen as great for combatting bi-erasure, and also a step forward for bi representation. Many bisexual characters on television are brought in as plot devices, with stories focusing on their sexuality, rather than them as a person.

Writing in *GQ* magazine, about being a bi woman marrying a heterosexual man, Beatriz pointed out how bi people often feel like imposters in the LGBTQ+ community for not being 'gay enough'. She also discussed how many bi people have to come out repeatedly as they 'pass for straight'. Beatriz closed by saying, 'In October, I will marry a heterosexual man – till death do us part. But I'll be bi till the day I die...'

APRIL ASHLEY

1935–2021

In her obituary in 2021, the *New York Times* described April Ashley as 'a model and socialite who rose from poverty in Liverpool to the heights of London society'. Ashley was also one of the first British women to undergo gender reassignment surgery, which was undertaken by Dr Georges Burou, a gynaecologist in Morocco, in 1960.

Before her surgery, Ashley had spent time in a mental hospital where she was subjected to conversion therapy involving electroshock therapy. She had also served in the navy and was a dancer at the Paris nightclub, Le Carrousel.

After some years of modelling, mixing in high society and working as an actress, Ashley's story was sold to a newspaper. As a result, her work dried up and she fled to Spain.

Ashley only returned to the UK in 2005, when she put in a request to then deputy prime minister, John Prescott, an old acquaintance, for a birth certificate that recognised her as female. Thanks to the Gender Recognition Act of 2004, she got her wish and was further recognised when, on this date 2012, she was honoured with an MBE for services to transgender equality at Buckingham Palace in London.

CLARE BALDING

B. 1971

Anyone in the UK watching TV coverage of the Olympic Games, the Paralympic Games, the Winter Olympics, Wimbledon tennis, horse racing or even the dog show *Crufts*, will be familiar with broadcaster Clare Balding. She began presenting sport on the radio for the BBC in 1994, and since 1998 has regularly presented major events, both sporting and non-sporting, for various television networks.

When Balding came out publicly as a lesbian in 2003, she discussed how her fears of losing work and being discriminated against were unfounded, although sadly it did affect her relationship with her grandmother. Balding entered into a civil partnership with Alice Arnold in 2006 and the pair later married in 2015.

Balding, who became the BBC's lead horse-racing presenter in December 1997, has twice been named Sports Presenter of the Year by the Royal Television Society, and has also received a special BAFTA to honour her work on London's 2012 Olympics and Paralympics. She uses her position to advocate for equal coverage of women's sport. Arguing against the unfairness of exclusively reporting men's sports, she also highlights the positive benefits women's sports can have on young women's attitudes to their own bodies.

In 2022, she was appointed Commander of the British Empire (CBE).

BARBARA GITTINGS & KAY LAHUSEN

1932–2007; 1930–2021

On this date in 1973, homosexuals in America were 'cured en masse by the psychiatrists'. This ironic quote came from Barbara Gittings, an early and significant member of the lesbian activist group, the Daughters of Bilitis. Along with her partner Kay Lahusen, Gittings campaigned tirelessly to have the American Psychiatric Association (APA) remove its definition of homosexuality as a mental disorder, which it finally did on this date.

Gittings and Lahusen initially stormed meetings of the APA, but eventually worked *with* them to organise a panel discussion on the subject, and even convinced a psychiatrist to take part (in disguise), to support their argument.

During the early part of the 1960s Gittings was the editor and Lahusen was art director of the *Ladder*, the magazine for the Daughters of Bilitis. As a photographer, Lahusen captured many of the movement's earliest demonstrations, providing important historical documentation of LGBTQ+ activism. Gittings continued her passion for the written queer word later in life when she worked with the American Library Association to ensure LGBTQ+ literature was well classified. This made it easier for people to find and further their knowledge on the subject.

In 2012, the city of Philadelphia named a section of Locust Street 'Barbara Gittings Way' in memory of the activist often referred to as the mother of the gay rights movement.

KANAKO OTSUJI

B. 1974

When Kanako Otsuji ran for parliament with the Constitutional Democratic Party of Japan in 2007, she was the first openly gay candidate to take part in Japanese national politics. Although unsuccessful that time, she told supporters, 'I hope to continue until I see the day that we look back and say, "This is a historic day in the history of sexual minorities."'

Otsuji, born on this date in 1974, said she became a politician because of the pain and isolation she suffered when coming to terms with being a lesbian. She publicly revealed her sexuality in her autobiography *Coming Out: A Journey to Find My True Self*, which was published in 2005.

In June 2007, despite same-sex marriages not being legally recognised in Japan, Otsuji publicly married her partner, Maki Kimura, at the Nagoya Lesbian Gay Revolution festival with 1,000 guests!

In May 2013, the resignation of a party house member enabled Otsuji to move up the ranks and win a House of Councillors seat. This made her Japan's first openly gay member of the National Diet, Japan's bicameral parliament, if only for a few months, as her term in office expired in July that year. She was later elected to the House of Representatives in 2017.

QUENTIN CRISP

1908-1999

The *Guardian* newspaper obituary of Quentin Crisp described him as a 'performer, raconteur and self-styled high priest of camp'. Crisp was a familiar sight in London's Soho in the 1950s and 60s. Defying gender norms and openly living a flamboyant queer lifestyle, Crisp was no stranger to controversy: human rights activist Peter Tatchell (see 12 Apr) recalls how in 1974 Crisp commented on Tatchell's Gay Liberation badge: 'What do you want liberation from?... What is there to be proud of? I don't believe in rights for homosexuals.' Crisp was often abused verbally and physically for his appearance but he never changed, keeping his consistently iconic style into his nineties.

His autobiography, *The Naked Civil Servant*, was published in 1968, and on this date in 1975 the made-for-television film of the same name was broadcast in both the US and UK. It dealt openly with Crisp's homosexuality, his parents' handling of it, his struggle to find employment and acceptance in social circles because of his appearance and his rejection from the military. Tatchell paid tribute to Crisp in his obituary by saying, 'there is no doubt about his courage in coming out and his bravery in flaunting his effeminacy. Prior to decriminalisation it was a very difficult and dangerous thing to do.'

LI YINHE

B. 1952

In China, sexual acts between people of the same sex were only decriminalised in 1997 and same-sex marriage remains illegal (although couples can enter guardianship agreements with similar, yet limited, legal benefits). The sociologist and sexologist, Li Yinhe, has been fighting to change this, and other laws regarding sex, for years.

Yinhe gained a Sociology PhD in the US in 1988. When she returned to China she realised how 'medieval' the laws and attitudes pertaining to sex, relationships and queer issues were in her home country, and she conducted the first major study of homosexuality there. Although she struggled to find people willing to talk openly about

their sexuality, she interviewed 120 people, and published her findings in her 1992 book, *Their World: A Study of Homosexuality in China*, later revised and published as *Subculture of Homosexuality* in 1998. As well as works on the sexuality of Chinese women, marriage and sadomasochism, the sexologist also wrote a study on bisexuality that publishers in China refused to print for years.

On this date in 2014, Yinhe revealed in a blog post that she was in a long-term relationship with a transgender man, and she countered accusations that she was a lesbian by explaining her heterosexuality in another blog post that has been read hundreds of thousands of times.

PROUD ALLY

JEAN GENET

1910–1986

Abandoned by his mother as a child and forced to embrace a life of crime, Jean Genet, born in France on this date in 1910, first put pen to paper while he was in jail. His first written piece was 'Under Sentence of Death', a poem that immortalised a fellow prisoner, executed for murder, in literature.

Genet's writing was often controversial. It was steeped in homosexual content, depicted the world of criminals and poetically portrayed the lives of the debauched. His 1949 autobiographical novel, *Journal du voleur* (*The Thief's Journal*), tells the story of his life as a tramp, pickpocket and male prostitute in various European cities.

In *Miracle of the Rose*, which chronicles the writer's experiences in Mettray Penal Colony as a teenager, Genet describes men who resort to violence because they do not possess the language of intimacy, beautifully romanticising their plight.

Genet was revered by French philosopher and writer Jean-Paul Sartre, who wrote a book about him, and also caught the attention of artist Pablo Picasso, and writer and feminist Simone de Beauvoir. When Genet was again convicted of theft in 1948 and threatened with life imprisonment, a group of well-known writers helped to get him 'pardoned in advance' by the French republic.

C.M. RALPH

B. 1955

Tracker McDyke is a fictional lesbian detective searching for her friend, drag queen Tessy LaFemme, who has gone missing from the Castro, an historically gay neighbourhood in San Francisco. These characters were invented as part of *Caper in the Castro* by artist C.M. Ralph in 1989, now known to be the first LGBTQ+ video game.

Ralph originally released the game as 'Charity Ware', meaning it was essentially free. Those downloading it were simply asked to make donations to an AIDS organisation of their choice.

After its initial success, Ralph 'straightened out' the original game, taking out all queer references, renamed it *Murder on Main Street* and sold it to Heizer Software. 'I took out all the references to the Castro, all the inside jokes,' Ralph said. 'It always cracked me up that these people were loving this game and…had no idea it was actually an LGBT game.'

Caper in the Castro was thought to be lost, but Ralph found the original floppy discs in 2017 and worked with Professor Adrienne Shaw of the LGBTQ Game Archive and Andrew Borman, Digital Games Curator at the Museum of Play in New York, to emulate the original game and were able put it online on this date in 2017.

ELTON JOHN

B. 1947

Singer/songwriter and pianist Elton John is known just as well for his fabulous dress sense, often comprising platform shoes, feathers, wigs and sequins, as his musical accolades. He was already one of the bestselling music artists of all time when he married Renate Blauel, a German-born sound engineer, on Valentine's Day 1984 in Australia. The pair divorced four years later; as John described, 'It wasn't meant to be. I was living a lie.' By 1992, Elton had come to accept his sexuality, telling *Rolling Stone* he was 'quite comfortable being gay'.

Fast forward twenty-one years, to this date in 2005 when John entered into a civil partnership with partner David Furnish. This was the very day the Civil Partnership Act came into force in England and Wales, meaning John and Furnish were one of the first couples in the UK to enter into one. The pair then had two children via a surrogate, and later married, again on this date in 2014, when same-sex marriage became legal in England and Wales.

In 1992 John began one of his biggest and longest-running projects outside of music, when he set up the Elton John AIDS Foundation. The foundation has raised millions of dollars for AIDS education and prevention across the world.

LANA & LILLY WACHOWSKI

B. 1965; B. 1967

The Wachowski sisters, Lana and Lilly, are the successful Hollywood duo who co-wrote and directed 1999 movie *The Matrix*, starring Keanu Reeves and Carrie-Anne Moss. Two further films in the series followed after the first was a huge box-office success and won four Academy Awards. The fourth film, *The Matrix Resurrections*, released in the US on this date in 2021, was directed and co-written by Lana along with David Mitchell and Aleksandar Hemon; Lilly had decided she did not want to 'go backwards' in her career.

The sisters are both trans women. Lana transitioned in the early 2000s, making her the first major Hollywood director to do so, and was awarded the Visibility Award by the Human Rights Campaign in 2012. Lilly came out as trans in Chicago's *Windy City Times* in 2016. In 2020, she explained how *The Matrix* was a trans metaphor, citing the character Switch as someone 'who would be a man in the real world and then a woman in the Matrix'.

The sisters also co-created *Sense8*, a sci-fi drama that aired for two seasons on Netflix. The series was praised for its LGBTQ+ characters and stories, and won the Outstanding Drama Series Award at the GLAAD Media Awards in 2016.

PAULI MURRAY

1910-1985

The Pauli Murray Center for History and Social Justice lists its namesake's many achievements as 'human rights activist, legal scholar, feminist, author, poet, Episcopal priest, labor organizer, and multiracial Black, LGBTQ+ community member'. Murray spent most of their life in New York, and became the first Black person to earn a JSD (Doctor of the Science of Law) degree from Yale Law School. Murray had several relationships with women, but did not necessarily see themself as homosexual, potentially viewing their identity in more masculine terms, and preferring an androgynous style of dress.

Murray was active in the civil rights movement and, in 1940, was famously arrested for refusing to move to the segregated back of a bus. Murray authored poems, articles and books, including *Proud Shoes: The Story of an American Family* (1956), a biography of their grandparents' lived experiences of white supremacy.

Murray criticised the civil rights movement for not including women's rights in its activities. In 1961 Kennedy appinted her to the Presidential Commission on the Status of Women, and in 1966 she founded the National Organization for Women with Betty Friedan. Murray also became the first Black American, perceived as a woman, to be appointed an Episcopal priest. On this date in 2016, the Pauli Murray Family Home was designated a National Historic Landmark.

ALAN TURING

1912-1954

'Father of computer science, mathematician, logician, wartime codebreaker, victim of prejudice' reads the memorial dedicated to Alan Turing in Manchester, UK. After completing his education, Turing joined the Government Communications Headquarters. During World War Two, building on earlier work by Polish codebreakers, Turing was able to develop a code-breaking machine known as the Bombe, which provided the Allies with vital military intelligence. He and his team are credited with dramatically shortening the war, saving millions of lives, and in 1945, Turing was awarded an OBE for his work.

Turing was convicted of gross indecency for homosexual acts in 1952. He bravely pleaded guilty and was given a choice of prison or probation, with the condition that he received experimental chemical castration as a 'treatment'. He accepted the treatment. The criminal conviction ended his civic career and a year after his prescribed hormone doses he was found dead in his home. The coroner ruled the death as suicide by cyanide poisoning.

On this date in 2013, 59 years after his death, Turing was granted a royal pardon by Queen Elizabeth II, and in 2017 more than 50,000 men convicted of similar sexual offences received pardons too. The amendment to the Policing and Crimes Bill, which pardoned these men was informally known as the Alan Turing Law.

ALBERT D.J. CASHIER

1843–1915

Albert D.J. Cashier, born on this date in Ireland and assigned female at birth, moved to the US as an adolescent and is thought to have begun wearing male clothes to get a higher-paid job.

Cashier enlisted as a man in the Union army during the American Civil War in 1862. While small in stature at around five foot tall, and generally quiet, Cashier's fellow soldiers testified that he was hard working, courageous and well liked. Multiple unverified stories attest to Cashier's bravery during his time with the 95th Illinois Infantry Regiment, which served in almost 40 engagements across more than 9,000 miles.

After his military service, Cashier continued to live as a man, leading modern historians to believe he was a trans man, as opposed to being someone who simply wished to serve their country at any cost. Towards the end of his life, he suffered dementia, which resulted in his story being discovered by doctors when he was hospitalised. Nevertheless, when he died, Cashier was granted a funeral with full military honours and was buried in uniform beneath a flag, near to his home in Illinois, which has been restored as a Civil War site for visitors.

CHRISTINA, QUEEN OF SWEDEN

1626–1689

Christina, Queen of Sweden abdicated in 1654. It is unclear why she no longer wanted to rule after 10 years on the throne, but her conversion from Sweden's state religion of Lutheranism to Catholicism and the fact she openly admitted having no interest in marriage both probably played a part.

As she left Sweden and headed across Europe, Christina's unusual appearance did not go unnoticed. One shoulder was higher than the other, and she wore a black wig and men's shoes. Her unapologetic, strong-willed personality was considered unorthodox for a woman at the time, and even more so when she later endeavoured to become queen of Naples. After this plot failed, she attempted to lay claim to the crown of her second cousin John II Casimir Vasa in Poland.

Christina's sexuality and gender have long been discussed, with some historians claiming that she may have been intersex. Others believe her 'distaste for marriage' and feeling 'nothing for all the things that females talked about and did', which she revealed in her autobiography, along with her close relationship with Ebba Sparre, with whom she shared a bed, are evidence of her lesbianism. On this date in 1933, the film *Queen Christina* premiered, starring Greta Garbo. Although it featured a highly fictionalised story, it did accurately portray her habit of dressing as a man.

MARLENE DIETRICH

1901–1992

Marie Magdalene Dietrich was born to a wealthy family in Schöneberg, Germany on this date in 1901. She changed her name to Marlene Dietrich and began singing and acting both on stage and screen. In 1930 she was cast in one of Germany's first talking pictures, *The Blue Angel* (*Der blaue Engel*), directed by Josef von Sternberg.

Dietrich moved to the US aged 28 to pursue her acting career and there Von Sternberg directed her again in a film called *Morocco* (1930), which features a scene in which Dietrich performs as a cabaret singer, dressed in a man's tuxedo and top hat, and kisses a woman in the audience. Both the outfit and the kiss were provocative for the period, but this image cemented Dietrich's trademark style of gender fluidity and wearing masculine clothing. The film also earned Dietrich her only Academy Award nomination and is heralded as one of the most progressive films about gender to come out of Hollywood before the Hays Code, a strict set of rules prohibiting nudity, sexual persuasions and violence, was introduced.

Dietrich was bisexual and reportedly made no secret about it, having multiple affairs with women, both in Germany and Hollywood, while married to her husband Rudolf Sieber. She has been romantically linked to Anna May Wong and, most notoriously, fellow Hollywood actress Greta Garbo.

LILI ELBE

1882–1931

Lili Elbe, who was assigned male at birth on this date in 1882 and named Einar Wegener, is thought to have first dressed in female clothes to fill in for a model who was late for a sitting with her wife, the artist Gerda Gottlieb. The pair met at the Royal Danish Academy of Fine Arts, married in 1904 and both worked as artists in Copenhagen.

As Elbe became the subject of more of Gottlieb's work and word got out about her cross-dressing, the pair moved to the more liberal city of Paris. After living as a woman for 20 years, Elbe took the brave decision to undergo what was then pioneering gender reassignment surgery. After consultations with the German sexologist Magnus Hirschfeld, she had a number of operations, including removal of the testicles and a uterus transplant to create a vaginal canal. The experimental surgery tragically led to her death when the transplanted uterus became infected.

Elbe kept diaries which were turned into an autobiography called *Man into Woman: The First Sex Change*, published posthumously in 1933. In 2000, a fictional account of Elbe's life was published by David Ebershoff and later made into *The Danish Girl*, a 2015 film starring Eddie Redmayne.

BILLY TIPTON

1914-1989

On publication of her book, *Suits Me: The Double Life of Billy Tipton*, author Diane Middlebrook said that the American jazz musician, Billy Tipton, was 'not a lesbian, because the women she was with didn't know she was female. She occupied an undefinable space. She was someone who worked creatively in the gap between biology and gender.' Living life as a man – in a way we would understand as trans, today – Tipton's assigned female sex at birth was only discovered upon his death.

Born on this date in 1914, Tipton had numerous relationships with women, who seemingly were never aware of his transgender identity. Later in life, Tipton married a stripper named Kitty Kelly and the pair adopted three sons.

Tipton was a successful jazz musician who played the piano and saxophone, and sang. At the peak of their career, Tipton's band, The Billy Tipton Trio, recorded albums for Tops Records and was offered a residency at a hotel in Reno, Nevada, where, had they accepted, they would have opened for big performers such as Liberace (see 7 Jun). Tipton turned this down and moved to Spokane, Washington, where he continued performing and lived out the rest of his days.

CHARLOTTE CUSHMAN

1816–1876

Charlotte Cushman, born in Boston, Massachusetts, was a descendant of Robert Cushman, one of the *Mayflower* Pilgrim Fathers. When her father died, leaving the family impoverished, Charlotte left school to pursue a career in opera, after earlier music lessons had helped reveal her remarkable contralto voice.

Her success as an opera singer was short-lived after her voice failed during performances in New Orleans, so Cushman turned to acting, performing as Romeo to her sister Susan's Juliet. Their first performance as the star-crossed lovers took place at Haymarket Theatre, London on this date in 1845. Acting in Europe and America, Cushman played both male and female roles on stage. She was praised for her performances of Hamlet, and won over audiences when she played Nancy, the prostitute, in Charles Dickens' *Oliver Twist*, after studying real-life 'women of ill repute' in the notorious neighbourhood of Five Points, New York.

Cushman reportedly had numerous female lovers and seems to have been fairly open about her relationships, even dressing the same as her long-term partner, writer Matilda Hays, when they lived together in Europe. When Cushman died of pneumonia aged 59, she was one of the most famous women in the world, and thousands of people held candlelit vigils for her on the streets of New York and Boston.

SANDI TOKSVIG

B. 1958

In the late 1980s, comedian, author and TV presenter Sandi Toksvig performed at the very first night of the Comedy Store in London, as part of the improvisational comedy team, The Comedy Store Players. Over 40 years later, Toksvig is still performing on stage. Her lengthy broadcasting career includes hosting BBC Radio 4's *The News Quiz*, quiz shows *QI* and *Fifteen to One* and being a regular contestant on shows such as *Call my Bluff* and *Whose Line Is It Anyway?* In 2017, she and comedian Noel Fielding took over as presenters for *The Great British Bake Off*, winning the hearts of the nation as an unexpectedly perfect coupling.

Nowadays often described as a National Treasure by the British public, when Toksvig came out in 1994 she says that the tabloid press painted her as 'Cruella de Vil' figure. They had threatened to out her so, under pressure, she revealed her sexuality to the *Sunday Times*. As a result, she was forced into hiding with her children for two weeks, after receiving death threats amidst what Toksvig described as a frightening media storm.

On this date in 2013, it was announced that Toksvig would be awarded an OBE in the New Year Honours list.

FURTHER RESOURCES

FURTHER RESOURCES

LGBTQ+ FIRSTS

Victim (1961)
The first English-language film to use the word 'homosexual' and sympathetically present queer characters on screen, starring **Dirk Bogarde**.

Caper in the Castro (1989)
Play **C.M. Ralph**'s game in this online emulation: archive.org/details/hypercard_caper-in-the-castro

The Line of Beauty (2004)
The first gay novel to win the Booker Prize, written by **Alan Hollinghurst**.

'The Transgender Tipping Point', *Time magazine* (9 Jun 2014):
Time.com/vault/issue/2014-06-09/page/1/
Laverne Cox becomes the first openly transgender person to grace the cover of American news magazine, *Time*, with her interview inside.

Pose (2018)
The first TV show to have an almost all lead cast of trans actors and characters, produced by **Ryan Murphy** and written and directed by **Janet Mock**.

ART & CULTURE

Medallion (YouWe) (1937)
Gluck's painting depicting lesbian love, which was used on the cover of the reprint of **Radclyffe Hall**'s book *The Well of Loneliness* (1928)

Peter Getting Out of Nick's Pool (1966)
Acrylic-on-canvas painting by **David Hockney**. Currently held at the Walker Art Gallery, Liverpool, UK.

'Martha', from *Cables to Rage* (1973)
In this remarkable poem, **Audre Lorde** revealed her sexuality for the first time.

The Celluloid Closet (1981)
Vito Russo's pioneering book on queer representation in film.

Paris is Burning (1990)
This documentary on the Harlem Ball scene, featuring **Willi Ninja**, shone a light on voguing and the communities who dance it.

LGBTQ+ HISTORY

Making Gay History podcast and website:
makinggayhistory.com
Listen to and read about the people who made queer history through **Eric Marcus**' interviews.

The Autobiography of Alice B. Toklas (1932)
Gertrude Stein's celebrated book that takes the form of an autobiography of her partner.

'1,112 and Counting', *New York Native* (27 Mar 1983)
Larry Kramer's essay calling on gay men and health professionals to act on the impending AIDS epidemic.

They Just Disappeared... Fragments of Gay History (*De forsvant bare ... Fragmenter av homofiles historie*) (1985)
Kim Friele's book about gay people from the Old Testament to Nazi Germany.

Stone Butch Blues (1993)
Leslie Feinberg's fictional work exploring life as a gender-non-conforming, queer person in 1970s America.

Pride (2014)
This feel-good film tells the story of an unlikely union between miners and queers against the Conservative government in the UK in the 1980s. **Mark Ashton** was a pioneer in the movement.

IDENTITY & SELF-ACCEPTANCE

Kellgren-Fozard's YouTube channel:
www.youtube.com/JessicaKellgrenFozard
Search Queer Sign Language to learn some LGBTQ+ signs in British Sign Language.

'A powerful poem about what it feels like to be transgender' (2015):
youtube.com/watch?v=S8DwxjDrNNM
TED Fellow, **Lee Mokobe**, explores identity and transition.

Born Both: An intersex Life (2017)
Hida Viloria's eye-opening memoir of gender identity, self-acceptance and love.

God's Own Country (2017)
Francis Lee's award-winning film of a young farmer's journey of love and self-acceptance.

'Thanksgiving', *Master of None*
(Season 2, Episode 8; 2017)
Lena Waithe writes and stars in this episode partly
based on her own coming out as a lesbian to her mother.

Queer & Muslim: Nothing to Reconcile (2019):
youtube.com/watch?v=8IhaGUImO_k
Blair Imani's TEDx talk.

Nanette (2019)
Hannah Gadsby's Netflix stand-up show that deals
with homophobia, sexism and violence.

CRIME & INJUSTICE
Miracle of the Rose (1946)
Jean Genet's semi-autobiographical work about his
time spent in a penal colony.

'A Day For A Lay', aka 'The Platonic Blow' (1948)
W.H. Auden poem he deemed too dirty for publication.
An unauthorised version was printed in 1965.

'Howl' from *Howl and Other Poems* (1956)
The poem by **Allen Ginsberg** that sparked an
obscenity trial.

The Death and Life of Marsha P. Johnson (2017)
The documentary in which activist Victoria Cruz
probes the suspicious 1992 death of her friend
Marsha P. Johnson.

LOVE & LOSS
Lovers: Ten Years On (1984–86)
Sunil Gupta's black and white photographic portraits
of gay and lesbian couples, taken in 1980s London.

A Single Man (2009)
Tom Ford's beautifully shot, heart-wrenching romantic
drama based on **Christopher Isherwood**'s 1964 novel,
which was inspired by the writer's own relationship with
a college student in the 1950s.

The Secret Diaries of Miss Anne Lister (2010)
A film about the diaries of heiress **Anne Lister**, later
known as Gentleman Jack, which gave an insight into
her private and love life.

Heartstopper (2022)
The joyous TV adaptation of **Alice Oseman**'s young
adult graphic novel about young queer love.

FEEL-GOOD & CELEBRATIONS
'Do You Come Here Often?' (1966)
The B-side on which **Joe Meek** overlaid campy
gay chat.

Tales of the City (1978)
Armistead Maupin's first novel that introduces you to
the residents of Barbary Lane, San Francisco – who
you can't help but fall in love with.

'You Make Me Feel (Mighty Real)' (1978)
The dance club hit by **Sylvester**.

Live Aid (Jul 1985)
Freddie Mercury performing Queen hits in Wembley
Arena to an international audience of 1.5 billion
people. Available on YouTube.

The Little Mermaid (1989)
The animated Disney musical in which **Howard
Ashman** steered animators towards basing the sea
witch, Ursula, on drag legend, Divine.

'Outside' (1998)
George Michael's song and music video which made
light of his arrest for cruising in LA.

Living with Pride: Ruth C. Ellis @ 100 (1999)
A documentary about **Ruth Ellis**' life.

'Honeymoon', *Schitt's Creek*
(Season 1, Episode 10; 2015)
The episode of *Schitt's Creek* (co-created by and
starring **Dan Levy**) in which characters Stevie and
David have a charming discussion about liking 'the
wine and not the label'.

'Without Further Ado', *Queer Eye*
(Season 4, Episode 1; 2019)
Jonathan McDonald Van Ness returns to his
hometown in Quincy, Illinois to make over his
high school music teacher.

TO LEARN MORE ON LGBTQ+ RIGHTS, HISTORY AND
POLICY IN THE UK HEAD TO STONEWALL.ORG.UK.
IF YOU'RE IN THE USA VISIT HRC.ORG (HUMAN RIGHTS
CAMPAIGN) FOR SIMILAR INFORMATION.

ABOUT THE AUTHOR

Originally from Derbyshire, **Lewis Laney** headed to the bright lights of Blackpool in his teens and began writing queer fiction. After having his first short story published in *The Next Wave: The Gay Times Book of Short Stories* (2002) at the age of 18, he went on to write for various publications, including the iconic music magazine *The Face*. His first book *The Little Book of Pride* was published in 2020 and immediately topped Amazon's LGBTQ History category. Lewis works in publishing and lives in London, where he works with local establishments to provide safe spaces for queer meet-ups.

AUTHOR ACKNOWLEDGEMENTS

Thanks to everyone who has played a part in getting this book out into the world and thanks to you, the reader for buying a copy.

My editor, Laura Bulbeck, guided me through the process in the most calm and unfaltering manner, extending my deadlines and gently nudging me to get a move on when needed. Her organisation, expertise and encouragement has been invaluable. Thank you.

Jenny, Julia, and Lesley did a wonderful job of checking things, tidying up my overly long text and making helpful suggestions, while Guntaas gave it the sensitivity seal of approval. Thanks to Rohana in production, and to Mel and Steve and to the army of Quarto folks who each have a hand in getting the book out there.

Much love to Jessica and Zara for commissioning the book, what feels like a lifetime ago, and thanks to Andrew for joining the team at the end and helping to get it over the finish line!

Thank you to Leonardo and Renata for the wonderful design and also to Angus Hyland for his expert eye. I definitely feel like I've made it; having a book art directed by Pentagram Design!

But of course, the main person who has made the book such a feast for the eyes is Charlotte MacMillan-Scott, with her wonderful illustrations. Thank you, Charlotte, for bringing these people to life in such a bright and uplifting way.

Thanks to all the queers and all the allies out there and in this book who fight the fight and make a difference.

And finally, thank you to Ben for making me coffee when I got up to write at 6am and for making my dinner when I was still writing at 8pm. You lift me up, support, feed and encourage me. This book's for you. x

ABOUT THE ILLUSTRATOR

Charlotte MacMillan-Scott is a UK-based illustrator and designer working in mainly digital illustration. She currently works from her studio in Frome. A self-taught artist, she began her career experimenting with screen printing before deciding to branch out into freelance illustration. As well as her popular portrait work, she covers a wide range of mediums, from printmaking, to products and murals. A lover of bold colour, Charlotte brings energy, vibrancy and a playful approach to all of her work. She did her first exhibition at The London Illustration Fair in 2019, and was nominated as one of five talents to look out for.
@charlottemsscott_illustration
www.charlottemacscott.com